949-507 SM

SMITH, E.D.

VICTORY OF A SO

1.

D1374627

JM

Hertfordshire
COUNTY COUNCIL

Community Information

0 7 NOV 2001

−8 JUN 2002
2 9 JUN 2002

2 0 JUL 2002

7/12

Please renew/return this item by the last date shown.

So that your telephone call is charged at local rate, please call the numbers as set out below:

	From Area codes 01923 or 0208:	From the rest of Herts:
Renewals:	01923 471373	01438 737373
Enquiries:	01923 471333	01438 737333
Minicom:	01923 471599	01438 737599

L32b

VICTORY OF A SORT

The British in Greece, 1941–46

E.D. SMITH

ROBERT HALE · LONDON

© *E.D. Smith 1988*
First published in Great Britain 1988

Robert Hale Limited
Clerkenwell House
Clerkenwell Green
London EC1R 0HT

British Library Cataloguing in Publication Data

Smith, E.D. (Eric David), *1923-*
  Victory of a sort ; the British in Greece,
  1941-46.
  1. Greece. Political events. Role of British
  government, 1941-1946. Great Britain.
  Government. Role in political events in
  Greece, 1941-1946
  I. Title
  949.5′074

ISBN 0-7090-3290-0

HERTFORDSHIRE
COUNTY LIBRARY
949.
5074
2 4 OCT 1988

Maps by EDANART

Photoset in North Wales by
Derek Doyle & Associates, Mold, Clwyd.
Printed in Great Britain by
St Edmundsbury Press Ltd, Bury St Edmunds, Suffolk.
Bound by WBC Bookbinders Ltd.

Contents

'Freedom can't be bought for nothing.
If you hold her precious,
you must hold all else of little worth.'
Seneca

Illustrations

Archbishop Damaskinos with Frank Macaskie
KDG's 'Thanksgiving Service'
Celebrating the 'Second Round' victory, January 1945
George Bagnall, member of the TUC delegation, January
    1945
Four ELAS delegates signing the cease-fire
General Sarafis at the armistice negotiations, February 1945

Maps

Credits

All photographs reproduced by permission of the Imperial
    War Museum

Foreword

by the Lord Hunt of Llanfair Waterdine KG CBE DSO

The deliberate destruction of the economy of Greece and the brutal treatment of its Greek citizens ranks among the major war crimes perpetrated by the Axis Powers during the last war. I was one of those who witnessed the wholesale wreckage of roads and bridges, railways and rolling stock, ports and villages in the wake of the German army's withdrawal in 1944, as the war in Europe approached its climax. I saw evidence of the massacre of civilians, epitomized by the village of Kalavrita in the Peloponnese. I met very many Greeks who had lived through those experiences, and survived. I formed then, and have retained ever since, a profound admiration for the indomitable spirit of the Greek people in the face of such adversity.

But there was also a darker side, even among the Greeks themselves, which was revealed in the aftermath of the departure of the common enemy. I was soon made aware of another calamity, for which those years of oppressive occupation provided a preface and a pretext, and which brought out the worst as well as the good qualities in the Greek character: a civil war. Its outcome would determine the divide between the rival ideologies of communism and the free world in the peace which was to follow the global clash of arms.

During the sixteen months of my service in Greece, I discovered that I was embroiled in an issue of crucial importance to the ideal of individual freedom. It was, perhaps, appropriate that such an issue should be resolved – at least for many years to come – in Greece, the cradle of democracy. I was not alone in having no conception of what lay ahead when the battalion I had commanded in Italy and the Indian Division to which I was promoted, were both diverted from the final drive northwards to the River Po, in order to bring succour to Greece. There was among all of us, Indian and British soldiers alike, a sense of bathos and frustration, a lowering in our morale, on being relegated to this backwater on the strategic map of Europe.

How wrong we were! Suffice it to say that I have never, before or since, been subjected to greater stress. Nor have I ever felt so proud to be associated with my fellow men, in peace or war, as I felt for the soldiers under my command. They were called upon to cope with situations, well nigh intolerable in themselves, of which they had no previous experience. They managed those situations magnificently, with patience and forbearance, tact and compassion.

Birdie Smith has rendered a valuable service in placing the Greek story during and after the war in its true perspective and with painstaking attention to detail. I welcome this opportunity to pay tribute to the Greek people and to the men and women of the Allied forces who helped them in their years of need.

John Hunt

Acknowledgements

The author and publishers are grateful for permission to reproduce copyright material from the following books:

W.S. Churchill, *The Second World War, Vols. V-VII* (Cassell plc)
John Hunt, *Life is Meeting* (Hodder & Stoughton Ltd.)
Jeanne Tsatsos, *The Sword's Fierce Edge* (translated from the Greek by Jean Demos, Vanderbilt University Press)

Acronyms and Terms

AFHQ	Allied Forces Headquarters
ANDARTES	Guerrilla troops
BEF	British Expeditionary Force
BLO	British Liaison Officer, attached to Resistance bands
BMM	British Military Mission to Resistance bands
Caserta Agreement	Arranged by British authorities and signed on 26 September 1944. Placed ELAS and EDES under authority of the 'Government of National Unity'. Resistance organizations put under command of Lt.-Gen. Sir Ronald Scobie.
CRA	Commander Royal Artillery
DAPM	Deputy Assistant Provost Marshal
DCLI	Duke of Cornwall's Light Infantry
EAM	National Liberation Front
EAS	National Liberation League, clandestine Leftist organization established by EAM in Middle East
EDES	National Republican Greek League, organization commanded by Napoleon Zervas, chief rival of ELAS
EKKA	National Socialist Liberation Group, Republican Resistance organization destroyed by ELAS in the 'First Round'. Led by Colonel Psarros and George Kartalis.

ELAS	National People's Liberation Army, EAM's military arm and principal formation of armed resistance
First Round	Considered by some as first phase of the Civil War or first Communist attempt to seize power by force (depending on point of view). Waged during autumn and winter of 1943.
Force 133	SOE forces in the Balkans with headquarters in Cairo
Force 140	British Forces for the liberation of Greece under Lt.-Gen. Sir Ronald Scobie
GHQ	General Headquarters
GR	Gurkha Rifles
HLI	Highland Light Infantry
KKE	Communist Party of Greece
KRRC	Kings Royal Rifle Corps
Lebanon Conference	Meeting of Greek political factions and Resistance organizations, held in May 1944. Although differences remained, it led to formation of Prime Minister George Papandreou's coalition 'Government of National Unity'.
MEF	Middle East Forces (Allied)
Mountain Brigade (also known as Third of Rimini Brigade)	Formed in ME during spring 1944, following mutinies in Greek armed forces
Operation Manna	Allied plan for return of Greek Government and relief of country
Operation Noah's Ark	Allied plan to harass German withdrawal
OPLA	Teams for Protection of the People's Struggle, EAM/ELAS security and terror organization
OSS	Office of Strategic Services, American wartime intelligence/sabotage agency

PEEA	Political Committee of National Liberation, shadow Government, formed by EAM in March 1944.
RAMC	Royal Army Medical Corps
RASC	Royal Army Service Corps
RSR	Raiding Support Regiment
RTR	Royal Tank Regiment
RV	Rendezvous
Sacred Squadron	Greek military unit, formed in Middle East, consisting mostly of former army officers
SBS	Special Boat Section
Second Round	Considered by some as second phase of Civil War or second Communist attempt to seize power by force (depending on viewpoint). Took place in December 1944 between ELAS and Government forces, primarily British, Indian and Gurkha troops
Security Battalions	Military units formed by Government of Prime Minister John Rallis to serve as auxiliary to German Occupation Forces
SIS	Secret Intelligence Service (British)
SOE	Special Operations Executive, British wartime intelligence/sabotage agency
Third Round	1946–49 Civil War, regarded by some as third Communist attempt to seize power by force
UNRRA	United Nations Relief and Rehabilitation Administration
Varkiza Agreement	Signed on 12 February 1945, formal end to December 1944 fighting (Second Round)
X	An extreme Royalist underground organization. Attacked Leftist activities in the Athens area. Led by Colonel Grivas (later to appear in Cyprus).

Preface

'We Greeks are lovers of the beautiful, yet simple in our
taste, and we cultivate the mind without loss of manliness.'

Thucydides

Over forty years have elapsed since Greece suffered the
torment of invasion by first Italy and then Germany,
followed by brutal occupation by the two Axis Powers. Even if
the story had ended with liberation in late autumn 1944, the
country would have undergone a terrible ordeal, impossible
for non-Greeks to comprehend. The euphoria of liberation
in 1944 by the British was to be short-lived as civil war
permeated the troubled land, until British soldiers stood
shoulder to shoulder with Greek comrades; alas, this time
their opponents were Greeks and not Germans or Italians.
By the end of 1946, Britain had begun handing over
responsibility to the USA until the last of her troops left a
country still in the throes of civil war, a war that was far more
devastating than the Axis Occupation.

Controversy about the role played by Britain in Greece
between 1941 and 1946 has not diminished by the passing
years. 'It is impossible to write ancient history because we lack
source materials and impossible to write modern history
because we have far too many.' Those words, written by
Charles Péguy, are true, and an illustration can be found in
Greece in the 1940s, where the editor, John Latrides, has a
bibliography of over seventy pages! From such a granary it
should be possible to marshal impressive evidence in support
of a wide range of opinions on Greece, and this has been

17

done already. I leave that to others because, as the title implies, this account concentrates on the part played by Britain in Greek affairs between 1941 and 1946. An early injunction by my publisher not to make it too political reminded me of Anthony Eden's minute written on 5 November 1941: 'Greek politics is a hot and sticky porridge and I abhor the idea of putting my finger into this mess.' A few weeks later Eden became Foreign Secretary, and he was forced to keep his finger in Greek politics until the fall of Churchill's Government in the summer of 1945. Like Eden, I have found it impossible to cover British participation without being enmeshed in politics, even though I have tried to avoid going into too much detail.

For the officers and men of Britain's Armed Forces who went to Greece, the political undertones meant little or nothing, except to a very few. In 1940 they were sent to help an old ally against the Italians; a few months later Germany was the ruthless invader striking at Greece; from late October 1944 the 'baddies' were KKE/EAM/ELAS because – so British servicemen were told – their aim was to establish a Communist state by coercion and intimidation. When events moved inexorably from the military defeat of ELAS at the turn of 1944, towards a savage civil war between bitterly opposed factions, reluctant to show mercy, was it surprising that the British were chary about getting involved once again? In addition, they were puzzled by the fact that such a kind, hospitable people could perpetrate such cruel acts against their fellow-countrymen.

As the years have passed, there has been a strong resurgence of interest in those momentous years of tragedy, stimulated in 1974 by the fall of the right-wing Military Junta in Greece and by the release of British State Papers into the Public Records Office at Kew. Inevitably, academics, writers and one-time participants have sought new evidence to justify previous statements or to refute legends that had begun to be accepted as historical fact. I am certain that those holding strong and often diametrically opposite views will continue to argue for years to come, as became evident after the controversial *The Greek Civil War*, shown on Channel 4 a year or two ago.

As this is primarily a British story set in Greece, the State

Papers consulted, most of the books I have read and the correspondents who sent me their wartime or post-war experiences are in the main British. I make no apologies for this, because if I had delved in detail into the political, economic and social issues of Greece between 1941 and 1946, my bibliography like John Latrides, would have been a long one and this book several times larger than is the case.

Did the British save Greece or merely leave its people a chance to make their own choice? And if the latter, did Britain help to create conditions which made such a choice inevitable? Whatever the answers may be, I, for one, believe that the services of British soldiers, sailors and airmen were indispensable and that Britain was held in great affection by the majority of the Greek people. Most of us look back on our tours in Greece with pride and genuinely believe that we played our part in saving the lives of innocent people caught up in a tragic situation.

Edward Chapman, who lived among the Greek peasants and fought with an ELAS partisan group under the name 'Kiriakos', returned thirty years later to his old haunts and '... found it all too much. It was all unreal ... the welcome, the memories, the genuine love and affection of these people after more than thirty years was beyond description, imagination, or even understanding.'

Long may those ties of love and affection continue.

Sidmouth
May 1987

1 Greece in Peril – Divided Counsel

'Never trust the advice of a man in difficulties.'

Aesop

1941, a year of disasters for Britain, her Dominions and her Empire, was to witness a highly dubious military venture when a small Imperial Expeditionary Force was sent to the support of the Greek people. Both the venture and the decision were rooted in history. Churchill's predecessor, Neville Chamberlain, during April 1939 had reacted to Mussolini's Good Friday invasion of Albania by guaranteeing Greece British support in the event of an Axis invasion. The offer remained hypothetical until 28 October 1940 when, bent on scoring off Hitler for seizing oil-rich areas of Romania, Benito Mussolini launched an attack on Greece from Albania, after complaining about alleged Greek assistance to the Allies and demanding the right to occupy certain strategic bases in Greece. In face of the Italian ultimatum, the Prime Minister of Greece, General Metaxas, gave the answer, 'No', and made himself popular overnight in his own country.

Benito Mussolini's sudden move infuriated his Axis partner, Hitler, who had hoped to conquer the Balkans by political rather than military means. Churchill reacted with warm-hearted chivalry to the crisis faced by the small nation: 'We will give you all the help in our power', which at that time amounted to very little. But to the surprise of most of the world, the Greeks fought back like tigers and soon the Italians were in headlong retreat.

One of the first members of the British Military Mission, Stanley Casson, arrived in Athens on the same day as the Albanian city of Koritsa was captured by the Greek Army. It

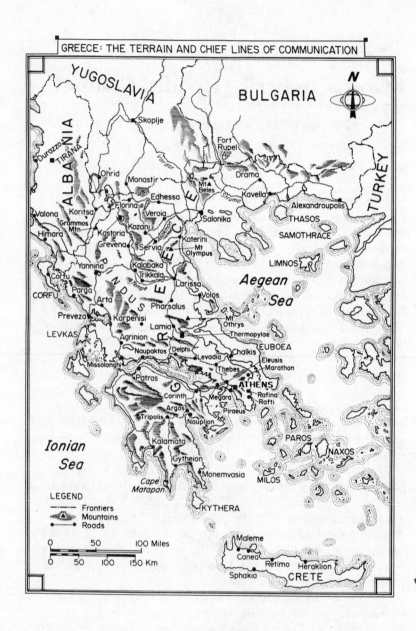

GREECE: THE TERRAIN AND CHIEF LINES OF COMMUNICATION

YUGOSLAVIA

BULGARIA

TURKEY

ALBANIA

Durazzo
TIRANA
Skoplje
Ohrid
Monastir
Fort Rupel
Drama
Valona
Koritsa
Florina
Edhessa
Mt Beles
Kavella
Grammos Mtn
Veroia
Salonika
Alexandroupolis
Himara
Kozani
Kastoria
Grevena
Servia
Katerini
Mt Olympus
THASOS
SAMOTHRACE
Corfu
Yannina
Kalabaka
Trikkala
LIMNOS
CORFU
Parga
Arta
Tempe
Larissa
Volos
Aegean Sea
Preveza
Karpenisi
Pharsalus
LEVKAS
Agrinion
Lamia
Mt Othrys
Thermopylae
Naupaktos
Delphi
Levadia
Chalkis
EUBOEA
Missolonghi
Thebes
Eleusis
Marathon
Patras
ATHENS
Corinth
Megara
Rafina
Rafti
Argos
Piraeus
Tripolis
Nauplion
PAROS
Kalamata
NAXOS
Gytheion
MILOS
Ionian Sea
Monemvasia
Cape Matapan

KYTHERA

LEGEND
— — Frontiers
Mountains
• • • Roads

0   50   100 Miles
0   50   100   150 Km

Maleme
Canea
Retimo
Heraklion
Sphakia
CRETE

N

was a masterstroke, as Koritsa was one of the main bases from which the Italians hoped to invade Greece. Casson later wrote that there were happy crowds everywhere, 'cheers and delight for the first and greatest victory'.

British help was not confined to the small number of RAF aircraft that eventually arrived. On 20 December a strong naval force entered the Adriatic and bombarded Valona with a hundred tons of shells. 'Prisoners told us that this alarmed the Italians more than any other attack that had been made on them by sea or air' (Stanley Casson).

Rarely recorded by British observers was the fact that a large amount of Italian booty captured in the Desert Campaign against Graziani was to be shipped to Greece for use against Mussolini's forces in Albania.

The Duce had expected victory within a few weeks, long before the Balkan winter set in, but from the start the Italian Air Force wasted its vast superiority in a series of raids against undefended islands and non-military targets. What was to have been a brief autumn campaign in Greece became a war in Albania, fought throughout the bitter months of winter in conditions of extreme hardship. By the end of 1940 the Greek Army had penetrated between twenty and thirty miles beyond the Albanian border and was pushing nineteen Italian divisions back towards the port of Valona.

What was not appreciated at the time by the majority of the Greek people, as well as the outside world, was the tremendous strain on the Greek Army during that bitter winter of 1940–41. Over 300,000 ill-equipped troops were operating in the Albanian mountains without adequate communications or transport to support them. Moreover, men serving in the forward areas were rarely, if ever, rotated with those in the rear because reserves of the correct calibre were virtually non-existent. By the time spring 1941 came, even if circumstances had allowed the majority of those Greek divisions to meet the German invader elsewhere, they would have had little to offer except courage and patriotism.

The Greeks' intense pride in their victories against the Italians overshadowed, to a certain extent, apprehension about a possible German invasion. Often heard was the cry: 'The Italians we can always beat to their knees, Germany never. But we will fight them till we die.' Not everyone in

Greece was involved in the war, a fact that caused bitterness and was to have repercussions in years to come. Over 600 ex-officers who had been dismissed in 1935 for having strong Republican views and opposing the King were not allowed by Prime Minister Metaxas to re-enlist and serve their country during this gravest of emergencies. That number included two men who were to play a leading role during the Axis Occupation and the civil wars that tore Greece asunder, Napoleon Zervas and Stefanos Sarafis.

It was hardly surprising that so little was known about the true state of their Greek ally, especially on the Albanian front, because British liaison officers were not allowed to travel freely, their visits being restricted to certain designated areas only. More often than not, they were required to wear civilian clothes and use pseudonyms. For example, the big, burly General Maitland Wilson, designated as C-in-C of any projected BEF to Greece, was called 'Mr Watt' by his hosts when he first paid a visit to Greece in 1941, a subterfuge that fooled no one, especially the alert Germans.

German vigilance was noted by Tom Joy, at that time an RASC corporal clerk, who had been seconded to the Royal Air Force in Greece under the command of Air Commodore (later Air Vice-Marshal) D'Albiac: 'The morning we landed was memorable. Before we got to Athens the streets were lined with cheering people, who had been warned by telephone from Piraeus and presumably hoped we were the first of many. In any case at that time Germany was not at war with Greece, and the swastika was flying from their embassy just a few doors from ours and all the others. They also had their shipping offices in the docks, openly noting arrivals of goods and arms from anywhere.'

Joy went on to say that the euphoria wore off because, 'The Greeks were disappointed at the smallness of our presence.' At the same time, in a diary entry, American Laird Archer made this comment on the RAF's arrival in late 1940 to help the Greeks on the Albanian front: 'If only the RAF had something more than skill, courage and typewriters! ... This morning twelve British Gladiators went up to meet 150 CR-42s and Italian Savoias over the Larissa base. They got thirty of the enemy and drove the others off. That precious dozen has been reduced to seven, I gather.'

Another early arrival in Greece during November was Alan Benjafield, then a sergeant in the RAF. Like Tom Joy he remembered the ecstatic welcome given by the people: 'Our reception was terrific, the Greeks turned out in mass and showered fruit, wine and flowers on us.'

Like other British servicemen, Alan Benjafield found that, while the Greeks were as one in their enmity towards the Italians, they were not so keen on opposing the Germans. His theory was that, 'The German diplomatic and propaganda services were doing a very good job. We were warned not to react to any German provocation.... Their favourite ploy, in a café, would be to say, in English, that England was finished and London was destroyed.' One further point the ex-RAF sergeant recalls was the behaviour of the Metaxas 'Blue Shirts': 'They were most arrogant in their dealings with the Greek people and I saw several ugly scenes.'

United though Greece was in face of Italian aggression, the country had remained divided since Metaxas had seized power in 1936, with the blessing of King George II. The divisions were deep-seated and, instead of disappearing during the years of Axis occupation that lay ahead, increased until it became difficult to find moderates in any walk of life. For such a reason, recent works on Greece during that period continue to reflect the depth of the schism between the political parties of Left and Right, Republican, Communist, Liberal and Monarchist.

During this period when Greece was fighting Italy, and as 1941 approached, Britain had little to offer except moral support, a fact that became apparent to Laird Archer in Athens: 'London explains over the BBC that Britain cannot help much, is alone in the West since the French defeat. Still the Greeks are cheered by arrivals of British ground support for the Air Force with some supplies: British boys picked up in streets and carried on Greek shoulders.'

Christmas Day 1940 was a black one for Corfu and a day of shame for the Italian aviators who visited that defenceless island. Laird Archer's cryptic diary entry explains why: 'Children of Corfu bombed today in the Public Square as they were opening Christmas packages dropped shortly before by British fliers. 400 are dead, scores wounded.' This action was one that was not to be forgotten. Even though the

Italians held the whip hand when, for over two years a large part of the country was under their military occupation, the Greek people tended to treat the Italian troops with scorn and open contempt.

Air Vice-Marshal D'Albiac had arrived on 6 November 1940, and he was followed over the next few weeks by two medium bomber squadrons, one mixed medium bomber and two-seater fighter squadrons – all Blenheim aircraft – and two single-seater fighter squadrons of Gladiators, trusty but slow-moving veterans. D'Albiac wanted to use his planes against the Albanian ports and Italian lines of communication, while the Greek General Staff asked his small force to give close support to the Army in its bitter struggle up in the mountains.

For a time D'Albiac's views prevailed, even though for political reasons he was not allowed to reconnoitre alternative airstrips or aerodromes, nearer the front line. Meanwhile units of his force continued to arrive during November and December, and by the end of the year the concentration was complete, pitifully small though it was. Indeed, it prompted D'Albiac into telling Cairo that Flight Lieutenant would be the appropriate rank for the AOC if more planes could not be spared!

The Blenheims continued to strike at targets in or near the Albanian ports of Valona and Durazzo, but after New Year's Day 1941 weather conditions deteriorated over the front and Italian fighter opposition became stronger. That they achieved so much is remarkable, as the Mk I Blenheims were old and tired aircraft. To make matters worse, the British pilots, being based in the Athens area, had an approach flight of at least 200 miles before they even reached the theatre of operations. Although invariably outnumbered, the gallant crews never ceased to give battle, and their presence in the skies over the Greek Army was a great boost to morale. D'Albiac had envisaged his force increasing to some fourteen squadrons after 15 January and hoped to base some of his aircraft in or near Salonika, but once again Metaxas and his Cabinet were reluctant to agree. In retrospect, their reluctance seems strange as the British presence was never hidden from the Germans, who were able to report just about every arrival by sea or air.

Early in February the Greeks began another offensive in Albania with the aim of driving towards Valona, but bad weather intervened and the Italians were able to hold up the advance just north of Tepelene. During the February offensive, the Greeks asked for maximum close support for their troops in Albania: the morale of the tired soldiers had been badly shaken by the bitter weather and by a disappointing lack of progress in the mountains against fresh Italian troops. D'Albiac agreed and belatedly was allowed to move the wing headquarters of his bomber force to the grass strip of Paramythia nearer the Albanian front. The efforts of the gallant Blenheim pilots were recognized with gratitude in the official communiqués, and for the few days that remained before the Germans invaded the country the prestige of the Royal Air Force was higher in the minds of the Greek nation than at any other period during the war. But to keep British aid to Greece in perspective, up to the end of February 1941 the total force, RAF and supporting Army troops, was barely 5,000.

Before leaving the part played by the Royal Air Force and turning our attention to the political moves that led to the despatch of the main Imperial Expeditionary Force to Greece, we should note that the first six Hurricane aircraft that arrived were a welcome reinforcement because the ageing Gladiators had been easily outpaced by opposing Italian fighters. During their first sortie over Greece, the Hurricanes shot down four Italian aircraft on 20 February and eight days later, in conjunction with the Gladiators, destroyed a further twenty-seven aircraft without loss. Having been in Greece since November 1940, D'Albiac well understood the agonizing dilemma the Greek Government faced before they decided to accept the Imperial Expeditionary Force on their soil. In his *London Gazette* report after the War he wrote: 'If they allowed British fighting troops to enter their country, war with Germany was ultimately unavoidable. To their lasting credit, however, they preferred to accept such a situation rather than have to submit when the time came to abject capitulation in face of overwhelming odds.'

The Greek premier, Ionannis Metaxas, continued to decline Winston Churchill's early offers of troops to resist the

Germans should they invade his country. He was striving to
perform a difficult feat because, while determined to defeat
Italy, he wanted to avoid provoking Hitler into coming to the
aid of his Axis partner. Moreover, the friendly relationship
which had hitherto existed between Greece and Germany
encouraged the premier into thinking he could succeed.
Outside the country, others were not so sanguine. General
Wavell, Commander-in-Chief in the Middle East, accurately
forecast developments when he wrote in November 1940: 'I
am quite sure Germany cannot afford to see Italy defeated –
or even held – in Greece and must intervene.' Unknown to
Wavell, Greece had been mentioned for the first time by
Hitler in his secret Military Directive 18, and on 13 December
he was more specific, giving his intention '... to establish in
the coming months a constantly increasing force in southern
Romania, and on arrival of favourable weather – probably in
March – to move his force into Bulgaria to occupy the
north-east coast of the Aegean and, should this be necessary,
entire mainland of Greece.'

On 1 January Laird Archer, who was to head UNRRA
after the 1944 Liberation, noted: 'The New Year dawned
with the great question in the minds of the Greek people and
their Western friends: if Germany comes to the aid of Italy,
will the Greek Government with its pro-German members
order resistance just as in October? Where does Metaxas ...
stand in the face of increasing Nazi threat?'

Of course, Archer could not know that Metaxas had less
than a month to live, worn out by work in the High
Command and in the Foreign Office – 'A combination of
diabetes, intestinal trouble and 'flu got him and the old heart
finally gave out.' The death of Metaxas, the man who had
spoken the famous 'no' to the Italian Ambassador, Count
Grazzi, plunged the whole of Athens into gloom. German-
trained, astute, brilliant, Metaxas had forced the Axis
war-machine to stop and overhaul its programme.

When General Wavell and Air Vice-Marshal Longmore,
AOC Middle East, went to Athens in early January 1941,
Metaxas asked for nine British divisions, to be assembled in
the Mediterranean for shipment as soon as Hitler attacked.
Even if the British had such a force – and they had nothing
like it in any theatre of war at that time – the logistical

problems would have been totally beyond their resources. Consequently, Wavell and Longmore were not impressed. Nor, indeed, had Anthony Eden been when, as Secretary of State for War, he had dismissed the thought of any military intervention in Greece as being 'strategic folly' (diary entry). He was to change his views dramatically after becoming Foreign Secretary on 23 December 1940.

Metaxas' refusal of the first British offer was received in London on 16 January. Churchill commented rather sarcastically, 'One cannot force little dogs to eat mutton.' The Greek premier still wanted the British to prepare plans, to hold troops in reserve but not send them 'until they could land in sufficient numbers to act offensively as well as defensively'. Nevertheless, at the end of the first Anglo-Greek conference, he said: 'We fight not for victory, but only for our honour,' and that, 'We prefer destruction to dishonour.' A few days later, when Metaxas died, he was succeeded by the Governor of the National Bank, Alexander Koryzis, who, after receiving reports of German preparations from several sources, decided to re-open negotiations for British help on 8 February. Such a decision came at a most opportune moment because General O'Connor's Desert Army captured first Tobruk and then Benghazi so that by 7 February all Cyrenaica was in British hands. For the first time in the war, Britain had the prospect of a few additional troops being available for use, even though Wavell continued to be very much against any major commitment in Greece.

Like many military experts, British and Greek, the C-in-C of the Greek Army, General Papagos, albeit armed with hindsight, in 1946 stated that the British should have continued their offensive in Africa and cleared the whole of Libya. At the time, however, the situation that faced the Governments in Athens and London was complex and bedevilled with imponderables. To complicate matters further, in January 1941 over 80,000 German troops appeared in Romania, which prompted a Foreign Office memo that stated: 'If we are unable to come effectively to the assistance of Greece, there is a real danger that she may be tempted to make a separate peace if reasonable terms are offered to her, and this is no doubt what Germany is trying to bring about.' As a consequence, the initial conferences between the British and Greek delegations were held in an atmosphere of distrust: the Greeks suspected that the British were trying to involve them in a war with Germany; the British were afraid the Greeks were toying with the idea of making a separate peace with Italy.

At first Churchill was convinced that British intervention was both necessary and inevitable, and in a telegram to Wavell on 10 January 1941 he set out his views: 'Destruction of Greece will eclipse victories you have gained in Libya and may adversely affect Turkish attitude, especially if we have shown ourselves callous of fate of Allies.' Despite his earlier misgivings, Wavell was to change his mind on this point and told his staff to prepare plans so that Greece could be given all military aid possible. Although post-war criticism has been that the despatch of the BEF to Greece was very much Churchill's concept – and blunder, Wavell as Commander-in-Chief changed his stand and loyally supported his prime minister. After his initial visit to Athens, Wavell decided that, 'Providing conversations with the Greeks show that there is a good chance of establishing a front against the Germans with our assistance, I think we should take it.' Not everybody agreed with him – in Whitehall, on that same day, the Socialist Cabinet Minister Hugh Dalton voiced his disquiet to Sir Alexander Cadogan in the Foreign Office: 'Might it not be better to allow the Greeks, under pressure, to make a separate peace ... better than having the country devastated to the last and better than putting in some of our own troops and having them not even evacuated but trapped and destroyed?'

Such doubts and fears were raised in the next War Cabinet, and later that day Churchill himself preached caution in a cable sent to Eden, who was out in the Middle East, shuttling from Cairo to Athens and thence to Ankara: 'Do not feel yourselves obligated to the Greek enterprise if in your hearts you feel it will only be another Norwegian fiasco.' The inference was obvious: the Prime Minister was not wholly convinced and thus he awaited advice from Eden and Wavell. That signal horrified the British Minister in Athens, Sir Michael Palairet, but his fears were to be proved groundless as Eden was bent on having his way. On 22 February, after a series of meetings with King George II of the Hellenes and his advisers, Eden, backed by Wavell and Dill (the CIGS), behaved to the Greeks like a high-pressure salesman, promising them 100,000 men, 240 field guns, 202 anti-tank guns and other weapons. Those figures were not inflated, even if, naturally, the troop total included administrative personnel. The Greeks, who had stoutly declared their intention of fighting the Germans whether the British helped or not, were greatly moved by the gesture their old ally, Britain, was making. On 23 February Koryzis, showing considerable emotion, formally accepted British aid to Greece.

After the war, Wavell's part in this decision was queried by General Sir Hastings (later Lord) Ismay, Assistant Secretary to the War Cabinet: 'I can't help thinking Wavell allowed political considerations to influence his military judgement.' At the time Wavell, too, countered criticism from his own staff in Cairo with Wolfe's comment: 'War is an option of difficulties.'

Typically Wavell, in the *London Gazette* published on 2 July 1941, did not try to make any excuses, although he did point out that accurate intelligence about German troop movements in Italy and North Africa was almost non-existent. For such a reason he and his staff did not anticipate that there could be any major German offensive in North Africa until May, at the earliest. Like everyone else, he was to be totally surprised by the comparatively unknown German General Erwin Rommel and his Afrika Korps.

Foreign Secretary Eden's hopes of creating a Balkan bloc to stop any German move southwards – 'the only chance to prevent the Balkans being devoured piecemeal' – came to nothing. The fact that Hungary and Romania had made common cause with the Axis and that already Bulgaria was wavering gave few grounds for optimism. His promise that British intervention in Greece would stiffen the resolve of Turkey and Yugoslavia meant little in those countries, especially when they knew that the British stood alone, and weak, in the war against the Axis powers. The former Vice-Chief of the Imperial General Staff, Sir Henry Pownall, wrote after the war: 'Looking back, it seems to me that in our efforts to form a Balkan bloc, we were attempting to build reality out of illusion.' In the event, Metaxas' views of his

Balkan neighbours were far more realistic than Eden's, because from the onset he doubted whether Yugoslavia would, or even could, resist German demands when these were presented to them. After Eden's hopes of forming a Balkan bloc had been dashed, his colleague Hugh Dalton, Minister for Economic Warfare, commented that they were 'little people waiting to be eaten one by one, and fear of Germany outweighed any moral support that Britain could offer'. Promises of moral support meant little to any Balkan country, threatened by Germany, especially when the ruthless destruction of defenceless cities, in the Netherlands and elsewhere, by the Luftwaffe served to remind them of what happened to those who defied Hitler.

One factor that could hardly be denied, even by the critics, was that an Expeditionary Force in Greece, however foolhardy it might be from a military point of view, would do much to convince the United States that Britain was still a contender worth backing in the fight against Germany and her reluctant ally, Italy.

Several accounts of what happened during the momentous conference held at Tatoi Palace on 22 February have been recorded by British sources, but we have only one Greek account, that kept by the C-in-C, General Papagos, which he published after the war. It is clear that Koryzis indicated that he was resigned to accepting decisions affecting the fate of his country, even if those were against his own judgement. He reminded the British that, 'To send an insufficient force might be worse than nothing at all', so that Eden's promise of 100,000 men was accepted by the new Greek Prime Minister with grave misgivings. British intervention in Greece now became a fact and, as a result, in the Western Desert General O'Connor's advance was stopped and his magnificent army disbanded. Churchill summed up the implications of such a decision when he sent an instruction to Eden: 'It is our duty to fight, and if need be, suffer with Greece.' The die was cast.

However, by this time Eden had become enthusiastic for the venture, sharing Churchill's view that, 'To stand idly by and see Germany win a victory over Greece, probably a bloodless one at that, seems the worst of all courses.' We can see that their reasons were political rather than military but it is true that Britain would have lost the respect of the neutrals, and probably the practical goodwill of the United States, at a time when the Lease-Lend Bill was under discussion, if she had not kept her promise to Greece.

Another gravely worried man was the Australian Prime Minister, Robert Menzies, who had been told that more than 17,000 of the troops offered to Greece would be Australian, with a further 16,000 New Zealanders joining them in an Anzac Corps. When he asked the British War Cabinet if they felt that the enterprise had a substantial chance of success, Churchill's reply was equivocal, even if it struck at the heart of the matter when he included the statement: 'If we forsook Greece, it would have a bad effect in the United States.' After three days of deliberations, Menzies and his advisers reluctantly agreed, while insisting on one condition: a contingency plan was to be drawn up to ensure that evacuation (if it became necessary) could be successfully undertaken. Even then, the officer who was to command the Australian and New Zealand troops, General Sir Thomas Blamey, was most unhappy about the immediate future. In a message to the Australian Government, Blamey signalled that, 'It was a military operation extremely hazardous in view of disparity between opposing forces and training.'

Once it was learnt that a final decision had been made in Athens, on 7 March there was a consternation among Churchill's planners in Whitehall. Major General Sir John Kennedy, Director of Operations, saw it as a major error, 'a very wrong policy ... another Winston lunacy'; while Lord Beaverbrook gave a soothsayer's warning: 'Remember three words – Gallipoli – Narvik – Dunkirk.' In contrast, the effect the decision had on America was certainly favourable, although the risks being taken were well understood. Admiral Stark minuted that, 'This has so weakened the British Army in Egypt that the Germans will have little difficulty in regaining all of Libya.' To Stark's minute, the Chief of Navy's War Plans, Rear-Admiral Turner, replied that, 'Abandoning Greece to its fate could have been an action so base and immoral – reinforcing them was necessary, regardless of its influence on the future of Britain.' Admiral Turner's minute was an accurate reflection of British motives in pressing military assistance on the reluctant Greek Government.

Discussions between the British and Greek military commanders were complicated by their ignorance of Yugoslav intentions. For historical reasons the Greek defensive positions had been constructed with Bulgaria in mind as the potential enemy, so that the Metaxas Line, a defence system of fortresses, covered the Greek-Bulgarian border of eastern Macedonia and Thrace but did not extend to the Greek-Yugoslav border of western Macedonia. If Germany violated Yugoslav neutrality, or if the Yugoslavs formed an alliance with Germany or allowed her troops to pass unmolested through their own territory, the unfortified Greek-Yugoslav frontier would have to be held by the Allies – particularly to the north of Florina, where a defile through the mountainous border country provided an entrance known as the Monastir Gap.

Unfortunately for the British, throughout the period of planning General Papagos was strongly influenced in his decisions by the desirability of having Yugoslavia fighting alongside Greece. Papagos was much concerned to defend the Metaxas Line, which was about a hundred miles in length, running along part of the Greek-Bulgarian border from the Beles mountains near Dojran to the mouth of the River Nestos, with isolated fortresses to the east in Thrace. There was another defence line which ran behind the first along the River Strimon but both these positions lacked depth and, even if they were held, in any strength whatever, the Bulgarian airfields were only fifty to a hundred miles away from Salonika, the second city of Greece and a port without any anti-aircraft defences, which could be bombed into uselessness within a matter of hours.

A much stronger position in northern Greece was the Aliakmon Line, some sixty miles in length, which ran from the mouth of the river of that name, near Mount Olympus, across to Veroia and on to the Yugoslav border. Mountain barriers, crossed by three defiles, provided a natural defence, and the position had the advantage of covering its supply line to southern Greece, as well as giving excellent observation over the open Macedonian plain. If Yugoslavia did not join the Allies, the Aliakmon Line offered the best chance of resisting the Germans, provided that Yugoslavia denied passage to the Wehrmacht. However, if the Germans violated

Yugoslavian territory, this line was vulnerable as it could be outflanked, thereby completely exposing the Greek Army in Epirus.

During the long discussions held at the royal palace at Tatoi, Yugoslavia's future intentions were unknown to British and Greeks alike and held the key to the puzzle. Papagos was on the horns of a dilemma. If he withdrew the bulk of his army at once to the Aliakmon Line, such a move would destroy any chance of Yugoslav intervention on the Allied side, especially after the key port of Salonika had been abandoned. The alternative was to risk waiting until the last moment in the hope that the Yugoslavs would join the Allies. General Papagos decided to take the latter course. He and his top advisers also appreciated that their small army could not oppose two major Axis Powers at the same time, so that in the event of a German invasion the main Greek effort would continue to be exerted on the Albanian front. No matter how the situation developed, the Greek Army should not jeopardize its position as victor against the Italians. National pride dictated this – even if it contravened normal military strategy as seen by the British commanders at the time.

The British felt that such a plan invited disaster unless the Yugoslavs decided to co-operate and resist the Germans. From the British records available of the Tatoi discussions, supported to some extent by Papagos' *The Germans' Attack on Greece*, it seems clear that Eden and Papagos had different recollections of what they thought had been agreed during their discussions; the misunderstanding persisted to the last, even into the published memoirs of both men. Wavell and Dill, too, were under the impression that the Greek C-in-C would begin withdrawing some of his troops from eastern Macedonia to join the BEF once it had moved up to the Aliakmon position after disembarking at Piraeus. It was only on 2 March, when members of the British mission returned once more to Athens, that they learnt the disturbing news that the Greeks had not begun to withdraw troops in any substantial numbers to the Aliakmon Line. Papagos insisted that the earlier agreement was that a final decision would be taken only after both Governments had discovered what the Yugoslavs intended doing. As no reply to Eden's telegram to Belgrade had been received (it had gone to Ankara not

Athens), Papagos had not ordered troop movements to the Aliakmon. Moreover, he said, it was now too late to do so because the Greek units might be caught on the move by the Germans. He also stressed the damaging effect on military and civilian morale if large areas of the country were evacuated and left undefended. In his post-war book, Papagos commented on this aspect: 'This only goes to show once again that in wars involving coalitions, political considerations were frequently opposed to those of a purely military nature and that they even over-ride them.'

It is of interest that the monacled, French-speaking Major-General Heywood, the British Liaison Officer in Greece, supported Papagos' account of the agreement – or disagreement – that followed. (Heywood took the minutes at the meeting at Tatoi.)

Once more Wavell was hurriedly summoned from Cairo, another round of discussions began and finally, under the immediate threat of a German invasion, agreement was reached. This time the Greek and British delegates signed a statement setting out their final decisions. That Wavell did not know about the failure of the Greeks to begin moving units to the Aliakmon Line can be explained by the fact that Major-General Heywood and his small team of liaison officers were still subject to niggling restrictions on travel that from the start had been imposed upon them. Communications in Greece during this era also made travel slow and difficult, whether by road or rail.

In accordance with the new agreement, the BEF would man the Aliakmon Line with the Greek contribution to the main defensive position being some twenty-three battalions, instead of the thirty-five originally sought. Such a shortfall left General Wilson with little time to adapt to a much more difficult predicament. The Anglo-Greek discussions had not been easy, and it was reported that Papagos was unaccommodating and, at times, defeatist. Eden went further when he said the allocation of Greek soldiers to fight alongside the British against the Germans had been achieved 'by a process which at times painfully resembled the haggling of an Oriental bazaar'.

The truth was that the Greek Government still felt they were being pushed into a situation not completely of their own choosing. On the other hand, the British suspected that overtures had been made to the Germans by one or two senior officers of the Greek Army in an attempt to avoid military intervention by Germany. On 12 March such an unofficial offer had been passed to Berlin which caused the German Foreign Secretary, von Ribbentrop, to draft the following telegram: 'The Greek Government, which is at war with our Allies ... and is drawing more and more English forces into its country, is mistaken if it assumes that it can pass on to us the responsibility for taking the initiative in terminating the conflict.' In the event, the telegram was not sent because by that time the British Expeditionary Force had begun disembarking in Greece in comparatively large numbers.

Later in 1941, the Germans were to claim that they had been forced to attack Greece in order to expel the British but after the war Papagos refuted that statement as being propaganda, a mere excuse for their invasion. He said that the two real reasons for the German assault were: one, they needed to secure and protect their right flank before launching their attack on the Soviet Union and, two, it was essential to seize the southern Balkans so that they could command the eastern end of the Mediterranean, vital for any future thrust against British interests in Egypt and elsewhere in the Middle East.

Both British and Greeks may have been suspicious about each other's intentions but now there was to be no turning back, even though in London some of Churchill's advisers continued to be against the expedition. In contrast, the American Secretary of State, Sumner Welles, thought it 'one of the wisest decisions taken during the War'. Be that as it may, the long-serving American Ambassador in Athens, Lincoln MacVeagh, predicted to his President that, 'The best that the Allies can look forward to is a succession of Thermopylaes ... with the Luftwaffe taking the place of the Persian arrows, darkening the sun, and British tenacity and Greek devotion would fight in the shades.' When Eden reported back to London that British forces were about to be engaged in operations more hazardous than it had appeared a week before, the War Cabinet became more reluctant than ever to support a campaign that had now little or no chance.

On 5 March, when most of his Cabinet stated they were against the venture, Churchill read out a telegram from the British Ambassador in Athens, Sir Michael Palairet, which ended with the following words: 'How can we possibly abandon the King of Greece after the assurance given him? This seems to be quite unthinkable. We should be pilloried by the Greeks and the world in general as going back on our word.' Such a prediction could not be dismissed lightly, especially by the emotional, chivalrous Winston Churchill.

Meanwhile the Greek war with the Italians continued unabated. On 3 March the Italian Air Force added to its unsavoury reputation when, in the words of Laird Archer: 'Larissa, Queen of the Thessaly Plain, which had been the heaviest bombed of all Greek towns because of the British air base nearby, was shaken to the ground by an earthquake at dawn. And today the Blackshirts have again bombed the city.'

Such uncivilized behaviour by the Italians was not to be forgotten or forgiven by the Greek people. Even when the Italians held the whip hand, occupying much of the country conquered by their German partners, the majority of the Greek people treated them with open contempt and disdain.

2 A Military Disaster

'There is not a fiercer hell than the failure in a great
object.'

John Keats

General Maitland Wilson, Commander of the Expeditionary
Force in Greece, arrived in Athens on 4 March. In a few
weeks he and his staff had to collect information which
should have been collated immediately after the British
guarantee to Greece had been given. An intelligence
organization had to be quickly established while Wilson's
senior administrative officer, Brigadier G.S. Brunskill, made
a rapid survey of port, road and rail facilities. The Greek
railway system was totally inadequate for wartime needs; for
example, the country's main line between Athens and
Salonika was a single track only. The road from Athens to
Florina – the country's main highway – was in many places
not wide enough for two vehicles to pass.

In spite of these difficulties, the British established an
advance base at Larissa where supplies for sixty days were
assembled. Forward depots were sited at Livadhion, Servia,
Kozani, Veroia, Edhessa and Amindaion, and by the end of
the first week in April 14,000 tons of engineer stores,
supplies of petrols and lubricants sufficient for thirty-eight
days, and ordnance stores for twenty days, had been
unloaded and moved up to the forward bases. During all this
period the German Legation continued to send reports back
to Berlin. Compton Mackenzie was to comment later: 'Their
Military Attaché, who spoke faultless English, did the rounds
of the cafés talking to the British soldiers, asking them their
unit etc.'

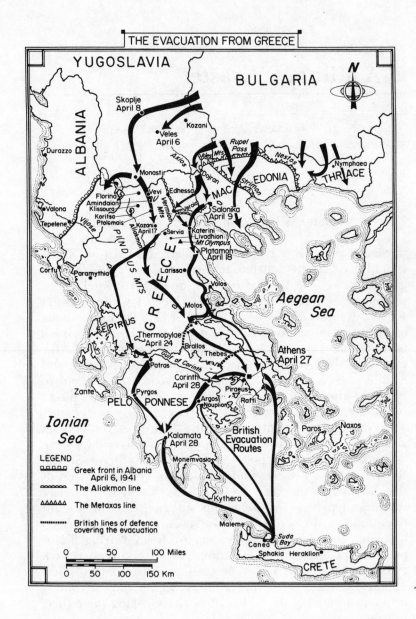

YUGOSLAVIA

BULGARIA

N

ALBANIA

Durazzo

Skoplje
April 8

Veles
April 6

Kozani

Monastir

Florina
Amindaion
Klissoura
Koritsa
Ptolemais

Vevi

Edhessa

Vermion Mts

Rupel
Pass

Valona

Tepelene

Viose

PINDUS MTS

Kozani
April 17

Aliakmon

Neraidha

Axios

Dojran

Salonika
April 9

Vslesa Mts

Nestos

Strumon

MACEDONIA

THRACE

Nymphaea

Corfu

Paramythia

Servia

GREECE

Katerini
Livadhion
Mt Olympus
Platamon
April 18

Larissa

Volos

EPIRUS

Molos

Aegean
Sea

Thermopylae
April 24

Brallos

Thebes

Athens
April 27

Patras

Gulf of Corinth

Corinth
April 28

Piraeus

Rafti

Zante

Pyrgos

PELOPONNESE

Argost
Nauplion

Ionian
Sea

Paros

Naxos

LEGEND

Kalamata
April 28

Monemvasia

British
Evacuation
Routes

Greek front in Albania
April 6, 1941

The Aliakmon line

The Metaxas line

British lines of defence
covering the evacuation

Kythera

Maleme

Suda
Bay

Canea

Sphakia Heraklion

CRETE

0   50   100 Miles

0   50   100   150 Km

An ex-sapper, D.W. Luckett, recalls how HMS *Bonad-venture*'s disembarkation was being scrutinized: 'We noticed that two large black Mercedes cars had been drawn up some little way off and the occupants were watching our arrival. One was a white-haired individual and rumour had it was von Papen, the German Ambassador. Be that as it may, the street in which the German Embassy was situated was placed "Out of Bounds" to all ranks.'

Many observers reported that the atmosphere in Athens was invigorating: grim, yes, but full of pride and confidence. The Greeks had taken heart again after initial misgivings – the new invader, when he came, would be beaten like the first.

The novelist Olivia Manning wrote that, 'When the first lorry loads of British troops, and the first tanks with their desert markings arrived in Athens, there was some dismay in the city but the Greek tradition of '*philoxenia*' (friendship towards a stranger) overcame early doubts.' Wherever the British troops went, some in overcrowded railway wagons, some in army trucks through the beautiful Greek country-side, the people welcomed them with smiles and gifts. Olivia Manning singled out the Australians: 'A wild lot, who are popular with the Greeks who admire their uninhibited behaviour'. During those few days before the Germans struck, the Greek people alternated between heady optimism and a fatalistic despair that shortly their country was going to be overrun by the two Axis Powers.

Not everyone radiated optimism, however. When WO 1. Arthur Macey, serving with 1st Armoured Brigade's armoured workshop, landed at Piraeus from the cruiser, HMS *Bonadventure*, naval ratings shouted out: 'We'll be back to pick you up!' Memories of Dunkirk were still fresh in the minds of sailors and soldiers alike. Within a matter of days, Arthur Macey was to be evacuated from Greece but, instead of reaching the safety of Alexandria, the ship on which he was travelling was hit by dive-bombers and had to limp into Crete's Suda Bay. His respite on that island was to be a short one – as it was for thousands of Allied servicemen.

On paper, the W Group, as the Allied Armies on the Aliakmon Line were known, was to consist of just over seven divisions: three Greek, four British and the Polish Brigade.

However, the Aliakmon was never held in such strength because Papagos continued to hope that Yugoslavia would join the Allies. Once again, he urged General Wilson to consider moving forward and defending the Metaxas Line. Wilson refused but when the 1st Armoured Brigade (less one tank regiment) arrived in the first convoy, it was deployed well forward of the Aliakmon position to act as a delaying force between the rivers Axios and Aliakmon.

Organizing the defence of the Aliakmon Line was not helped by the piecemeal arrival of the British convoys at Piraeus. By early April some troops had dug in, others had not yet reached the forward positions, while others were still in Egypt. For example: on 5 April the experienced 6th Australian Division had one brigade (the 16th) in the forward area, with two battalions of its 19th Brigade still moving up from Piraeus, while its headquarters staff sailed next day, and the 17th Brigade following five days after that. Wintry conditions still prevailed in northern Greece, and it was bitterly cold, even on low ground, so that many of the Dominion troops now saw snow for the first time.

When the Greek 19th Division was moved forward to the Axios Plain, the New Zealand Division had the difficult task of holding a sector of over 23,000 yards. The Australian 6th Division stood in the Servia Pass in the valley of the central Aliakmon, with its 16th Brigade ready to move up to Veroia in support of the Greek 12th Division in the mountains nearby. One regiment of the Greek 12th Division was on the left flank of the New Zealanders in the Pieria Mountains while the 20th Greek Division was near Edhessa in the Viermion Mountains to the north.

On the map the dispositions appeared sound and logical but after the British had made contact with their Greek comrades, the weakness of their allies became apparent. The number of divisions gave no indication either of their actual manpower or of the state of their equipment and transport available. Brigadier Charrington, commanding the 1st Armoured Brigade, found that the 19th Greek Division, reputedly a mobile formation, had 'no possible prospect of fighting as a mobile force with their few bren-carriers, motor cycles and small cars'. The Greeks had shown themselves to be courageous and stubborn fighters in the mountains against the Italians but it was obvious to British observers that they could not fight and hold a well-equipped enemy in a war of movement. They possessed few field or medium guns, and their only anti-tank guns were those captured from the Italians. Moreover, as mentioned before, the Albanian front had sucked in nearly all the reserve manpower and available equipment the Greek Army possessed. It was a situation which did not augur well for the struggle with the powerful and well-equipped Germans which was about to begin.

Once the BEF began arriving on Greek soil, D'Albiac reorganized his small force into three wings. He still had to provide air support for the Western Greek Macedonian Army (fifteen divisions) which was being attacked with great ferocity in the Albanian mountains. For this purpose, the RAF western wing consisted of one bomber and one Gladiator fighter squadron. For the Macedonian front, the eastern wing was to operate in support of the Greek Eastern Macedonian Army (three divisions and the equivalent of two brigades) and was based on improvised airstrips near Larissa which were still soft with rain. The third wing, consisting of one bomber and one fighter squadron, together with an Army co-operation squadron, was based at airfields near Athens, and when a few Swordfish aircraft of the Fleet Air Arm arrived in March, these were sent to Paramythia. The total British air strength based on Greek soil amounted to some eighty aircraft of varying vintage. Against this, the Luftwaffe had 400 bombers and 380 fighters and reconnaissance aircraft readily available, while their Italian allies had some 300 planes operating in the Albanian sector. D'Albiac's problems were compounded by the fact that communications between the wings were often unreliable, so that for a variety of reasons his airmen would face insuperable odds when the Germans attacked – and that now seemed inevitable.

After the British had decided that the expedition to Greece had to take priority over the Desert Campaign, on 27 March Rommel struck and within hours his opponents were falling back in disorder and in places without a fight, as fast as the Italians had when General O'Connor swept forward earlier in the year. Back in London, Winston Churchill did not appreciate how depleted the Desert Army had become and in disbelief that disaster threatened cabled Wavell: 'I presume

you are only waiting for the tortoise to stick his head out far
enough before chopping it off.' However, the retreat became
a rout so that the head of the tortoise was not chopped off,
although on the left flank of the Afrika Korp's advance the
garrison of Tobruk stood firm and, by so doing, upset
Hitler's long-term plans for capturing Cairo and the Suez
Canal.

While this was going on, another chapter in the Balkan
tragedy was being enacted in Belgrade. On 25 March Prince
Paul, Regent of Yugoslavia, and his ministers took the
decision to align their country with the Axis powers by
signing a Tripartite Pact on that day. The signing of such a
pact had seemed inevitable ever since a chastened prince had
come back, on 5 March, from a meeting with Hitler at the
Berghof. On his return Prince Paul had jibbed and called a
council meeting but in truth there was little for them to
discuss. The Allies were unable to promise any military or
material help, only calls to resist. But once the pact became
public knowledge, a group of young service officers, with the
encouragement of British diplomats and agents (Julian
Amery took an active part), led a popular uprising to
overthrow the Government. The Council of Regency was
dissolved, and the chief Cabinet ministers were arrested:
Prince Paul went into exile, and seventeen-year-old King
Peter's accession was proclaimed on 27 March. The
celebrations were to be short-lived, because unfortunately
there was no time to organize the country to meet the storm
that was about to break, the revenge of an angry dictator
whose original plans had been rebuffed and thwarted.

While the news had been greeted with acclaim in London,
Hitler, shaking with rage, declared he would clean up the
Balkans 'good and proper'. His decision to destroy
Yugoslavia caused rapid changes to be made in the overall
German strategy in the Balkans. The invasion of Yugoslavia
was delegated to Field Marshal von Weichs, in command of
II Army, which was strengthened by transferring formations
from List's XII Army. In Greece, the news of the Yugoslavian
change of heart came too late for Papagos to persuade
General Wilson to move any formations forward to the
Metaxas Line, some 125 miles away. With a German attack
now imminent, Wilson knew that the new defence line would

be overrun before the Anglo-Greek force could reach the area and dig itself in. Greece would be on her own because against Yugoslavia, which had not yet mobilized, twenty-seven German divisions, seven of them armoured, would strike simultaneously from Austria, Hungary, Romania and Bulgaria.

For the invasion of Greece, General List had under his command three corps, consisting of six infantry, three motorized and two tank divisions, with some 200 tanks, and a further two divisions in reserve. Hitler had wanted Operation Marita to begin on 1 April but heavy rain swamped the Bulgarian airfields and List did not consider the weather good enough to ensure maximum support from the Luftwaffe until 6 April. At 05.15 hours on that day, the German XII Army began its attack on Greece. It was Palm Sunday. Meanwhile over Belgrade the Luftwaffe began bombing the naked, defenceless city. More than 1,500 tons of bombs rained down, with sticks of incendiaries following and turning the centre into an inferno. Although the first raid lasted barely an hour, an even more severe one followed at 11 a.m. Thereafter, for almost seventy-two hours, waves of bombers moved back and forth across Belgrade until 10,000 buildings had toppled and over 17,000 civilians lay dead among the ruins.

Hitler had taken his revenge. The Yugoslav *coup*, coming as unexpectedly as a thunderclap in winter, had forced him to change his plans at the last moment. As always, the key to his Blitzkrieg against Yugoslavia was unremitting speed. The six separate Serbo-Croat armies, although totalling about a million men, were unco-ordinated and went into battle against the Wehrmacht with primitive equipment and transport that often depended on ox-carts. By the morning of 12 April, the swastika flew once more over the German Legation in the rubble that was once Belgrade. The nation's will to resist had gone and there was no alternative but to surrender.

Palm Sunday in Athens was a fine morning. The majority of Athenians had feared there would be an air raid on their city, but it did not come – which was just as well, because the streets were crowded with excited people, behaving as if there had been another victory. After dark there was an air

raid on Piraeus but Athens itself was untouched. From the
city, the sky over Piraeus was aglow until, in the small hours
of the morning, a gigantic explosion, which flung people out
of bed, was followed by a series of tremendous rever-
berations.

When morning came, it was learnt that a merchant ship,
carrying a cargo of TNT, had exploded. The port of Piraeus
had been devastated by the explosion of the munitions ship
Glen Fraser. The ship should have been unloaded on Sunday
morning but through inefficiency it had been left with its
dangerous cargo. At the time there were rumours of
sabotage but post-war records confirm that at 9 p.m. on the
night of 6 April a low-level attack by German bombers hit the
ship and caused the terrific explosion, which smashed
windows seven miles away and closed down the entire port
for ten days. Eleven ships, totalling 41,489 tons, were lost.
The port was in ruins; even after urgent repair had been
effected, no more than five out of its twelve berths were
brought back into operation. Admiral Cunningham called it
'a shattering blow', for the raid deprived the Allies of their
only well-equipped port through which supplies to W Group
could be passed. The accuracy of the Luftwaffe raid was
attributed later to the presence of German agents in Piraeus
who had been allowed to watch convoys unloading and thus
knew the nature of the *Glen Fraser*'s cargo.

A small measure of consolation came when it was
announced that, on the same night, six Wellingtons from No
37 Squadron RAF had destroyed an ammunition train and
railway installations at Sofia, while Blenheims of No 84
Squadron had damaged railway equipment further south;
brave gestures both, which were not to be repeated when the
war swirled swiftly into Greek territory, and the Luftwaffe
ruled the skies by sheer weight of numbers.

Next day, in western Thrace, stubborn Greek resistance
against vastly superior forces was finally overcome when,
among other positions, the fort at Nymphaea was destroyed
by a concerted attack of dive-bombers and flame-throwers,
used by German infantry. Throughout the day the Luftwaffe
kept up a constant attack against the Greek units manning a
series of forts along the Metaxas Line. The defenders did not
give in without fierce resistance, and typical of the struggle

was the action at Kelkayia, which was held by men from the Greek 18th Infantry Division. Throughout the day the Germans attacked again and again, only to be met with counter-attacks by Greek soldiers outside the fort which were twice successful. Severe losses were inflicted on the attackers until the fort fell on the following day – but only after the Germans had brought up special equipment that manufactured thick smoke which, in conjunction with flame-throwers, brought Greek resistance to an end. Towards noon on the 7th, the garrison was compelled to surrender, but the high reputation of the Greek Armed Forces had been upheld by its courage. The threat to Salonika intensified as the Germans turned the Metaxas Line until on 8 April the Greek Army in eastern Macedonia was forced to capitulate. Then it was merely a question of hours before the Germans reached Salonika to occupy the city, something that had been inevitable once the Yugoslav Southern Army had withdrawn and left the Greek flank fully exposed. German armour drove into the silent city of Salonika on 9 April.

During this time, the citizens of Athens were kept in ignorance of the true state of affairs at the front because, as a precaution against panic, all communiqués said next to nothing, although wild rumours seeped back and the population knew that the Germans were breaking through with speed. So far, W Group had not been in contact with the Germans but news coming out of Yugoslavia indicated that Skopje had fallen to the German IX Armoured Brigade which was advancing southwards. As a consequence, Wilson made preparations to modify the Aliakmon Line and also had in mind a second defensive position across Greece further south, which he hoped would include Greek troops withdrawn from the Albanian front. Meanwhile, in front of the BEF, the ill-equipped Greek 19th Motorized Division was unable to prevent the swift advance of German armour. Light tanks of the British 4th Hussars (1st Armoured Brigade) on the west of the River Axios escorted demolition parties which blew up road and rail bridges over the river and withdrew, under General Wilson's orders, through the Edhessa and Veroi Gaps to Kozani. Here they joined the blocking force to defend the Vevi Gap.

With the fall of Salonika and the immediate threat to W

Group, General Papagos, who during the previous day had
ordered an offensive on the Albanian front in conjunction
with Yugoslav forces, now called off the attack. The Greek
Army in Albania was in danger of being cut off by the
German Motorized Group, moving towards the Monastir
Gap.

Formal capitulation of Greek Forces in east Macedonia was
negotiated between the German commander of II Armoured
Division and General Bakopoulos, commander of the
Eastern Macedonian Army. As a result, there was no
alternative but to begin redeploying W Force if it was to avoid
being cut off without any chance of being evacuated. Papagos
was consulted and agreed to a new line of defence which was
to run, initially, from the Aliakmon-Olympus position on the
right flank, across to the south of Servia and then up to
Klissoura. A more permanent line further south would be
from Servia along the River Venetikos, thence across the
Pindus range to the Adriatic. By adopting this defensive
position, the Greeks would have to give up all the territorial
gains they had won in Albania, as well as the whole of
Macedonia. Up to that moment, Papagos had refused to
withdraw units from their positions, fearing that such a
withdrawal would cause a collapse of morale. By delaying
such a decision, half the army in Thrace had been lost
already and the other half cut off in Albania. In a matter of
hours, discipline and cohesion disintegrated as men drifted
away or sought refuge in remote villages.

The main point of entry into Greece from Yugoslavia is at
its narrowest at Vevi, where the road winds through a pass.
In the pass, it was hoped that well-sited guns, supported by
infantry machine-gunners, would hold up the leading
German column and thus allow the bulk of the Anglo-Greek
force time to get back to the new defence line, where it had
been anticipated that some units from the army in Albania
would be able to come back and join them. For such a reason,
it was vital the Germans should be denied access to the pass
for as long as possible.

During 8 April, forward tank patrols near the bridges fired
on the leading elements of the German columns, then blew
the demolition charges and retired. The headlong rush of
the Germans was slowed down, and the advance became

more cautious, thus giving General Wilson valuable time to create as orderly a defence as was possible under the circumstances. He already had the 19th Australian Brigade with some units of 1st Armoured Brigade under command (Mackay Force) in the Monastir area, and during the night of 8-9 April he added a company of New Zealand machine-gunners, as well as bringing in the remaining tanks and anti-tank guns. In addition, the newly arrived 17th Australian Brigade, which had been struggling up the narrow, jammed road from Athens, was sent for in a hurry.

The 17th Brigade had already spent seven gruelling days in bitter weather without proper rest or a hot meal. Early on 10 April one battalion was detached and, by forced marches through the mountains, managed to reach Vevi Pass just before darkness fell. The battalion was directed to a dangerous, exposed position on the forward slope and told to dig in, an order that was virtually impossible as the rocky ground was frozen hard. With a German attack at first light thought likely, the Aussies worked hard to scrape holes or shallow trenches. The temperature continued to drop, and some men collapsed with exhaustion and frost-bite.

The tank regiments and the Northumberland Hussars (anti-tank gunners of the 1st Armoured Brigade) formed the reserve, with the Royal Horse Artillery coming up in support with their 25-pounders. The small force held some twelve miles of mountainous country. Their orders were simple: the pass had to be denied to the Germans for at least two, probably three, days.

At about midnight, the infantry on the forward slopes heard noises and movement ahead and, according to the Australian Official History, voices shouted to them: 'All right – friendly patrol here.' 'Put that gun down, Steve. It's only me.' These reassurances had come from specially trained SS men who had infiltrated between the widely spaced patrols. By such a trick the Germans captured a number of prisoners and ensured that the defenders went without much sleep thereafter. The snow, driving sleet and bitterly cold wind made life miserable for men who had come straight from the Desert, with only greatcoats and one blanket each to sustain them.

Next morning, 11 April, the weather was wild, with the

wind whipping the snow and mist into a screen which reduced visibility to less than a hundred yards. Taking advantage of this, German tanks moved forward but they were stopped when two were blown up in a minefield. A little time later, some German 105mm guns arrived and shelled the forward slopes where the Australian anti-tank gunners and infantry had tried to find cover. Just before the winter light failed, two battalions of German infantry attacked astride the road, only for accurate artillery fire to stop them. After dusk they tried again and got to within 300 yards of the forward Australian line, where they dug in during the hours of darkness. Once again they attempted the ruse of the night before, only to find that the Australians were not to be deceived twice.

During the following day it was thought that German tanks were moving around the flank, and a squadron from the 3rd Royal Tank Regiment was sent to counter this threat. R.J. (Bob) Crisp, the South African Test cricketer who was one of the troop officers, described what happened in *The Gods Were Neutral*: 'Sleet battered my eyelids as the tank ploughed through cultivated mud and I ordered tank commanders not to attempt any turns till they were on firm ground. The squadron nevertheless left behind a trail of broken-down tanks and when, after a freezing night, news came that the enemy armour report had been a false alarm, and we went back, we counted the toll of the purposeless advance. Five tanks were lying with hopelessly broken tracks, two more had fractured pistons. There were no more spare parts, so the tanks were destroyed.' 3 RTR had been sent to Egypt with new 1937-model tanks (A13s) but, on being detailed to go to Greece, were ordered to exchange their new tanks for A10s – slower 1935-model cruisers – veterans which already had just about worn out their tracks in the desert. All fifty-two of these A10s were to be left in Greece, fifty-one having broken down and only one, a victim in battle, knocked out by the Germans.

S.S.M. Aris (no relation to the ELAS leader due to appear later), who served in the same regiment as Major R.J. Crisp, has thrown more light on those infamous tank tracks. According to him, the new ones held in the Ordnance Depot, Port Said, were found to be made of cast iron instead of steel.

Proving useless, the A10s of 3 RTR were refitted with the old
and much-worn tracks before embarking for Piraeus. Aris
also mentioned that there was only one local map with each
squadron – not the best way to conduct armed warfare
against a mobile enemy!

The Australians and their supporting units were to hold
the Vevi Pass for nearly three days, until on 12 April sheer
weight of numbers and complete exhaustion defeated them.
The position would have been overrun before that had it not
been for the gunners of the Royal Horse Artillery, who stood
firm, firing over open sights until the German tanks and
infantry were about 400 yards away. Then they withdrew,
bringing all their guns out with them. Their cool gallantry
had saved the day.

It had been a costly stand and all three Australian
battalions were badly mauled, with many men being taken
prisoner. As the result of a planned but sudden local
withdrawal, a whole company of the Australian 2/8th
Battalion was captured by the SS on the Sotor Ridge, in the
area of the pass. Their captors marched the Australians
forward during the night, only to abandon them in a field in
front of the British sector. The cold-blooded SS intended
that the Australians should act as a shield in the event of a
British counter-attack. Inadvertently the British did open
fire at the group, killing and wounding several Australians.

Without wireless sets at infantry company level during this
campaign, it was not surprising that in the fog of war, and
especially during the most difficult of military operations, a
withdrawal by night, sub units and individuals failed to
receive orders and were left behind on more than one
occasion.

Following the collapse of Yugoslavia and the fall of
Salonika, General Wilson decided that the long Aliakmon
defensive Line could no longer be held. Like Leondidas of
Sparta before him, he felt that the only chance of a
prolonged stand was at Thermopylae, some hundred miles
back to the south. If the retreat was to be an orderly one and
not a rout, it required a series of determined rearguards to
hold each position until the withdrawing troops were
through, and then to slam the door, ready to move further
back. Even without German pressure from the ground and

even more important from the air, it was asking a lot, especially from the Anzac soldiers, who had covered many miles already over difficult country: one Australian battalion was defeated by sheer exhaustion and began to disintegrate.

The Australians on the Veroia Pass had to move over thirty miles, scaling the 3,000-foot Imathia range before descending into the Aliakmon Valley and facing yet another climb. The passes in and around Mount Olympus were to witness several stirring battles fought by rearguards, all attempting to hold up the German advance for as long as possible. One of these was just south of the small town of Ptolemais where the main road to the south crossed a dyke and then ran alongside a river and between two ridges – a natural ambuscade. Here the rearguard was the responsibility of the 4th Hussars, reinforced by a squadron of 3 RTR's cruiser tanks, two troops of Northumberland Hussars' anti-tank guns, two companies from the Rangers who had fought with distinction with Mackay Force, and the Royal Horse Artillery, still intact with their reliable 25-pounders.

The 4th Hussars had their pre-war light reconnaissance tanks, Mk VIBs, weighing only five tons and equipped with nothing but two machine-guns. In open battle they could be no match for the big German tanks, but the Hussars had a long history of dash and aggression, and they were to display those qualities on 13 April, after the last of the infantry had passed through their position. When the first German pursuers came in sight, the artillery fired off a barrage and withdrew, followed by the heavier tanks which passed through the screen of 4th Hussar tanks, who waited to make sure that all had gone through them.

Their delay was almost fatal, as it was an armoured division with artillery support that was leading the German advance and not infantry. The little reconnaissance tanks rushed back with shells bursting around them, and as soon as they were over the dyke, the bridge was blown. An officer of the Hussars described the scene thereafter: 'We get our first view of the enemy. It's not very different from our own – same pace, same intervals, but all armour and a great deal bigger. I count over 200 as they disappear into the dip where apparently they are concentrating. Then two tanks and a motor-cyclist come down the road to the blown bridge. As they reach it, everything opens up on them from our right, streams of tracer, anti-tank and machine-gun. The anti-tank shells just ricochet off the German tanks. The motor-cyclist dismounts and takes notes. More tracer opens up – the range is about 1,500 yards. The motor-cyclist remounts and rides quietly back. The tanks lumber after him. An impressive show.'

The commander of this rearguard, Colonel Lillington, had ordered his big guns to hold their fire to encourage the Germans to close up, and his plan worked. Not until the column of German armour was nose to tail down the road was the order given to fire. The Germans suffered heavily and their casualties were increased when six Blenheims, on their way to bomb the Monastir Gap, swept low and machine-gunned the column, to the enthusiastic cheers of the watching British. (The story of those six Blenheims of No 211 Squadron will be told later, on p. 54.)

The Germans appreciated that only a full-scale attack, supported by artillery and mortars, could blast a way through this small, determined rearguard under Colonel Lillington. Such an attack tried to find a way round the left flank, where it was engaged by two squadrons of the Hussars, supported by anti-tank guns, manned by the Northumberland Hussars. Once again the German heavy tanks were forced to withdraw. At 1900 hours, when it was learnt that all the retreating infantry had passed through Kozani, some sixteen miles to the south, the rearguard was given the order to disengage. While doing so at Ptolemais, there was another brisk action which involved a squadron of cruiser tanks of 3 RTR, reinforced by the Northumberland Hussars, and once again the Royal Horse Artillery fired over open sights. Fifteen German tanks were knocked out; the fighting was so fierce that the official German report of the action maintained that Ptolemais was held by a British armoured division. On a small scale, it had been a model action, in a campaign that was too often chaotic.

The respite gained was to be short-lived, and with IX Panzer Division pressing them hard and the Luftwaffe dominating the sky, units of the Expeditionary Force were forced to continue their retreat – otherwise they faced certain destruction. Vic West of the Rangers (King's Royal Rifle

Corps) wrote in his stirring account: 'Here was the Luftwaffe and for the rest of the campaign, they were never to leave us, ever-present, hovering about like evil, metal crows.' Those survivors who were in the retreat remember the succession of long, sleepless nights which sapped their endurance, together with the cold and hunger, all made doubly worse because they were going back and back.

With only eighty planes, of varying ages, available to face the Luftwaffe and the Italian Air Force, boasting a combined total of over 700 planes, D'Albiac's tiny force could do little to help as the crisis worsened. Despite the crippling odds, countless sorties were flown between the 9th and the 15th, even when the gallant few were badly outnumbered. On the first day of the German invasion, twelve Hurricanes had met twenty ME109s and shot down five of them without losing a plane. Bombing raids continued to be carried out by Blenheim and Wellington aircraft from Athens and Larissa, and because there were no specialist planes to help Army reconnaissance, Blenheims were used for such a role, even though their pilots had no previous training in appropriate techniques.

So to the story of the lost Squadron, the six Bristol Blenheims which flew on Easter Sunday, 13 April 1941, from Paramythia, not far from the Albanian border. Their story has been told by a surviving air-crew member of the Squadron, Flight Lieutenant J.B. Dunnet, at that time a nineteen-year-old sergeant observer with 211 Squadron, the most experienced of the Royal Air Force Bomber squadrons in the Middle East. Daily the squadron had flown on operational sorties over the River Kalamos, which in Greek mythology was the legendary River Styx, across which the boatman Charon ferried the souls of the dead. Around three o'clock on that fateful Easter Sunday, Dunnet watched the six Blenheims, loaded with mixed fragmentation and 250 lb bombs, climbing into the afternoon sky and setting course for the target – German troops and armoured fighting vehicles in the Florina area. In his words: 'We waited until the purple shadows descended into the Valley of Legends as Paramythia was known, and in the chill of the evening air, we all knew that our Squadron had crossed the Styx for the last time.'

In *The History of the World War II in the Middle East*, the record states briefly: 'On one mission, all six Blenheims of No 211 Squadron were shot down with the loss of the Squadron Commander and the Commander of the Western Wing.'

Forty years later a chance report in the magazine of the RAF Association led to Dunnet's long and patient investigation, including interviews with relatives of the dead air crew, and visits to northern Greece to talk to eye-witnesses who remembered seeing one or other of the Blenheims shot down. By using the latest computer techniques, it has been possible to recreate the last flight of this squadron.

It was these planes which caused the 4th Hussars to raise a cheer as, sweeping low, the Blenheims used their forward machine-guns and strafed the German columns. Minutes later, Messerschmitt 109 fighters from Jagdgeschwader 27 stalked the Blenheims and began attacking them. One by one the slow-moving aircraft were hit, set on fire or crashed. After the three rear Blenheims had been shot down, the fighters concentrated on the leading trio, and within five minutes the last of the gallant aircraft, flown by the commanding officer of the squadron, Squadron Leader Irvine, crashed near the small hamlet of Vigla. Of the two pilots who baled out, one was killed during the following day and the other died later in a mid-air collision. In 1979, as a result of the long, meticulous investigation carried out, the bodies of those airmen that could be found were laid to rest under headstones made of Italian marble in the Phaliron War Cemetery near Athens.

From 15 April onwards, the Luftwaffe switched its main effort against the few British planes that were still capable of flying. After ME109s destroyed some Hurricanes while they were taking off, it was decided that the dwindling air effort should be concentrated in the Athens area. Before the German invasion began, D'Albiac had considered that a general withdrawal from Albania in the Koritsa area would be expedient, but the Greek General Staff had refused on the grounds that it would upset the morale of their soldiers: when such a withdrawal was forced on them, it was too late. Reliant upon mule and bullock transport, the spirit of the Greek Army on the Albanian front collapsed and organization quickly disintegrated. There was a feeling of numb, weary resignation; after a long and terrible winter, the realization that the Germans had stabbed them in the back filled the soldiers with impotent rage.

In Athens there was to be no respite for the RAF with the whole weight of the Luftwaffe directed against the aerodromes there. The remaining Blenheims operated only at night before they were forced to be ferried back to Crete. On 20 April approximately 200 twin-engined Messerschmitt 110s and single-engined 109s attacked Athens, to be met by every single serviceable Hurricane left in Greece, a total of twelve aircraft.

One of those twelve gallant pilots was the author Roald Dahl, who has described his experiences in *Going Solo*. During the three days prior to 20 April, Dahl made eight sorties, on each occasion on his own, a single Hurricane against whatever the Luftwaffe sent against him. On 20 April, at ten o'clock in the morning, the dozen planes in formation flew over Athens, under the leadership of that great Middle East fighter ace Flight Lieutenant 'Pat' Pattle. With the sky suddenly filled with German fighters, it was to be every Hurricane pilot for himself and, in Roald Dahl's words, 'Wherever I looked I saw an endless blur of enemy fighters, whizzing towards me on every side.'

Five Hurricanes were shot down and the great 'Pat' Pattle met his end. The seven Hurricanes that survived were barely serviceable, but between them the original dozen had shot down twenty-two Messerschmitts.

Two days later the remaining Hurricanes were strafed at Argos so that only five planes survived to be flown to Crete. The surviving pilots, Roald Dahl among them, were flown to Egypt in a DH Rapide. They were, Dahl wrote, '... tremendously lucky, the odds were strongly against any of us coming out alive'.

In his subsequent report, Sir John D'Albiac stated that pilots were taking off in aircraft which had been riddled with bullets, and under any other circumstances they would not have been airworthy. He added that the courage of those men never failed, no matter how exhausted they were and despite flying against great odds.

While facing such a heavy onslaught, the Imperial Expeditionary Force had no air support during their last few days in Greece, which saw the Australians and New

Zealanders fighting side by side, reviving memories of their association as part of the famous Anzac Corps, twenty-six years after Gallipoli. During the night of 17-18 April, after the main body had withdrawn well to the south, the Anzac defenders of Servia, hidden by a thick cloud of fog, quietly left their positions. It was only next morning that the German patrols discovered that the pass was no longer held.

From 18 April onwards that was to be the story in Greece – small, gallant rearguards holding the German advance just long enough to allow the main body to retreat, until eventually there was nowhere else to go, as the front contracted in a radius around the Gulf of Corinth.

On 17 April Wavell flew into Athens to consider the possible necessity of an evacuation. He was accompanied by Rear-Admiral Baillie-Grohman, who was to be given that responsibility if the decision to evacuate was made. By this time Greek resistance on the Albanian front and in Epirus had virtually ceased. As a consequence, Wavell did not hesitate to cancel the sailing of the Polish Brigade and the Australian 7th Division, which meant that only 58,000 of the 100,000 troops originally promised by Eden had actually landed to participate in the short campaign. On 21 April the 140,000-strong Greek Army in Epirus surrendered – under suspicious circumstances as far as the Army Commander, General George Tsolakoglou, was concerned. Not long afterwards he was appointed the first collaborator Prime Minister under the Axis Occupation, and his name is one that has not been forgotten in Greece.

The Greeks' pride in their wonderful exploits against the Italians on the Albanian front – where Mussolini's forces lost 100,000 men – shone even in defeat, when they issued one of the last of their war communiqués, the 181st: 'It is satisfied that at the moment of the capitulation no Italian troops had succeeded in entering Greek territory but were kept in Albanian territory.' The Greek General Staff's obsession with hard-earned gains, won from the Italians, is one that was well understood throughout the country even in the throes of defeat. That Germany should have forced its soldiers to withdraw in face of the despised enemy, Italy, was an act no Greek could endure.

During those last days Papagos vacillated between

optimism and despair and seemed completely out of touch with his field commanders – which, with primitive communications and with the Luftwaffe in full control, was probably inevitable.

On 20 April Papagos told his King that continued resistance could only result in the complete devastation of Greece, and advised the immediate evacuation of the Imperial Expeditionary Force. By that time disaster after disaster had meant that such a resort was unavoidable. The collapse of Yugoslavia and the driving of a wedge between the Greek Army in Albania and the Anglo-Greek Forces, the surrender of the Army of the East, the disintegration of the Army of the Centre and finally, the suicide of Koryzis, the new Prime Minister, all added to the totality of defeat. Koryzis shot himself after he had heard about the true position of the Greek armies in Epirus. Their surrender, reported a British observer later, left the Greek soldiers in total confusion, thoroughly ashamed that they had been ordered to stop fighting when the British were still trying to save their country.

The sudden switch from trying to get men and supplies forward to the Expeditionary Force to ensuring their evacuation added to the bewilderment of the citizens of Athens. Olivia Manning wryly commented; 'As for the British Forces, it seems that they had scarcely reached the front before they were on their way back again.' Two or three days later another observer noted that a British overnight camp had been set up and was the scene of 'a remarkable come and get it folks' demonstration'. The Anzacs opened up stores to the poor, distributing blankets and other equipment while scores of small boys began stripping trucks after their tyres had been removed by the troops. Also coming back in droves were haggard Greek soldiers who had returned after their capitulation in Epirus, in tattered uniforms and asking for food. 'These are the victorious heroes who a few weeks ago were greeted with bands and banners but now there isn't even an organization to supply them with cigarettes and coffee,' commented Laird Archer.

Once the decision had been made to evacuate the Expeditionary Force, nine days were originally allocated for the operation, but the worsening military situation made it necessary to reduce this to five. The British Mediterranean Fleet, on its way back from bombarding Tripoli, was not expected in Alexandria until the day before the evacuation was to begin – and Alexandria is some 600 miles from Greece. As a result, it was decided to use not battleships but destroyers to carry the soldiers. Small craft were collected from every available source, and a force of seven cruisers, twenty destroyers, nineteen troopships and two infantry assault ships, with their own powered landing craft, was duly assembled. On 22 April the Joint Planning Staff went to Crete, and details were worked out with the Navy planners. Techniques and lessons learnt the hard way at Dunkirk were to be put into operation. At the same time, the German propaganda machine was boasting that not only were the British facing another Dunkirk but this time few would escape from the shores of Greece.

For the British, the biggest handicap, compared with Dunkirk, was the fact that the Luftwaffe had complete supremacy in the skies over Greece – over Dunkirk, the RAF had kept the air clear and thus protected, to a large extent, the armada of large and small ships as they sailed back to safety in Britain. As a consequence, the decision was made to use six beaches as far to the south as possible, which also had the advantage of being much nearer to Crete, where it had been decided to take the men first so that ships could make a quick turn-round and return to collect more.

The plan called for all administrative and base personnel to be moved out of the area around Athens to the Peloponnese so that fighting troops could then move in. The wounded, the convalescent and nurses were to go first, followed by combat troops. With no protection against air attacks, it meant that movement had to be carried out by night to dispersal areas where bodies of troops would remain quiet and hidden from the dive-bombers during daylight hours. After dark they went to the beaches where, apart from their personal arms, all pieces of heavy equipment had to be destroyed. The ships would come in one hour after sunset and embark as many as possible, with orders to leave not later than 0300 hrs, so as to be away from land by dawn. Time was needed to organize an operation of enormous complexity, and this meant that the last rearguard would have to hold

Thermopylae, so that detailed plans could be finalized.

Into the Thermopylae position came the dog-tired men of the fighting rearguards. As the evacuation was due to begin during the night of 24 April, it meant that the position had to be held until 23 April. The defenders there had expected a major German attack as early as 20 April – before they had a chance to strengthen the position – but, to their surprise and enormous relief, the Germans had outrun a long, tenuous supply line, so that it was to take them some four days before they had fresh troops and guns and ammunition with which to continue the advance. This delay meant that on 23 April the defenders at Thermopylae were thinned out. One of the three New Zealand brigades, the 5th, after destroying their guns and heavy equipment, moved off to the beaches, while the 4th Brigade was sent back sixty miles to prepare the last rearguard action at Thebes. This left the old Thermopylae Pass at Molos to be defended by the 6th New Zealand Brigade with some Northumberland Hussars and Royal Horse Artillery in close support. At Brallos the Australians also sent about half their numbers away.

At 0730 hrs on 24 April, the day the main evacuation started, the long-awaited attack on the Thermopylae position began with a heavy artillery bombardment, intense dive-bombing and spotter planes searching for gun positions. The rearguards' guns were well camouflaged and stopped firing whenever aircraft were overhead, so that the Germans did not have much success in knocking them out. The Australians and New Zealanders held firm throughout a day which witnessed much bitter fighting and fierce clashes – but no break-through.

The Germans then tried to force the position with a massed tank attack – a tactic which had brought them much success in the past. The battle report of the I/XXXI Panzer Regiment recounts what happened: 'Nineteen tanks in file charge along the road.... On our right the hills, on our left the dreaded Thermopylae swamp. We had to push on, go on, do anything but stop.... Suddenly we came under fire from six or eight guns ... shells burst on all sides, a few Tommies ran across the road, and several machine-guns chattered. A heavy tank was hit direct ... in the middle of the road are three others on fire ... before long there was not a single tank in going order, and only two still able to shoot.'

The artillery from the New Zealanders, the Royal Horse Artillery and the Northumberland Hussars had waited for such an opportunity, and the tremendous German attack was stopped in its tracks. Late that night, breechblocks were removed, guns were destroyed and the entire force quietly fell back through the last rearguard, to hide all the next day from the Luftwaffe and then, at night, to go down to the beaches to await evacuation.

Events were now moving fast. On the same day the action at Thermopylae had been fought, General Papagos resigned his command, the Greek Army capitulated, the King was flown out to Crete by the RAF, Anzac HQ closed down and the Australian and New Zealand commanders were ordered to leave. General Freyberg pointed out that his 4th Brigade would be fighting the last rearguard and asked who was to command them; when he was told, 'Movement Control', he sent his own HQ away and remained behind himself. Such a gesture was typical of one of the bravest officers of his generation.

General Wilson stayed in Athens until the last minute, arriving at the Corinth Bridge just before dawn on 26 April. The evacuation had been going well: the 5th New Zealand Brigade, which had been sent away from Thermopylae, had embarked during the night of 24 April, as had nearly 7,000 base troops. During the next night about half the Australians had left – in all during the first two nights over 18,000 had been evacuated. But nearly 40,000 remained.

The Corinth bridge area was obviously a most vulnerable spot, but now it was guarded by only three tanks and a few Australian infantry. After dawn on 26 April there was a heavy air attack on the Corinth bridge. By this time it was clear that, in the main, the Germans were trying to stop the evacuation by using the Luftwaffe rather than their ground troops. They made one last effort to seize the Corinth Canal road bridge when the accurate air attack knocked out every anti-aircraft gun around the canal, and this was immediately followed by low-flying Junkers 52s in groups of three: soon the sky was dotted with coloured parachutes. Then, while a thousand paratroops dropped, gliders crash-landed near the bridge, men jumped out, overwhelmed the pickets and raced to clear the explosives. Dramatically the charges exploded, killing all the Germans in the *coup-de-main* party and dropping the bridge neatly into the canal.

What caused the explosion? Controversy still exists to this day. Captain J. Phillips (Devons) and Lieutenant J. Tyson (Royal Engineers) were firing their rifles at the charge when it exploded, and they certainly believed they were responsible. However, experts say that wet gun cotton could not be detonated if hit by a bullet in such a manner. On the other hand, the Germans believed that either the explosives went off as they were being hurriedly dismantled or some TNT was set off by a shell splinter. But there were no guns firing at the time, and therefore the most likely explanation is that the two officers did indeed cause the explosion. Whatever the cause, this action provided a welcome respite so that, south of the canal, the evacuation went on unhindered.

About this episode, one ex-gunner officer (the late Major R.G. Burnell) wrote: 'The following morning my Battery Commander (122 Battery LAA) was with his staff car and driver, just south of Corinth Bridge, when the Germans dropped a large number of parachutists armed with machine guns and grenades. They overran our guns and captured the BC and his car. Our gun crews were unequipped to offer resistance once the parachutists had landed as they had no small arms – not even one rifle per gun crew, and the guns were quite inappropriate for ground defence. One crew was largely demolished and the sergeant and several gunners killed but most were taken prisoner.'

Meanwhile the Germans north of the bridge, escorted by a captured tank, drove triumphantly into Corinth on 26 April, where a Greek-speaking German officer relieved the mayor of his responsibilities. All over Greece similar scenes were taking place. Tanks and carriers, full of dusty, grimy soldiers, clanked into apparently deserted towns. Slowly the Greeks came out of the houses and walked up and down, staring at their conquerors. Within a few days everyone knew about Reichsmarks, and business was brisk.

The captured Corinth Canal meant that the 4th New Zealand Brigade, units of the 1st Armoured Brigade and Autralian gunners, forming the rearguard at Thebes, now could not embark from beaches in the Peloponnese, so that they were directed to fall back to the beaches near Athens.

Three full days were to elapse from the time the Germans seized the Corinth Bridge until the last of the Expeditionary Force was evacuated, and during that time another 30,000 British and Australians were embarked. The large number evacuated was due, in part, to British organization and discipline, in part to the fact German units did not follow up their victory. On the other hand, the Luftwaffe continued to show the greatest activity, dive-bombing and machine-gunning along the southern shores wherever they saw any movement, and sinking many ships. S.S.M. Aris was to comment, years later, that, 'The dive-bombing made one very religious!'

C.M. Woodhouse, a name that will appear many times during the story of the Axis Occupation of Greece, tells this anecdote about the British commander of the BEF: 'On the quay I saw General Wilson, calmly elephantine, with a few disconsolate staff officers.

"What are you going to do now, sir?" one of them asked him.

"What many generals have done before me," he replied. "Sit on my luggage!" '

Wilson was to return to Cairo, and Major-General Bernard Freyberg, holder of the VC won in World War I, was selected to command the garrison that was to remain in Crete.

In such little ports as Nauplion and Monemvasia, the scene was a familiar one, with the long line of patient troops silhouetted at the shore line; motor barges black and low-slung, chugging from the water's edge towards waiting corvettes and destroyers; muttered interchanges between captains and beachmasters: 'I can take a hundred – tell them to get a move on.' As the ill-starred British Expeditionary Force was brought out, a wry jest passed through the ranks: the initials BEF really stood for 'Back Every Fortnight'.

On 27 April the infamous swastika flew from the west wall of the Acropolis a few hours after Radio Athens had broadcast its last free words: 'Greece will live, brothers. Have courage and patience.' The whole nation was to need those qualities in large measure before war and violence were to disappear, not four years later, when the German Reich fell and most of Europe celebrated, but nearly eight years later, when the devastating civil war in Greece came to an end.

For those who fought in Greece and were fortunate enough

to be evacuated, the memories they recall are strangely similar. Most remember Greek civilians still giving the thumbs-up sign, with shouts of '*Nike, nike*' ('Victory, victory') as their last farewell to the departing Allies. Vic West's comments have been echoed by many: 'The Greek population had turned out in force ... to clap and cheer every passing truck of the departing English. We had been beaten, and they knew it.... They cheered as though we'd won a resounding victory.... Dusty and dirty, as we were, we sat bolt upright in salute to their unquenchable spirit.'

One or two ex-servicemen report that a small handful of the local population did turn against them during the retreat, feeling that they, the Greeks, had been let down, but their experiences were not shared by the majority. Even in the bitter hour of defeat the acting Prime Minister, Tsouderos, when broadcasting to the nation about the Armistice, paid a warm tribute to the departing Imperial Force: 'Greece will ever be grateful to the great and noble British people whose sons have come to our land on their own initiative – to fight for us in the cause of justice.' Within hours Tsouderos accompanied his King, first to Crete and from there to Cairo, to begin four years in exile.

The final stages of the evacuation gathered speed, and at first everything went according to plan at several ports. Kalamata was to be the one black spot but those who arrived there on 26 April were evacuated safely. Rob Bewshea, then a corporal in the Royal Signals, remembers the dramatic way a destroyer sailed into the harbour with searchlights ablaze, lighting up the quay and the soldiers waiting to embark. In a matter of minutes all were aboard and the destroyer turned to sail for Alexandria – and safety. On 28 April, however, fortunes changed at Kalamata when the advance guard of V Panzer Division overwhelmed a small 4th Hussars perimeter-guard, burst into the town to capture the naval embarkation officer and his signalman and thus cut communications with the approaching ships. The thousands of Allied soldiers in the town were not organized for defence – indeed, only about 800 of them were fighting troops, the rest belonging to base units. Inevitably there was great confusion and very little resistance when the Germans crashed into the town, and soon large numbers of prisoners were rounded up. It took great determination and courage to fight under those circumstances, and it was here that New Zealander Sergeant J.D. Hinton, after being wounded, led a party of his countrymen in attacks on one German position after another. Months later, in a prisoner-of-war camp, he learnt he had been awarded the Victoria Cross.

The confused fighting in Kalamata ended in a temporary victory for the Allied soldiers, whose hopes of being evacuated were raised once more. A Royal Naval squadron of two cruisers, *Perth* and *Phoebe*, and six destroyers had been on the way in when the fighting broke out, and a signal-lamp warning was flashed to them, 'Boche in Harbour'. Captain Sir Philip Bowyer-Smyth, on the *Perth*, seeing tracer fire and hearing explosions in the town, decided that the number of men now likely to be saved did not justify risking his ships. He ordered his force to withdraw and, although another signal lamp flashed out a message to say that firing had ceased and evacuation was possible, he did not alter his decision. In his defence, appearances on shore might well have seemed much worse than they were. Whatever the reason, over 7,000 men were left behind to their fate.

Among the remnant was Driver Reg Simmons from 312 Company, RASC. Like many others he had hoped to be evacuated, hiding in the hills by day and coming down to the water by night, but on 29 April the Germans captured most of the survivors. As a POW, Simmons spent some six weeks in Corinth. He was one of several who confirm that, after becoming a prisoner, the Greek civilians' attitude did not change towards the defeated Allies, helpless though they were. Men, women and children risked dire punishment and even their lives to hide or help Allied soldiers still at large, or to give them small gifts after they had been captured. Simmons was to spend another four years as a POW in Austria before being reunited with his wife.

S.S.M. Aris was another whose active war-time service ended when German paratroopers captured a large number of his unit, not far from Nauplion. After four years as a POW, he escaped on Palm Sunday 1945 and, following an epic journey, met the advancing Russians – and eventually found freedom.

For the Royal Navy, defeat in Greece was as bitter a pill to swallow as it was for the other two services. At the end of March 1941 the sea battle of Cape Matapan had given them virtual command of the sea in the eastern Mediterranean, and as a result the Italian Navy never interfered with sea operations and around Greece and Crete. If they had, it could have been disastrous for the Imperial Expeditionary Force, as well as for the Royal Navy. Unfortunately, sea power alone could not offset the complete command of the skies enjoyed by the Luftwaffe.

The bare statistics cannot tell the full story of such a campaign. It is clear that Adolf Hitler wished to avoid heavy casualties: The Germans reported that they lost 1,500 killed or missing, with a further 3,700 wounded. Of more significance, perhaps, the Luftwaffe lost over 200 experienced airmen. As far as the British Imperial Force was concerned, about eighty per cent were evacuated either to Crete or back to Egypt. 12,000 casualties (more than half from the United Kingdom) included 900 dead, of whom over 600 were Australian and New Zealanders, and over 1,200 wounded, of whom some 900 were Anzac. The RAF, completely outnumbered, lost seventy-two aircraft in combat and 137 destroyed on the ground, either in Crete or on the mainland, having flown in for specific missions. The Royal Navy, whose skill and daring enabled such a large proportion of the BEF to escape, lost two destroyers and four transports, with twenty-one other ships being sunk. To offset these grievous losses, one cruiser, six destroyers and four submarines of the Greek Navy escaped to Alexandria, thereafter to fight under the overall command of Admiral Cunningham and his successor. Inevitably the Army lost nearly all its heavy equipment, including 104 tanks, 400 guns and some 8,000 vehicles.

Militarily, the decision to go to Greece's aid had ended in disaster – it had been a gamble without hope from the beginning. But was there any alternative? General Papagos summed it up well: 'For Greece to be crushed without a single British soldier striking a blow in her defence would have meant a flagrant breach of the promises so repeatedly given. Also it would have certainly had an unfavourable effect on American public opinion. The Greeks did not ask for a British Force, and did not expect one. It was offered for several reasons that involved primarily British reasons.'

From that moment on, Britain had a moral obligation to help her ally until the Nazi occupation ended. In political terms, it meant that the British Government would not abandon its traditional interest and influence in Greece. Air Vice-Marshal D'Albiac in his final *Gazette* wrote: 'I suggest that it would have been difficult to refuse her [Greece] this help, and our conduct would have been most reprehensible in the eyes of our countrymen and those of important neutrals had we failed to do so.... We will never forget the brave and courageous spirit of the Greek people, whose kindness and sympathy towards us were as great when we finally had to leave Greece to the occupation of the Germans, as when we arrived in November 1940 in the fever and anxiety of the opening days of the war against Italy.'

3 Crete – Mission Impossible

'If fate means you to lose, give him a good fight anyway.'

William McFee

The Greek people were stunned by the speed with which disaster had struck and left them at the mercy of the Axis powers. Field Marshal von List arrived in Athens on 30 April and quickly named a Greek puppet Cabinet to govern on behalf of the Reich. General Tsolakoglou, who had commanded and surrendered the Army in Epirus without informing his superiors, was nominated Prime Minister of a Cabinet about which Laird Archer was to write: 'The ageing Archbishop of Athens with sublime courage has refused to administer the State of Oath to the new Cabinet. He said it is not the will of the people that Greece should be governed by men appointed by the enemy.'

Germany wanted her experienced front-line troops for the next act, the attack on the Soviet Union, and despite promises made prior to the invasion that Greece would not be handed over to her Axis partner, on 2 May Italian soldiers began arriving in Athens. The reception in the city was predictable: 'With pompous strides the officers, marching ahead of the troops, entered Zonaras last night and they were greeted not with the scowl that the Germans got but with ribald laughter.' The laughter was soon to be muted, for a day or two later, arrests and even executions for various violations of the Nazi code began. A number of these were for harbouring and helping Anzac and British soldiers, of whom it was estimated there were nearly 4,000 at large, somewhere in southern Greece. By now the Axis-controlled Press and radio were full of tirades against members of the Metaxas regime, blaming them for the war and for the nation's lack of preparedness, for misusing funds and, the worst crime of all, for inviting the British to come to Greece.

Away from Athens, across the sea in Crete, the next round between the British and Germans was about to be enacted. With British naval power a mighty force in the Mediterranean, to uninformed observers Crete appeared to be an island that could be defended. Moreover, there were some 44,000 men on the island, on paper a formidable obstacle for the Germans to overcome. But only 8,700 had come fresh and fully equipped from the Middle East: after evacuation from the mainland, 29,000 British and Dominion troops and 15,000 Greeks had been flung together as an improvised defence force, many of whom were demoralised by the defeat in Greece, some had been wounded, and several lacked even rifles; so many supplies and armaments of war had been left behind in Greece that even seasoned troops would have found the going hard. One New Zealander, Second Lieutenant Charles Upham VC of the 20th (NZ) Battalion, called Crete 'a pauper's campaign, mortars without base plates, Vickers guns without tripods'.

Lest we blame the commanders on the spot unduly, it must be remembered that Generals Maitland Wilson, Freyberg (nominated as GOC Crete) and Weston (Royal Marines) in turn expressed pessimism about the task of defending the island with the resources available. Wilson, during his short 'stop-off' in Crete before returning to Egypt, signalled his belief that the island could be held only '... if there were three serviceable airfields, three fully equipped brigade groups and adequate anti-aircraft support'. To those demands, the Chiefs of Staff in London merely replied that Crete must at all costs be denied to the enemy but that no air reinforcements would be available for some time (COS Signal of 9 May 1941).

The Chiefs of Staff, armed with the benefit of their Ultra intercepts about future German intentions, were lulled into complacency, forgetting that possession of fresh, accurate intelligence was of little use to the defenders of Crete if they lacked the requisite aircraft, heavy weapons and adequate communications for use against the assault when it came.

There were other factors that weighed against Freyberg's conducting a successful defensive operation. Prior to his arrival there had been six different commanders within a matter of months, so that no one had been there long enough to ensure a measure of continuity in defensive planning. In addition, the bitter fact that the Luftwaffe had ruled the skies over Greece was soon to be repeated over Crete. Despite optimistic predictions in the British Press, Crete was virtually indefensible from the start. The island is 170 miles in length, but in 1941 there was only one major narrow road which followed the long coastline. The port facilities at Suda were limited – only two ships could berth at a time, while at Canea unloading was feasible only by lighter. Anti-aircraft, artillery and tanks were woefully short, and of the twenty-one tanks that could be spared from Egypt, all proved defective, lacking cooling systems for their guns and even reasonable wireless communications. No air cover was possible from North Africa, 400 miles away. To cap it all, on 19 May the last of the RAF fighter planes, three Hurricanes and three obsolete Gladiators, were flown back to Egypt. The ground troops were to be at the mercy of the Luftwaffe once more; indeed, the volume of air attacks increased day by day, well before the assault on the island was launched.

Also on 19 May, detailed orders for the attack on Crete were being given out in Athens by General Kurt Student, the commander of the Seventh Air Division. A dedicated professional soldier, Student had enthused about and worked for the plan until he knew it down to the last detail. Crete was to be attacked by paratroops at four different points simultaneously. The main objective of the Luftwaffe was given to the Assault Regiment, whose target was Maleme airfield, whose capture was essential to Student's overall plan. The 3rd Regiment was to seize Canea, the capital of the island. At the same time, the 1st Regiment was to strike at the town and airfield at Heraklion, while the 2nd Regiment was allotted identical targets at Retimo. It was to be the biggest airborne operation ever attempted, with 10,000 parachutists making the initial strike and a further 750 landing in gliders. After the airfields had been seized, a back-up force of 5,000 would land in JU52 transports while, for mopping up isolated groups of defenders, a seaborne force would be landed on D-Day 2. It was an immaculately planned operation for which local security was absolute. One factor had been drummed into each battalion commander at Student's 'orders group' in Athens: it was vital that at least one airfield be captured quickly and securely held thereafter, thus enabling follow-up troops and supplies to be flown in, otherwise the momentum of the attack would falter and allow the defenders to concentrate on mopping up the parachutists.

In private, the GOC Crete, Bernard Freyberg, had never been anything more than realistic about the outcome. For example, on 30 April he pointed out in a signal to Wavell that his ill-equipped force, without air support, was not adequate for the task, ending up with, 'Decision to hold Crete [should] be re-considered.' But it was too late for such a reversal of policy and, having made his point, the loyal Freyberg got on with the job and, in his words, 'didn't belly-ache'.

As a consequence, some historians have tended to be critical of Freyberg, and certainly one of his signals to Churchill expressed buoyant optimism. 'Am not the least anxious about an airborne attack' was despatched on 5 May, after he had positioned the majority of his troops in strongpoints strung along the coast. Freyberg's decision to do this is puzzling because, through Ultra intercepts, precise details of Hitler's Directive No 28, including troop strengths, timings and dispositions, had been made available to him, even though he did not know the source of the intelligence or the existence of the 'Enigma' machine. Despite this information, the GOC Crete failed to grasp that the airfields would be prime targets; instead, he made his dispositions to meet what he considered would be the main threat, a seaborne assault. To complicate matters even more, communications between his four main groups were so unreliable and primitive that each virtually operated on its own, in a vacuum and often in the dark. After the war, one military commentator suggested that, if there had been one hundred field-wireless sets in Crete, the island might have remained in British hands.

The unflappable Freyberg was having his breakfast on Tuesday, 20 May, when at 7 a.m. the first gliders loomed silently overhead, whereupon he remarked, "They're dead on time." In a few minutes the defenders stood mesmerized as hundreds of parachutes opened above them. Behind them, the German bombers moved in their wake, softening up the opposition, while the gliders disgorged their soldiers at various parts of the island. 'We watched hundreds in a daisy shower, dropping rapidly to earth from no great height.... The eye is aghast with the spectacle. There must be 500 transports at least up there. They line up to disgorge now, without ceasing' (Vic West).

Although subsequently the British Chiefs of Staff were to assure Churchill that '... the enemy entered Crete as a conquering power', the majority of Germans who took part in the early phases of the operation had a very different impression. Many paratroopers jumped too soon and landed in the sea, others hit drop zones far from pre-planned positions, planes crashed, and gliders that did land often hit the ground with such an impact that their passengers were killed or badly injured. The 3rd Battalion of the 1st Assault Regiment, landing east of Maleme, had a terrible time after landing, and by dusk only 200 out of the original 600 men remained alive. Top commanders proved as vulnerable as the soldiers, with two generals being killed when their gliders crashed in the early stages of the invasion.

By dusk on 20 May it was clear that General Student had made one fatal miscalculation: by striking at too many airfields simultaneously, he had failed to secure any of his objectives. This dispersal of effort had not been his original intention but had been urged on him by Hitler himself. Moreover, casualties were extremely heavy, between 4,500 and 6,000 – the estimate varies, and the loss of aircraft was equally disastrous, with the lowest estimate being 270 and the highest nearly 400. It is not surprising that, after the battle for Crete was over and an exhaustive inquest had been held, Hitler decided the day of the mass airborne assault was over, and that thereafter German paratroopers were normally deployed as elite infantrymen.

The turning-point of the campaign was really brought about by the dire lack of communications. Lieutenant-Colonel Lionel Andrew VC, commanding the 22nd (NZ) Battalion, had lost contact with three of his five companies, and his headquarters had been heavily mortared. He himself was hit by a shell splinter. Realizing that he could not hold the airfield and the slopes with some 200 men, Andrew decided he must withdraw the company from Pt 107. Unknown to him, in the immediate area, other units of the brigade had been having local successes and when he, as commanding officer, eventually contacted brigade headquarters, the Brigadier assumed that Andrew was merely adjusting his perimeter – anyway, the wireless then went dead. Andrew did not know that his three missing companies were still holding out. When he and his 200 men pulled out, into the gap walked the German Assault Regiment. Maleme airfield was taken and a few hours later the first JU52 landed at the airport. By that evening the Germans had established a shuttle service from Greece and were able to throw in troops at a breathtaking rate. One day later, planes were flying in forty men at a time and landing every three minutes. With the loss of Maleme, the fate of the island was sealed.

The impending loss of the island was as terrible a blow to Greece, as it was to the British, whose Commander-in-Chief in Cairo, Wavell, was close to despair. On the island, spirited, resolute little actions continued, yet inevitably they lacked cohesion. The Cretans showed extraordinary gallantry, many of them joining the British and Imperial troops, armed only with ancient firing pieces and other primitive weapons. Thirty-three-year-old Second Lieutenant Charles Upham of the 20th (NZ) Battalion made charge after charge near Maleme airfield and, although wounded in the shoulder, continued to fire at the Germans. Then he led a final rearguard action up a 600-foot ravine before he was persuaded to board a Navy destroyer. Upham won the first of his two Victoria Crosses for outstanding courage there. Another VC was awarded to Sergeant A.C. Hulme of the 23rd (NZ) Battalion for repeated acts of bravery.

It would be wrong to pretend that scenes of panic and disorganization did not occur during the last few days in Crete. A medical officer with the Cyprus Regiment recalled: 'I knew that I was taking part in a retreat. In fact, I wondered if it could not be called more correctly a rout.' That doctor saw naked panic that came close to breaking point, with more than one man tying on a field dressing to claim Red Cross evacuation as one of the 'walking wounded'. The same doctor added that a bitter jibe was coined on the sandy beaches: 'Every man taking part in the Cretan evacuation would soon receive a medal inscribed with the words, EX CRETA.'

Morale plummeted when the position became hopeless, and leadership at all levels was severely tested. Vic West came across a long column of men who had given up any further thoughts of fighting. 'There was every bit of a thousand there ... the silent men didn't look very wounded to us, no sign of bandages, no smell of blood ...

Among the assortment of glorious, inglorious and less reputable events shone the rearguard action which was the overall responsibility of Major-General E.C. Weston, Royal Marines, who was commanding a mixed force of his own marines and Anzac troops. Their task was to hold the Germans back as long as possible, which they did with remarkable resolution, in conjunction with Layforce, commanded by Brigadier L.E. Laycock. By means of stirring counter-attacks, the rearguard deterred the Germans from following up too closely and preventing the large-scale evacuation.

At the time it was estimated there were some 22,000 troops to be evacuated, and with German reinforcements arriving on the island in ever-increasing numbers, the growing pressure meant that the prospect of rescuing more than a small proportion did not seem good. As for the ships which were to embark the troops, Admiral Cunningham later described them as having been driven hard for more than two months without respite, adding that their officers and men were on the verge of complete exhaustion, physically and mentally. And the Luftwaffe saw to it that the evacuation was an ordeal under fire that the survivors were never to forget.

Thursday 22 May was a particularly sad day for a part of Admiral Cunningham's fleet. While making a daylight sweep in the perilous but vital task of preventing enemy seaborne landings, air attacks against the fleet began at 0700 hours and continued incessantly thereafter. With the Luftwaffe operating from bases less than thirty miles away, Admiral King's ships first engaged a convoy escorted by an Italian destroyer, *Fagittario*. The British cruisers and destroyers opened fire and turned the convoy back but did not press home the attack before they themselves pulled away to the west. Admiral King's decision was later criticized by his superior, Cunningham, but his reason for doing so was that ammunition expenditure had been heavy and still his ships were being subjected to fierce onslaughts by the Luftwaffe. Skilful manœuvring, together with lively anti-aircraft fire from King's ships, resulted in little loss or damage at first but the situation was to take a drastic turn later in this calamitous day. The air attacks increased in volume and intensity, and by darkness two heavy cruisers, HMS *Gloucester* and *Fiji*, and one destroyer, HMS *Grevant*, had been lost. Despite this setback, during that same night reinforcements bound for Crete were embarked at Alexandria on the *Glenroy*, because it was still intended that the island should be held – although the overall position had changed dramatically following the loss of the airfield at Maleme. The Royal Navy, however, had done its duty, and all enemy convoys by sea had been turned back from Crete.

From 23 May the Royal Air Force began to take a hand, albeit a limited one, and Maleme airfield was bombed by Blenheims, Wellingtons and Marylands. Unfortunately the whole effort was on too small a scale to be effective and, although scoring successes, the RAF lost far too many aircraft. On the same day, at about 0200 hours, King George II of the Hellenes, together with members of the royal household, embarked on a British destroyer. The King had narrowly escaped from his house at Perivolia shortly before it had been surrounded by Germans and had made an eventful, difficult two-day journey across the central mountains, escorted by New Zealand soldiers and accompanied by Colonel J.S. Blunt, British Military Attaché to Greece.

In Cairo, the decision to stop sending any more reinforcements meant that a signal was made to the *Glenroy* and she was recalled to Alexandria. By now Cunningham had signalled the Chiefs of Staff in London, to state categorically that it was no longer possible for the Navy to operate in the Aegean or in the vicinity of Crete during the hours of daylight.

By the afternoon of Sunday 25 May, the Germans had taken Galatas and broken through a defensive line composed of about 6,000 New Zealanders, Australians and Greeks, all of whom had been the target of unceasing air attacks for several days. The situation was partially restored by a bold counter-attack led by Colonel H.K. Kippenberger of the 10th New Zealand Brigade, a counter-attack that was described by General Freyberg as 'one of the great efforts in the defence of Crete'. Freyberg had come to the conclusion that it could be only a matter of hours before the island was lost, especially when the following day, 26 May, saw the situation in the Suda area rapidly deteriorating. He sent a message to General Wavell, informing him that troops in the western sector had reached the limits of their endurance after continual fighting and concentrated bombing during the preceding seven days. Within his command, communications had broken down and organized administration was virtually impossible – although, if evacuation was decided upon at once, the GOC felt that it ought to be possible to bring off a substantial part of his force.

Orders were given for a planned retreat to Sphakia on the south coast to begin on Tuesday 27 May. Detailed to carry out a rearguard action to cover the movement to Sphakia, the Rangers fought, died and, in Vic West's words, 'had our proud little battalion broken'. Unknown to these brave men, Wavell replied to Freyberg advising him to hold on as long as he could, adding that a cable had been received from Churchill which in spirit was gallant, even if totally unrealistic: 'Victory in Crete essential. Keep hurling in all you can.'

It was already too late, and by this time General Blamey, GOC Australian Forces in the Middle East, and Peter Fraser, Prime Minister of New Zealand, had met the Commander-in-Chief in Cairo to express their gravest concern about the fate of Anzac troops fighting so desperately in Crete. Could a proportion of the troops be withdrawn safely or had total surrender become inevitable? To that question Admiral Cunningham gave his classic reply: 'Whatever the risks, whatever our losses, the remaining ships of the fleet would make an all-out effort to bring away the Army.'

Once more it was to be an inglorious evacuation, and once more the Royal Navy lived up to the Dunkirk tradition. Regardless of loss or danger to the ships, the troops had to be moved out. For three days the evacuation continued, with the Luftwaffe carrying out relentless low-level strafing. In the end, the naval losses were severe, three cruisers and six destroyers sunk, with a further seventeen ships badly damaged.

There were bitter words in the House of Commons but even more critical were the messages received from Australia and New Zealand. Of the troops left behind in Crete, over 3,000 were Australians and more than 1,600 New Zealanders; now many Australian voices were accusing the United Kingdom of sending green, ill-armed troops to be butchered in Crete. Feeling between Churchill and the Dominion Governments of Australia and New Zealand was never to be the same again; the rift opened was never completely healed.

The last lift from Crete disembarked at Alexandria on 1 June to bring to an end a sustained ordeal for the Mediterranean Fleet that has no parallel in British naval history. For the officers and men who had participated, there was none of the inspiration of battle with the enemy to sustain them. Instead, they had to face unceasing anxiety in trying to bring back thousands of their own countrymen, many of whom were exhausted and dispirited, in ships that were completely overcrowded. All this was done with the Luftwaffe hounding them at every available opportunity. The Commander-in-Chief, Admiral Cunningham, summed it up: 'There is rightly little credit or glory to be expected in these operations of retreat, but I feel that the spirit of tenacity shown by those who took part should not go unrecorded.' The majority of the officers and naval ratings who took part in the evacuation of Greece, and then Crete, were serving for 'hostilities only', men who came from all walks of civilian life, with an average age in the mid-twenties only.

Both in Crete and on the mainland of Greece, hundreds of British, Australian and New Zealand soldiers remained at large, trying to evade capture and, in many cases, taking active steps to escape and make their way back to the Middle East. One story is singled out as it illustrates why the Royal Marines have been such an elite force for so long in the British Armed Forces.

Officers and men of the Royal Marine battalion that formed part of the rearguard fought to the last, knowing how slender were their chances of rescue. Eventually reaching the beach at Sphakia too late for the last lift, the battalion was disbanded by Major Ralph Garrett, Royal Marines. He then made it known that he would never allow himself to be taken prisoner, and that he intended to find a boat and make his way to Africa. Garrett went off in search of a boat and found a landing craft which had been abandoned earlier in the campaign. Swimming out to her, he found that the port screw had been fouled by a wire and the engines incapacitated but she did have some provisions on board and appeared to be seaworthy. The indomitable major then found a lance-corporal of the 2/7th Australian Battalion who had been a mechanic in civil life, and with the help of an Australian officer they got life into the engine and finally brought the lighter inshore. Ralph Garrett called for volunteers to join him on this desperate venture. To his cry 'Who goes home?', five officers and 134 other ranks responded. That total included Royal Marines, Australians, New Zealanders and men from other commandos who had landed a few days before. By 1 June they had collected some petrol, water-containers and rations and cast off.

First they went to a small island twenty miles south of Crete, Gavdapola, where a well was found and all water-containers were duly filled. By this time an engine-room staff had been selected and, in Garrett's phrase, 'All the troops were exercised in seamanship.' At 9.30 p.m. on 1 June they set sail for Tobruk, 180 miles distant, which they knew to be in British hands. They had no sextant, no knowledge of the deviation of a magnetic compass and only a small-scale atlas for navigation. Garrett estimated they had petrol for 140 miles.

After they had set sail, many things went wrong, including the steering gear, which broke down, before first one engine and then another packed up. Undaunted, Major Garrett made sail, the canvas being furnished somewhat inadequately by the winch cover. Their troubles increased when the sea rose and sea-sickness overwhelmed most of the passengers but the devoted engine-room staff, having stripped the engine down, got it under way next day. For twenty-four hours the engines kept chugging until stocks of petrol were exhausted. By this time passengers had to be rationed to a sixth of a pint of water, an inch and a half cube of bully beef and half a ship's biscuit per day, so that by 4 June they were all very weak, and still the African coast had not been sighted. In desperation, they contrived to make four blankets into a jib and stitch into a mainsail, but the lighter refused to answer to her helm. At times it was necessary for relays of exhausted men to plunge overboard in small parties and, by swimming with all the energy left in them, push the bows round onto the proper course again.

On 8 June two Australian private soldiers died from exposure and exhaustion and were buried at sea, only for land to be sighted later that day. Early in the morning of 9 June they ran onto a sandy beach and, after two Maoris had found a well of water some forty-five minutes away, the party discovered they had beached the landing craft some seventeen miles west of Sidi Barrani. Garrett's party had sailed over 200 miles.

On 10 June Major Garrett marched his force across the desert, to where lorries awaited them. His little band of intrepid men, bearded, gaunt and hollow-eyed, were still led by the officer who had taught them what the Corps motto meant; *'Per Mare Per Terram'* – 'By Sea, By Land'. Garrett received the DSO for his inspired leadership. Ironically, he was to drown, with his son, in peacetime some seven years later.

Thanks to the indomitable spirit shown by the Cretan people, many Allied soldiers escaped from the island in a variety of boats or evaded capture for weeks and even months. Before the German assault, two Cretan battalions were formed, with only a percentage of the volunteers being armed with rifles, and then with but five rounds of ammunition to fire. The others used clubs, knives and a variety of home-made weapons in defence of their homeland.

On 20 May these gallant men fought a skirmish with the Germans, captured seventeen prisoners and put them in the gaol at Kasteli Kissan. For nearly a week the Cretans fought heroically by the side of the New Zealanders and held up their assailants until sheer weight of numbers won the day.

The struggle took on an even uglier complexion when a major of the German paratroopers lined up the whole village and, after separating the men from their families, shot 200 of them in cold blood.

Acts of barbarism like this stiffened the will of the people to resist, even under the eyes of their conquerors. Vic West, a lance-corporal in the KRRC, was taken prisoner on Crete. While being marched to Suda, before being transferred to Salonika to begin four years in captivity, he recalls a grandmother threading her way through the marching ranks to hand out water to the prisoners, undeterred by the curses and threats of the German guards. At the side of the road stood her worried husband, anxious for his wife but ready to replenish her water-container. West ended that anecdote with the words: 'The Greeks were our true allies and I never heard a word or saw an attitude antagonistic to the British or Dominion troops.' Dozens of ex-servicemen have supported his assessment in accounts written after the war or in letters to the author.

The losses in the short campaign were staggering, and included nearly 12,000 prisoners, some of whom (about 1,000) did escape later to rejoin the Middle East forces with a further 1,737 wounded. It is true that some 15,000 men were ferried to safety but that represented only about half the total number of troops that were on the island before the Germans began their assault. The RAF lost forty-seven planes between 20 and 27 May, while operating at the extreme limit of their endurance. The experiment of fitting extra tanks on the Hurricanes, so they could operate from Egypt, was not successful as the fighters lost much of their manœuvrability and were at a grave disadvantage in the series of 'dog-fights' in the sky over Crete.

The story of Crete was a story of lost opportunities. The defenders had their chances, but the fact remains that the dominating feature of the battle lay in the almost unchallenged command of the air possessed by the Germans. Inevitably, the unceasing bombing and strafing, most of it completely unopposed – especially during the last few days – brought about an ever-quickening loss of confidence and morale. Moreover, complete air supremacy meant that the Germans had up-to-date intelligence and could detect major moves by the defenders, while the opposite was true as far as Freyberg and his subordinate commanders were concerned. All their problems were compounded by a severe shortage of transport, guns, ammunition and heavy equipment, as already mentioned.

So, was the determined resistance worth the price paid? In spite of their overwhelming air superiority, the Germans looked failure in the face, and it was not until they gained control of the airfield at Maleme on the second day that there was any glimpse of success. Then, with characteristic boldness, they threw in everything available, regardless of loss of life, with the result that the Flieger Korps XI, comprising elite parachute and airborne troops, was almost wiped out as a unit, together with its transport planes, gliders and equipment. Originally the Korps had been earmarked for Hitler's forth-coming attack on Russia, and in its place he had to use troops which he could ill spare, troops who might have played an important part in support of the Vichy forces in Syria or given much-needed help to the armed rising in Iraq.

Although the massive use of German bombers in a close-support role was a key factor in Crete, in the long term Hitler had to pay a heavy price, because one-fifth of the German Air Force was employed, which meant the attack on Russia, 'Operation Barbarossa', had to be delayed. The presence in Russia of the 170 JU52 transports lost and the 4,000 to 5,000 elite troops killed or missing in Crete might well have been decisive. In the long term, the German attack on Crete was a mistake as it diverted valuable troops and badly needed air-craft from the main theatre in order to gain a pyrrhic victory.

At the time, the loss of the island was considered a devastat-ing blow to British hopes of winning the war. Admiral Cun-ningham, in his book *A Sailor's Odyssey*, gave his opinion in these words: 'Had we defeated the German attack and held the island the problem of its maintenance and supply would have been extraordinarily difficult. We should undoubtedly have required a large garrison ... all the ports available for landing supplies were on the north coast within reach of enemy airfields ... The Royal Air Force would also have had to be maintained in considerable strength in Crete. This would have involved the construction of new airfields.'

Cunningham does present the other side of the argument

by saying that the retention of Crete would have relieved much of the strain in supplying the beleaguered garrison of Malta during the critical weeks that lay ahead for convoys and ships, escorted by the Royal Navy.

Even with hindsight, it is difficult to see how the outcome of the Battle of Crete could have been very different. It was a losing battle fought with grim determination from the start, but with the odds against a British success far too high because of the Germans' complete domination in the air. On the other hand, it gave Hitler and his generals much to think about, for they never attempted an airborne assault on such a scale again.

After Crete fell, in Athens a neutral observer wrote that, 'There is a sadness so deep that eyes are tearless and faces are stony, unable to capture emotion.' Spirits lifted when the RAF started attacking German shipping in Piraeus harbour. And on 6 July: 'Athens is rejoicing after a terrific British air-raid on the German-held air base at Tatoi. More Vs chalked on pavements and on walls.... Unfortunately some Greeks also perished. However, Athens had buried its dead, dried its tears, and chalked up again the signs of victory, in spite of severe penalties....'

No, Greece was not dead, only dazed and numbed with shock.

4 Stirrings of Resistance

'People demand freedom only when they have no power'

Nietzsche

In Athens, Jeanne Tsatsos, wife of Constantine Tsatsos, Professor of Philosophy at the University of Athens, had begun keeping a diary of life under the Axis occupation which twenty years later she presented with text unaltered under the title *The Sword's Fierce Edge*.

Her first entry was about an English officer whom a neighbour had hidden in her kitchen. The frightened woman went to Jeanne to ask for help: 'Every so often we hear of some Ally in danger or need. The working people help with all their hearts, but they have no way of aiding these men to escape, nor of feeding them. So we make up a chain of friends ready to support them.' Together with one of her middle-class friends and her husband, the intrepid Jeanne went to the house where the Englishman was hiding. 'He looks like a hunted bird. We exchange a few words and then go warily out into the street. I put my arm through his and we walk along unconcerned.... Every time we meet German patrols, I chatter Greek to him playfully.'

She soon learnt that the officer was in love with a Greek girl and did not want to leave Greece: all he wanted was to stay near his loved one. In the end, he was moved to another hiding place and thus passed out of Jeanne Tsatsos' life for ever. Two or three days later, the Italians seized the neighbour and her husband, accusing them of having helped and hidden Englishmen. 'The two of them are confessing nothing. No secret escapes them. In order to protect our

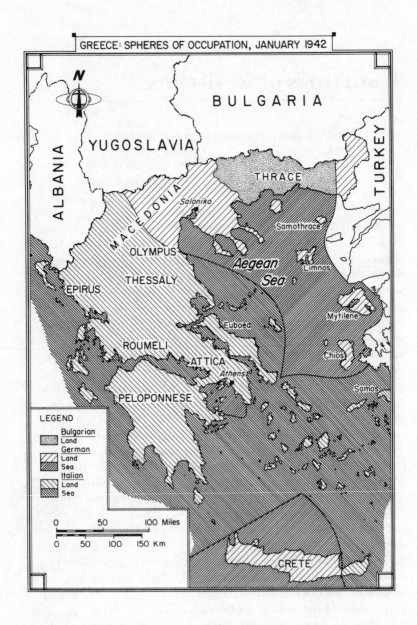

GREECE: SPHERES OF OCCUPATION, JANUARY 1942

N

BULGARIA

YUGOSLAVIA

ALBANIA

TURKEY

THRACE

MACEDONIA

Salonika

Samothrace

OLYMPUS

Aegean
Sea

Limnos

THESSALY

EPIRUS

Mytilene

Euboea

Chios

ROUMELI

ATTICA

Athens

Samos

PELOPONNESE

LEGEND

Bulgarian
Land

German
Land
Sea

Italian
Land
Sea

0   50   100 Miles

0   50   100 150 Km

CRETE

friends from ourselves, we try to know as little as possible. Just those things necessary for our work.'

Almost without exception and instinctively, the Greek people were helping the British and Dominion soldiers, feeding them and making arrangements for them to remain at large. For the Greeks it was the first form of resistance to the Axis Occupation, and it was not long before Germans and Italians began to take reprisals, ruthlessly punishing those who helped to hide or feed Allied soldiers on the run.

Until Hitler launched Operation Barbarossa on 22 June 1941, the unsuspecting Soviet Union was Germany's ally. As a consequence, many important members of the Greek Communist Party, the KKE, were released by the Nazis from prison or detention, where they had languished since the Metaxas regime had imprisoned them. Among them was a man who was to play a major role in Greek affairs during the next four years, George Siantos.

Siantos was a Moscow-trained Communist and, like most of his comrades, had been bewildered when Stalin made his infamous pact with the Nazi leaders of Germany. George Siantos was to have greatness thrust upon him, as successor to the Secretary-General of the KKE, Nikos Zachariades, who was whisked away by the Germans after their attack on Russia and for a long time it was presumed that he had died in a concentration camp. Only when the war ended was it known that he had survived Dachau. From late 1941 onwards Siantos acted as Secretary-General of KKE, a shadowy figure about whom little was known outside the Party. Gradually he emerged from the wings as the Occupation continued until events thrust him into the limelight towards the end of 1944.

Tribute must be paid to the handful of British who, at a great risk to their own lives, voluntarily remained in Greece or Crete to help organize the escape of their fellow-countrymen. One such was Frank Macaskie, who was wounded on Crete in May 1941 and captured. Soon afterwards he made the first of many escapes, this one from the prison camp at Kokkinia and, after accepting the hospitality of local Greeks, he took ship for Turkey and eventually reached Cairo. There he persuaded his superiors that many Allied soldiers were still at large in Greece and could be retrieved, so that he was back in that country by

November 1941, charged with the organization of escapes. He had arranged the evacuation of some fifty men before he was seized – in his words, 'We were bound to be caught sooner or later, for all Athens knew when a *caique* [a small boat] was leaving.'

It was the Italians who captured him, and the intrepid Macaskie escaped from Kithnos and gave them a fortnight's hunting before being caught once more. Bound with ropes, he was taken to Rhodes, where again he escaped, only to be apprehended. And so his saga continued. In turn, he was imprisoned on the islands of Samos, Leros and Rhodes and finally, in March 1943, in the Kallithea Prison in Athens. There Macaskie was charged with espionage and, as he had been captured in civilian clothes, he had no defence to offer against the indictment. Sentenced to death, he found himself incarcerated in the condemned cell of the Averoff Prison and for some three months remained there. His fortunes changed when Italy collapsed, and a judicious bribe enabled him to escape, to accept sanctuary offered him by Archbishop Damaskinos. For a fortnight he stayed with that remarkable prelate, who during the Occupation interceded on behalf of countless people and saved the lives of hundreds. Macaskie made his way back via Turkey to Cairo and, after a well-earned spell of leave in the UK, returned once more, this time by parachute, landing during May 1944 in Phthiotis. Thereafter his story, like that of many other British and Allied agents, echoed the momentous events that led to the liberation of Greece and the bloodshed that followed. There were other brave Englishmen in the same mould as Macaskie, men who loved Greece and were following in the Byronic tradition, inspired by their desire to help a ravaged land and its long-suffering people.

The winter of 1941 and the first few months of 1942 saw mainland Greece and her islands in the throes of a devastating famine. The occupying Powers were fully committed to the war in other theatres and were unable to do much to alleviate the suffering – even if they had wanted to do so. Macaskie was to write later: 'I saw the famine in the winter of 1941, when people were dying in the streets, and ate grass and thistles like myself; but everyone would share with me what he had.'

It has been estimated that 450,000, out of a total population of 7 million, died of starvation or from ailments directly resulting from a chronic lack of food and the bare necessity of vitamins. Throughout that winter the whole nation suffered the torments of hunger, scratching around to survive, and the effect was to last for months, even years. An important witness was Richard Capell, correspondent of the *Daily Telegraph*, who accompanied the British and Greek forces that liberated some of the islands in the Aegean during the summer of 1944. Capell was to write that the women were wan and that children looked like waifs after their ordeal. He went on to tell of the island of Samos, where the wayside children were wizened and the villagers looked at those who had come to liberate them with haggard faces and eager eyes. Although that was 1944, the famine they remembered was in early 1942, when hundreds died of hunger and all had felt themselves doomed. The village teacher told Capell how during that torment he used to gather weeds for his family and how, one day – when the dish again was only boiled grass – one of his children, a little girl, went and pressed her face against the window. She was weeping but would have wished that her father had not seen it. Two years later he wept again at the memory. Capell's verdict was to be echoed by hundreds of British who followed him into Greece, when he said that only the indomitable spirit of the courageous people had enabled them to survive. That impression would remain with him for ever.

Like the people of other countries that had been overrun and occupied by the Axis powers, the Greeks had to learn to exist under their conquerers. Men and women in many professions found they had no alternative but to co-operate, to some extent, with their German and Italian masters. In the vast majority of cases, doctors, lawyers and civil servants had little choice, otherwise there would have been total anarchy, and inevitably this was doubly true in Athens and the larger towns. The narrow line dividing those who were in this category from the comparatively few who collaborated for personal gain, wealth and positions of importance often became impossible to define. Those living in comparative freedom in the remote mountain villages tended to condemn those who co-operated in any fashion with the Fascist rulers.

However, a large proportion of the bureaucracy of the German-sponsored regime was a hold-over of the Metaxas era, and inevitably this fact was not forgotten in the years of bitterness that followed. Lists were prepared and, in due course, retribution was sought when the German forces began pulling out of Greece. Amidst the hatred and emotion, more often than not inspired by the hard-line political KKE supporters, there were senseless acts of revenge against innocent people. Journalist Richard Capell was to pose the question: 'Had it been a service for every administrative officer to resign and leave no buffer between the people and the tyrants?' Greece was not, of course, alone in this problem, as Resistance movements in other European countries also singled out 'collaborators, many of whom did not deserve that title'.

As far as the Allied war effort was concerned, Greece was near the bottom of the list of priorities when 1941 changed to 1942. In Africa Rommel had failed to take Tobruk, and after a long withdrawal his forces stood almost where they had been when he had assumed command eleven months before – in the great Sirte bend between Ajetabia and Tripoli. In the Far East, Pearl Harbor had been the first of a long list of disasters that were to shake the United States and Great Britain. The shifting of the war to the Far East was to end white dominion in Asia which had marked the last 200 years. Britain was about to lose an empire, which she recovered after much fighting only to hand it over after the war ended.

Against these dramatic events, which continued into the early part of 1942, it is no small wonder that Headquarters Middle East Command had little time to think about supporting or organizing a resistance movement in Greece, although some saboteurs had been trained before the evacuation in 1941 and about a hundred sabotage kits left behind. In the event, the first sparks of defiance came from Greeks themselves, and the British, almost by accident, were to find themselves inextricably involved without any agreed long-term plan or any real conception of the political problems that would stem from their first major act of sabotage in the Greek hinterland.

After the winter of 1941-2 was over, differing factions in Athens and elsewhere tried to decide how they were going to react against the occupying Axis Powers. The formation, in the previous autumn, of the National Liberation Front (EAM) had been treated with wariness by most established politicians in Athens, who suspected, with good reason as it was to transpire, that it would be controlled by the Communists. The one common denominator which seemed to be shared by politicians who had opposed Metaxas was their distrust of the exiled King George, and few were brave or foolhardy enough to support him in public. 'No return without the people's consent' was the cry.

While the politicians prevaricated, so too did the regular officers of the armed forces, the more senior of whom felt that guerrilla warfare in the mountains would achieve little and merely bring down the vengeance of the Germans or Italians on the heads of innocent villagers. Three exceptions were officers who had all opposed Metaxas and been punished for so doing: Bakirdzis, Sarafis and Zervas. In their different ways, each man was to play a major role in fanning the spark of resistance in Greece until it became a forest fire. In the end, their Republican beliefs were not strong enough to withstand pressures from the KKE or, in the case of Zervas, from the British, so that in time Sarafis and Zervas became bitter enemies. Bakirdzis, known as 'the Red Colonel', eventually followed Sarafis' example and joined ELAS, although he was to have second thoughts when faced with the prospect of having to use force against the British in Salonika in late 1944. Britain had honoured him with a DSO for gallantry in the First World War, and memories may have influenced him into negotiations rather than open strife. Bakirdzis was to become yet another casualty of the Civil War: he committed suicide in 1947 after being deported to Ikaria.

During the early stages of the Occupation, Colonel Bakirdzis, under the pseudonym of Prometheus, was an important Allied intelligence agent in Athens, with a radio link to Middle East Command and thus, indirectly, to the Greek Government in Exile. Over that clandestine link, continually sought by the Nazi secret police, reports about conditions under the Fascist regime and news of the first stirrings of revolt were relayed back to SOE (Cairo), and on occasion by SOE to the British Foreign Office. One major item was the birth of EAM on 27 September 1941, which was the first step towards setting up the Military Wing, the National Popular Liberation Army (ELAS), whose formation was made public a few months later. As both military and civilian elements were politically minded to a degree to be found only in Greece – and their members discussed any and every subject – it was not long before the title EAM/ELAS was used for the sake of simplicity until, eventually, the terms became synonymous in the minds of most people.

With thousands of Greek citizens, full of pride and patriotic feeling, just waiting for a chance to take a more active role against the invaders, the newly formed EAM/ELAS was in an ideal position to take the lead. Hounded by the Metaxas regime, the Greek Communists had learnt to survive and build up clandestine links, as well as forming local committees so that their Moscow-trained leaders could continue to further the KKE cause. To translate words into deeds needed *kapetanios*, guerrilla leaders, who could inspire the youth in the mountains to take up arms in a way the KKE's Central Committee could not achieve from their urban hide-outs.

The fact that EAM/ELAS were creations of the KKE was suspected by many Athenians but this was not generally realized elsewhere, so that the appeal to young men in the mountain villages, eager to fight and for the excitement thus offered, was a strong one. The tragedy was that so many who volunteered to join found themselves trapped, especially after the factions became polarized when deep, ideological cleavages and a vendetta-like atmosphere permeated every aspect of national life. The anonymity of the EAM leaders aroused the suspicion of Archbishop Damaskinos in Athens, a striking figure of a man who stood over six feet six and whose courage, energy and resolution acted as a buffer between his people in Athens and their German and Italian conquerors.

Damaskinos had been deposed as Archbishop of Athens by Metaxas and restored by the Germans to his high office. However, if the occupiers expected unthinking co-operation from His Beatitude, they were to be bitterly disappointed. First Damaskinos refused to swear allegiance to the puppet-Government. In the months that followed, he denounced the deportation of Greek labour to the Third Reich; the deportation and savagely inhuman treatment of the Jews, mainly from the Salonika area; and other draconian measures imposed by the Axis authorities. In time, his moral courage led to Damaskinos' being put under house arrest, but it did not stop his activities for Greece. By autumn 1944 he was a much respected, popular figure throughout the country and especially so in Athens.

The Archbishop's comments about EAM/ELAS were recorded by Jeanne Tsatsos in her diary: 'But what is this EAM, can't they give us a name? ... I hear about this EAM and I don't know it. I don't believe in abstract ideals – at least for our country. I must know who are the men who are fighting for them.'

Damaskinos had not met the first ELAS *kapetan* to gain national fame, Aris Veloukhiotis (whose real name was Athanasios Klaras). If he had, there is little doubt that His Beatitude's reservations would have increased. Prior to 1941, Aris had led a chequered life, with periods spent in gaol and in exile, which had left him a bitter opponent of Metaxas and his supporters. Stefanos Sarafis was later to write that the imprisonment exile and torture Aris had endured had embittered him, even though, '... despite certain defects in his character and an extremism, due to a feeling of inferiority because he had signed a declaration (of repentance) during the Metaxas Dictatorship, we worked together very well.'

Myers and Woodhouse, both of whom knew Aris well, described him as being of short stature and wiry, a man who radiated self-confidence that helped to make him a simple, persuasive orator, which, coupled with his profound knowledge of Greek history, had an immediate appeal to village audiences. Brigadier Eddie Myers added that Aris relaxed only after drinking, an interesting statement because one of his future ELAS colleagues, Sarafis, criticized him for '... carousing with them [the British] in the evening; wanting to put them all up against the wall next morning'.

In the long term, Aris was to find that his original renouncement of Communism, albeit under duress, was never to be quite forgotten by the Central Committee of his Party, and this fact was to inhibit him at one or two crucial moments. With hindsight, it seems a tragedy that Aris, who had the personality to win men over to the ELAS cause, often used brutal methods both to recruit and to prevent desertion, and rumours of his behaviour began to percolate back to the Greek community in Egypt.

Another important leader was Colonel Napoleon Zervas, who took to the mountains of his native Epirus in April 1942. The portly, smiling Zervas had been one of several officers with strong Republican views who had not been allowed to fight against the Italian and German invaders by the Metaxas regime during 1940-41. An ardent follower of the exiled Republican General Plastiras, Zervas' past was not without blemish: he had been a professional gambler and had a dubious reputation, the details of which have become a mixture of fact and fiction over the years. Woodhouse was to say that Zervas original selection as a Resistance leader, to be supported by Britain, was 'one of the more dubious decisions by SOE; but justified as events were to prove'. With his merry, sparkling eyes and enormous black beard, Zervas was to be a respected, popular figure with those British officers who came into contact with him. Brigadier John (now Lord) Hunt, who met him in the autumn of 1944, described him as 'a bluff, laughing cavalier', a description that has been echoed by others. Opinions differ as to why Zervas took to the hills in the first place – one theory was that he was more or less blackmailed into doing so by the SOE. Be that as it may, he was to show that he did understand guerrilla warfare and even in adversity was totally loyal to the British.

From the end of 1941 the trickle of those escaping from Greece to join their armed forces in the Middle East had increased but the expense involved in arranging such escapes meant that more ex-officers than other ranks actually reached Egypt. As quite a number of the officers had been appointed by, and served under, Metaxas, their attitude towards ELAS was bound to be antagonistic and at variance with the feelings of the majority of men they led. In March 1943 such differences came to a head when there were mutinies in the Greek Brigade stationed in the Lebanon. It was Ambassador Reginald Leeper's introduction to the minefield of Greek politics.

In 1941 the Foreign Secretary, Anthony Eden, had explained to Australian-born Leeper why he would not be

sending him as Ambassador to Athens. 'That is too easy for
you. The Greeks are so friendly,' were the words used by the
Minister, words that Leeper was to recall to Eden when they
were both in the British Embassy in Athens under siege in
December 1944, with Greek snipers firing at the building.
Having been appointed Ambassador to the Greek Government in Exile in 1943, Leeper was soon to find divided
counsel not only among the politically minded Greeks –
which meant just about everyone, military or civilian in Egypt
– but between the FO in London, the SOE and the military
commanders in the Middle East. Rarely did they have the
same views on how the Resistance in Greece was to be
encouraged and then supported. Subsequently Leeper
himself played a major role which has been criticized by
left-wing writers and politicians.

When the King of Greece and Prime Minister Tsouderos
arrived in London after their narrow escape from Crete, the
FO, supported by Winston Churchill, tried to persuade them
to establish themselves in Egypt, where there was a large
Greek community with links to their mother country. The
British felt that in Cairo Tsouderos would be able to keep in
closer touch with affairs in Greece, as well as being near to
the Greek armed forces based in the Middle East. It was only
after strong pressure from Whitehall that the Prime Minister
and his colleagues did leave the United Kingdom for Egypt,
where the King joined them afterwards. The relationship
between King George and his Cabinet was often a strained
one, as most of his ministers were Republicans, while one or
two of those who joined the Cabinet, after the Government's
return to the Middle East, were strongly opposed to the
King's retaining power after the war.

Months after the BEF had left Greece, British and Greek
servicemen continued to escape or to do their best to avoid
imprisonment. Civilians, too, were trying to flee from the
occupied homeland in order to fight the Axis enemy. One of
those was a future Prime Minister of Greece, Panayiotis
Kanellopoulos, who was another of those banished by John
Metaxas. Kanellopoulos reached Cairo in 1942 after escaping
in a small boat with his wife and two companions. As a
youthful champion of democratic freedom, he was promptly
appointed Vice-President of the Greek Council and Deputy

Prime Minister of the Government in Exile. Kanellopoulos had refused to join EAM, when approached at the end of 1941, but he leaned farther to the left than Tsouderos and his colleagues in the exiled Government.

Although the first twelve parachutists who landed on Greek soil towards the end of 1942 were loosely called British, two were New Zealanders, one was a young Greek, Themi Marinos, who originally posed and dressed as a British officer, with a temporary commission because the Greek guerrillas had specifically ruled out Greek officers for the mission, and twenty-year-old Indar Gill, who was half-Indian, half-Scot. (In post-war years he was to attain the rank of Lieutenant-General in the Indian Army.) It is important to emphasize that none of these men was a professional intelligence agent or had received any detailed political briefing about the situation that was to confront them in the weeks to come. Indeed, with the exception of C.M. Woodhouse, Marinos and two signals NCOs, who had been nominated to stay on in Greece after the mission, the others were to return to Egypt as soon as Operation Harling had been completed.

The purpose of Operation Harling was to blow up one of three giant viaducts on the single-track Athens-Salonika railway, following which eight members of the team were to make their way to the coast, to be picked up by a submarine. All the team were selected at short notice, so that those commentators who have alleged that the British sought to take over the Resistance from the very beginning are not supported by the last-minute selection and rushed preparation of the first SOE mission to Greece.

Both the leader of the group, Colonel (later promoted to Brigadier) Eddie Myers, and his deputy, Major (Chris) Woodhouse, have written that the briefing they received in Cairo was haphazard and sketchy, to say the least. Myers, a regular in the Royal Engineers, had been overseas for nearly seven years and was within two weeks of handing over his job before returning to the United Kingdom. He had been employed in a staff appointment and has stated he was far from fit after sitting at a desk in Cairo. He spoke no Greek – unlike Woodhouse, who was fluent, as well as having served in Greece and Crete during 1940 and 1941. But Myers had completed his quota of parachute jumps and, being an officer in the Royal Engineers, had a professional knowledge of demolitions; he also had the reputation of being a most efficient staff officer.

The selection and briefing of the Harling team was very much a last-minute affair. One of the volunteers had not parachuted before and, as time was so short, the first jump he ever made was 'for real' onto Greek soil at night. Another, Major Denys Hanson, was asked if he was prepared to go on the operation on Saturday 26 September, just two days before the party was due to be dropped. Having said 'yes' at SOE HQ, 'a secret place known to every Cairo taxi-driver', there was little time for him to prepare for an operation that was now being given the highest priority by the Commander-in-Chief, Middle East.

With plans for the El Alamein battle well advanced, it was vital that German supplies to North Africa were effectively stopped, which included the single-track railway that ran through Greece down to Piraeus, for the bulk of Rommel's supplies came from that port and then across the sea in coastal vessels to Tobruk and Benghazi. The twelve volunteers were tasked to blow up one of three major bridges over the Gorgopotamos Gorge as soon as possible after they had landed in Greece and carried out a reconnaissance of the target area.

Myers divided his team into three self-supporting groups, each consisting of a leader, a linguist, a sapper (all officers) and a signals NCO (sergeant). This precaution was taken in case only one group landed and reached the target area: being self-contained, they could still carry out the mission, provided they were able to contact guerrillas who were prepared to assist them. The precaution was a wise one because, although the three groups did arrive and eventually met up, it was to be several long, frustrating days before they did so.

All three groups met with a chapter of accidents from the moment they first emplaned in Egypt. Eddie Myers and his companions in one aircraft had to return after searching in vain for recognition signals from what the crew thought was the proposed dropping zone: they had been briefed that there would be twelve fires lit by the waiting *andartes*.

Feeling thoroughly deflated, the four parachutists had to return to Cairo, only to try once more two nights later. As before, the air crew searched in vain for twelve lights, but the sight of two fires, possibly lit by shepherds, was enough to prompt Myers to drop there and then. Many of the group's stores that followed the four men went astray – or, more accurately, fell into the clutches of local villagers. Even more worrying was the fact that nothing was known about Zervas and his partisans – which was not surprising as they were some fifty miles to the west of the dropping point! Myers and his three companions had landed on the slopes of Mount Oeta, near a location that GHQ Cairo had decoded from a message from Athens as being 'Pera Karsi'. A subsequent investigation revealed that the correct location should have been 'Sakaretsi' in Epirus, where Zervas, night after night, waited patiently for the British parachutists who never came, over ten days march from where Myers had been dropped in error.

Denys Hanson, one of Myers' group, was to describe the area where they landed as '... to the tourist strange and wild, primitive and beautiful. And, of course, to the guerrillas, apart from the food problem, it is a heaven-sent playground.' Eventually they met up with the second group, but for several days there was no news about the third. Major Chris Woodhouse, Myers' second-in-command, set off to try to locate Zervas, taking with him a remarkable old man, Barba Niko, who had helped to feed and look after the group as they hid in a cave from the searching Italian troops for days on end. The tall, broad-shouldered Chris Woodhouse was a man of tremendous stamina and, when a weary Barba returned to the cave, saying that Woodhouse had continued on his own, his comment was, 'What a walker that boy is. He has the wings of Hercules on his feet.' Myers reckoned Woodhouse covered nearly 200 miles while searching for, and then returning with, Zervas. The portly, ebullient guerrilla leader was overcome with joy at seeing Woodhouse, greeting him as '*Evangelos*' ('Angel of Good Tidings'). Without hesitation, he offered immediate support for Harling and, after selecting some of his best men, he and Woodhouse set off to join Myers.

Meanwhile, having emplaned and deplaned for four

Reprisals by the Germans – a roofless village destroyed by fire

Left to right: King George II, Air Vice-Marshal J. D'Albiac and General Papagos in March 1941

The Bishop of Canea blesses a British Bren-carrier before the British defeat in Greece, April 1941

A Blenheim in Greece. Though outnumbered, the RAF air-crews
fought with gallantry

A briefing by Colonel K. Tzigantes DSO, during operations in the Aegean, summer 1944

Sailing in for the Liberation. *Left to right*: General Scobie, Harold Macmillan and Rear-Admiral John Mansfield on HMS *Orion*

Planning the liberation of Salonica, led by Major Anders Lassan VC (*centre*)

Crowds welcome the RAF in Patras on 4 October 1944.
Note the wide variety of banners

What the citizens of Corinth thought about German (Nazi-style) civilization, October 1944

Liberation Parade in Athens. *Left to right*: Lieutenant-General Othonaiosi (Commander-in-Chief Greek Forces), Prime Minister George Papendreou and Lieutenant-General R. M. Scobie

abortive sorties over Greece – and each time not dropping for one reason or another, the third group eventually landed close to the Italian garrison at Karpenisi. While they were floating down to earth, the Italians opened up with tracer fire and mortars but somehow or other the four parachutists managed to escape, to be found by Aris and his party. It needed diplomacy and the interpreting skills of Themi Marinos to persuade the ELAS leader to take them to Myers' cave. Aris had about eighty men with him so that, with Zervas' help, there would be 150 *andartes* for the operation. At last, and after several setbacks, it looked as if Harling stood a chance of being successful.

The early distrust between Zervas and Aris was never to disappear, especially when, initially, the ELAS leader appeared reluctant to join the venture, claiming that he would first have to obtain clearance from colleagues elsewhere. Whether he merely changed his mind or did seek and receive such permission is a matter of conjecture, but after Aris had committed his men to the operation, both he and Zervas worked in close harmony with the British team.

Prior to that, Myers and Hanson had carried out a close reconnaissance of the three possible targets and selected the one at Gorgopotamos (Swift River) as being the most suitable one to attack, even though it was only a matter of degree: all three would have been fraught with danger. The viaduct was closely guarded by some sixty to a hundred Italian guards actually on the spot, and local villagers said that German troops, acting as a mobile force, were held in reserve nearby. Myers' plan involved a simultaneous attack on the two guardposts at the south and north ends of the viaduct, as well as cutting all communications with the outer world, including the destruction of the railway track in case the enemy tried to rush up reinforcements by train. While this was going on, and after the south end of the viaduct had been captured, Captains Tom Barnes and Denys Hanson would go in below the bridge with the demolition party.

Months after the mission had been completed, an ELAS myth was born which claimed that the whole operation had been the brainchild of Aris, a claim that has been refuted by Woodhouse and others who participated in the raid. After his initial reconnaissance, Myers had prepared an outline plan which subsequently he discussed with Zervas and Aris, when he changed certain details on their advice. Aris was astute enough to realize that, if ELAS did not participate in this, the first major act of sabotage in Occupied Greece, it would be extremely damaging to their reputation. If it became known that they had not co-operated with the British parachutists, much of their appeal to the uncommitted youth of the country would have been lost.

The spirit of harmony and comradeship caused Woodhouse to recall that, on the approach march, Zervas and Aris were '... lying side by side in a straw hut with their legs sticking out; they were exchanging anecdotes in an ebullient mood.' Unfortunately for Greece, they were never to do this again. When the attack was launched against the guardposts on the viaduct, composite bands of EDES and ELAS *andartes* were fighting side by side, and after a prolonged and furious exchange of fire the one at the south end was captured. Barnes and his demolition party then moved in underneath the viaduct. The attack against the north post was pressed home and after a long fire-fight the Italian garrison was overcome. Meanwhile from the north could be heard explosions and gunfire, which meant that the Germans in their reinforcement train had been ambushed successfully. Barnes' first demolition explosion saw two complete spans of the bridge rising a few feet in the air, which was the signal for celebrations as far as three men were concerned: 'Zervas, Aris and I joined hands and danced on our own. Being three of us, we sang trumpeting as we danced the Klepther Ballad of "The Three Lads of Volos" ' (C.M. Woodhouse). The second charge exploded and the thunderous noise reverberated around the gorge as the spans of the viaduct collapsed and its piers toppled over.

The operation had been a great success and in high spirits the British party, with the mixed band of excited *andartes*, withdrew towards Mount Oeta. After checking numbers, Myers found that four guerrillas had been wounded but no one killed, a small cost to pay for cutting the vital German supply line, especially when it was to take the Germans seven weeks to repair and erect wooden trestles over the gap – which almost immediately broke down and had to be rebuilt once more. Of equal, or even greater, importance, news of the daring exploit spread from village to village throughout Greece, bringing the first real ray of hope to a nation which had suffered greatly during a year of enemy occupation, made worse by the terrible famine of the 1941-2 winter. It was to be the first and last time the ELAS and EDES worked in amicable, close co-operation against their common foe.

Outside Greece, others were equally impressed by the destruction of the Gorgopotamos viaduct, the most important being Adolf Hitler himself. His adjutant noted that the Führer had stressed that, 'The recent blowing up of a bridge [Gorgopotamos) had shown how disagreeable for supplies such a disruption of traffic could be.... The enemy must be prevented from continuing their partisan war against the Axis line of communications, otherwise a catastrophic situation would arise.' Zervas and Aris were both honoured with OBEs from the British Government, an award declined by the latter, who said that he would prefer boots for his *andartes*.

Aris's cruelty was witnessed by Hanson when, after the viaduct operation, an Italian prisoner was killed in cold blood by a young lad of sixteen with a knife, as Aris stood by, 'smiling into his beard'. Later Hanson, drawing on his experiences as a BLO with ELAS, was to describe Aris as 'the most ruthless man I've ever met, and most cold-blooded, and the cruellest. He was an ex-schoolmaster, sentenced in Greece for homosexual offences and trained in the Moscow School of Communists, an intelligent, able man with no heart, without human pity ... a fanatical leader of men.'

Despite Denys Hanson's obvious hostility, he admitted that, 'Aris was very brave physically and he was a colourful and important figure in this period of Revolutionary Greek history.' That opinion was to be more than reinforced by Costa G. Couveras, a major in American Intelligence, when he came to Greece later in the war: 'Aris impressed me as the greatest of the EAM/ELAS leaders whom I met during my sojourn in Greece.'

Later Myers and his team heard that, although they had withdrawn from the Gorgopotamos Viaduct without any loss of life, thirteen hostages from the nearest village had been shot by the Italians, including a gallant man, Costa Pistolis, who had not only given them useful information but helped as a guide during the planning stages of Harling. He was tortured by the Gestapo and, steadfastly refusing to implicate others, was shot. Dozens of courageous Greeks were to suffer a similar fate, their loyalty to friends and relatives unbroken by torture and imminent death. The Germans took over responsibility for guarding the three viaducts in the area, one of which, Asopos, was to be selected as a target in the future, when it became the cause of further altercation between Myers and the ELAS leaders.

Myers and those due to return to Egypt by submarine began their long, laborious march towards the coast accompanied by an officer and some *andartes* from EDES. On 22 December, after circumventing several villages to avoid detection, they bade a warm farewell to the *andartes* who had escorted them. With their battledress in tatters, and boots torn and useless, it was only the thought of the submarine and the return to the fleshpots of Egypt that kept Myers and his companions going day after day. Security was always a problem, even when it was known that the village nearby was a friendly one. Myers was to reflect on how difficult it was for a Greek peasant to keep a secret to himself, a sentiment often repeated elsewhere by British servicemen in Greece during the 1940s.

At journey's end, the party awaited evacuation night after night: seven British officers, one NCO and two Cypriots kept a fruitless vigil, straining their eyes into the gloom, often imagining the hull of a submarine breaking surface. As each night passed, they were disappointed but not disheartened. When Christmas Day came, Myers wondered if he had ever spent, or would spend again, such a bleak and unhappy Christmas. That afternoon one of Zervas' men arrived, bearing a note from Woodhouse to the effect that there would be no submarine coming to fetch them. They were not going to be evacuated from Greece. Instead they were ordered to stay on. Woodhouse added that Bill Jordan, another New Zealander, who was a specialist signals officer, had parachuted in to organize the wireless communications which had rarely worked. The morale of the party, at hearing the bombshell from GHQ Cairo, was at rock bottom.

'We had marched our way to the coast and now we would have to march back again ... on nothing. In silence and bitterness we looked to our packs and our boots. We were going to live in Greece now, indefinitely ...' (Denys Hanson). As for volunteering to stay on, that request was met with mutiny in their hearts. It was not surprising. They had carried out their mission, magnificently – only to find that no one was coming to fetch them out. Subsequently Myers was told that the Royal Navy had already lost one submarine while trying to pick up an SOE group elsewhere, and reluctantly the Commander-in-Chief, Mediterranean, felt that another submarine could not be risked.

Wearily they began a nightmare march back during which Myers contracted double pneumonia, and for a day or two it looked as if he was going to die. He owed much to Themie Marinos, especially when the Italian troops moved towards the village of Skoulikaria. The sick officer had to be taken out in a hurry on a diminutive donkey, shortly before the Italians burnt down the village. At a crucial moment, an airdrop brought in medicines which helped to restore Myers to health once more. One of the party noted that the large container was marked in illiterate Greek, for which the English equivalent would have been 'For the Seeck Colonello'. It seemed incredible, to that observer, that the SOE organization at base could not find somebody to write the language correctly – if it had to be marked in Greek!

By early February Myers had recovered almost miraculously, and Edmunds, Indar and Hanson agreed to do what they could to help, during the time they were obliged to stay in Greece – but they still wanted to be evacuated at the first opportunity. By this time the thirteenth man, in the person of New Zealander Bill Jordan, had arrived and reported to Myers. He had been sent in primarily because no messages had been received in Cairo from the Harling group, so he had been told to find Myers as soon as possible and to brief him about the background to the sad fact that there was to be no evacuation in the foreseeable future; they were to stay on indefinitely. For Myers there was a new assignment, as commander of a military mission set up to co-ordinate action with any Greek partisans prepared to co-operate with the British against the Germans and Italians.

Bill Jordan has been described as a likeable, quick-tempered man, full of energy and impatient of sham. He was

also a first-class signals officer and, using the equipment he
had brought in with him, regular, reliable communications
were quickly established with Cairo which meant that, in one
important respect, Myers was better off, as supplies could be
requested and, within reason, dropped whenever the
weather, Luftwaffe and aircraft availability so allowed. Bill
Jordan and his NCO signallers worked extremely long hours
enciphering and decoding a string of messages, the volume
of which increased as the political ramifications that faced the
new BMM in Greece unravelled.

1943 was an exciting year in Europe, and one of hope for
the Allies in several theatres. In Greece, however, it was a
tragic one, because the temporary alliance forged at
Gorgopotamos between ELAS and EDES disintegrated and
relations continued to worsen until open civil war flared up
in the late autumn, to add a new and terrifying dimension of
suffering to an already ravaged country.

As resistance to the occupying force grew, so the savagery
of German and Italian reprisals in Greece escalated. Stung by
the Gorgopotamos sabotage, the Italians executed innocent
hostages at Lamia. In Athens the secret police continued to
exact retribution against anyone who violated, or was alleged
to have violated, the Axis code. Jeanne Tsatsos wrote at the
beginning of January: 'They hunt us down without ceasing.
Every day they kill.'

Into the city of tension and rumours came one of two
famous brothers, Major Yiannis Tzigantes, from Egypt, to
have talks with politicians and senior officers as well as
organizing resistance within the Athens-Piraeus area and, in
particular, sabotaging the Corinth Canal. The intrepid
Tsigantes' efforts attracted too much attention and gossip,
and after being surprised by the Italian Secret Police, he was
killed in a gun-fight. Keeping a secret in Athens was, as St
Paul discovered, difficult – 'For all the citizens, and the
foreigners who lived there, liked to spend all their time
telling and hearing the latest new thing' (Acts 17, verse 21).
Unfortunately several names of fellow-conspirators were in
Tsigantes' possession, and this led to some arrests and to even
more people going underground or having to leave Athens
in haste.

The majority of pre-1941 politicians prevaricated;

although keen to be recognized as patriots, prepared to strike a blow for freedom against the Axis, they had reservations about EAM's close connection with the Communists which could threaten their future positions. In contrast, the KKE Central Committee had no doubts whatever. At a secret meeting during December 1941 held in Thessaly, they drew up plans for a complete monopoly of the resistance movement, and to this end a massive recruiting programme was set in motion in most parts of the country – the north-west being the exception, Zervas' home territory. Following such a rapid expansion came requests for weapons and, although Aris made little attempt to hide his hatred of the British, he was prepared to accept BLOs with his groups, not only as a means of getting arms and supplies but to retain respectability in the eyes of the uncommitted Greek people, the majority of whom looked on the British as friends to be trusted. As Myers had been given specific instructions by SOE (Cairo) to direct and co-ordinate all *andartes'* action, he duly sent BLOs to work with ELAS, including the reluctant Denys Hanson, whose account of what happened is contained in *We Fell Among Greeks*.

In January 1943 Monty Woodhouse, better known as 'Chris' during his service in Greece, had managed to persuade Aris not to attack Zervas. After reporting this to Myers, Woodhouse set off for Athens on a mission ordered by SOE, the purpose of which was for him to contact an unofficial group of six colonels, with a view to enlisting their aid in organizing a national resistance movement. Even though Woodhouse spoke the language fluently, his height and colouring made it a dangerous undertaking for him to pass as a Greek, and it was a hazardous enterprise from start to finish. In the event, four of the colonels he met were reluctant to commit themselves. Of more importance, Woodhouse had talks with leaders of the KKE, in particular George Siantos, the Secretary-General, known as 'the Old Man', and Andreas Tzimas, former Communist deputy in Macedonia. Woodhouse's presence in Athens could not be hidden for long, and Tzimas helped to whisk the tall Englishman away before the Gestapo in Athens pounced.

Tzimas and Siantos were Communists whose ideas on how the movement was to progress were at variance on several occasions. Siantos, the orthodox Party man, wanted to tighten political control over the *andarte* bands throughout the country. Shortly afterwards, Tzimas set off for the mountains, where he became the political representative at ELAS GHQ. His influence was to exert a certain restraint on the erratic Aris while, at the same time, he was to establish a cordial relationship with Myers and Woodhouse, which was possibly one of the reasons that led to his eventual removal from the ELAS triumvirate. In Woodhouse's opinion, Tzimas was 'the only intelligent and reasonable Communist leader and his departure [on a mission to Tito in Yugoslavia] was a calamity for Greece'.

While Woodhouse was dodging the Secret Police in Athens, his SOE superior in Cairo, Brigadier Keble, had suggested he should remain in the city to co-ordinate intelligence and sabotage, a suicidal instruction to say the least! Meanwhile Myers was doing his best to encourage the formation of national bands of guerrillas who would operate, with British support, against the Axis. Aris refused to commit himself, pointing out that he would have to seek permission from Athens before joining, but two ex-regular officers with strong Republican views came forward as potential leaders of such groups, Colonels Psarros and Sarafis. Psarros had close links with a group of middle-class Liberals, among whom was Jeanne Tsatsos, whose diary entries stated that his group, EKKA, operating around Mount Parnassus in early 1943, contained many members who had republican, and even monarchist, sympathies.

Initially the much more Socialist-minded Sarafis, with his military bearing and general attitude, impressed Myers but the British commander later changed that favourable opinion: 'I should have paid far more attention to his rather weak chin and evasive watery blue eyes.' At first there was a degree of rapport between them, probably because Sarafis usually got on well with regular officers, a point he makes more than once in his memoirs.

Although Sarafis agreed to raise and command a band of guerrillas in Thessaly, it was not long before he began to have doubts. After the war, he wrote that a unified resistance movement was the only way to liberate Greece and he was not interested in helping the British war effort, if it was at the expense of the peasant people, left to the mercy of the invader. On the face of it, that was a noble sentiment, but if it had been carried out literally, there would have been different types of resistance movements in all the occupied countries during the Second World War because, sadly, the Germans invariably exacted retribution following acts of sabotage, and it was the innocent who suffered.

After Zervas, Psarros and Sarafis had agreed to co-operate as part of the national band concept (non-political, unified and under the overall command of the Commander-in-Chief, Middle East), there were long discussions with Myers about the appointment of a Greek commander of such a force. They agreed that the exiled General Plastiras would be a most suitable choice to lead such an enterprise. This recommendation, relayed back by Myers to Cairo, met with a rebuff when SOE, the FO and the KKE Central Committee all turned it down. KKE was not interested in sharing power in any form with Plastiras, while the British Foreign Office felt that the exiled general was 'too politically tainted as a Republican'. As yet unknown to Myers, the future of the exiled King George II was a powerful factor in shaping British foreign policy towards Greece, and unfortunately the FO often spoke with a different voice to the Service Commanders in the Middle East, whose aim was to win the war as soon as possible, without being hampered by possible political repercussions in the peace that followed.

Myers' plans were to suffer an even more serious setback when he was informed that Sarafis and some of his officers, after accepting hospitality from a local ELAS group, had been taken prisoner during the night and their men disarmed. His immediate reaction was to signal Cairo to stop sending any more arms to ELAS until the matter had been resolved: Zervas was much more belligerent and wanted to rescue Sarafis by attacking the ELAS group. In the end, Myers, accompanied by Themi Marinos, set off at speed for Porta in the south-west plain. On their way, the two men heard how the captured Sarafis had been led in handcuffs through villages to be greeted with shouts of 'Dosilog! Prodotis!' – 'Collaborator! Traitor!'. On arrival in the village, Myers learnt that Sarafis had been accused of collaboration with the Italians in Trikkala, an accusation that was to prove

about as accurate as the story spread by ELAS later that
Zervas collaborated with the Germans for gain – as opposed
to merely a local truce. After pleading for the life of Sarafis,
Myers obtained a stay of execution until the arrival of Aris
and Tzimas at the end of March. After the two ELAS leaders
had arrived, he once more explained that he was seeking
ways of co-ordinating the resistance movement throughout
the country. On this occasion, Tzimas was not helpful; he
accused Zervas of being a British puppet with ambitions to
become a dictator after the war, and he objected to BLOs
'running the Greek Resistance, with the long-term aim of
restoring King George II to the throne after the war was
over'. Such a cry was to be heard by BLOs on numerous
occasions, and it was to continue to be one of the main planks
of EAM/ELAS propaganda for months to come in Greece.

Sarafis was released but to Myers' astonishment the man
who had been marched from North Pindus to Roumeli in
chains had accepted the post of Generalissimo of ELAS. It
was an amazing *volte face*, about which Sarafis gives only the
barest of details in his memoirs. The British officers who
knew him best, Myers and Woodhouse, were inclined to be
more charitable than some of their subordinates, such as
Denys Hanson, who ended the war as a Lieutenant-Colonel
with an OBE and an MC. Hanson's comment was: 'Sarafis,
far from being grateful to us for having saved his life, became
our bitterest enemy.'

Thin, dark haired, rather intense, Sarafis was a big catch as
far as EAM/ELAS was concerned, for in a short time his
name attracted a number of much-needed regular officers to
commit themselves to ELAS. What is not clear is to what
extent he controlled the destiny of ELAS after he became its
first C-in-C. That the Communist leaders wanted someone of
his stature was understandable and proven by the fact that
the post of Generalissimo had first been offered to Zervas,
who had turned it down. Sarafis was to give two reasons for
his sudden conversion to the ELAS cause. Firstly, he felt that
only ELAS was big enough to unite all the Resistance
factions, adding that too many small organizations would
have been inefficient from the military point of view and
impossible to co-ordinate nationally. Secondly, he had not
been impressed by the discipline and bearing of Zervas'

guerrillas, which contrasted most unfavourably with the uniform, turnout and spirit of his ELAS captors.

An angry Myers accused him of being intimidated into joining ELAS, a charge that Sarafis hotly denied. Later the brigadier was to take a more charitable view by writing: 'He was an educated man and, although he may not have been blessed with many of the qualities of a leader, I believe that in his own mind he thought that what he was doing was the best thing for his country.' Woodhouse felt that Sarafis genuinely believed in a Socialist democracy as well as being a Republican, and was prepared to accept that the KKE did also. Whether Sarafis was just being naïve or was reluctant to face unpalatable facts is not easy to judge because his memoirs throw little light on some of the more controversial aspects of ELAS' bid for power. When compiling his story, Sarafis often ignored a contentious episode completely or dismissed it in a few bland words.

During the summer of 1943 ELAS' new GHQ consisted of the triumvirate Sarafis, Aris and Tzimas, and the three men remained together until the last-named was sent by the KKE Central Committee on a mission to Tito in Yugoslavia during the late autumn. Myers set up his own HQ nearby in the Pindus village of Theodharan. His task was made much more difficult by the apparent inability of his superiors in London and Cairo to appreciate that any attempt to impose the King's return on a reluctant Greek people was bound to fail; indeed, he strongly advocated that a statement should be issued, on behalf of the King, promising that he would not return until a nation-wide plebiscite had been held immediately after the war. Myers and his BLOs appreciated that EAM was portraying the King as a bogy-man in order to win support to themselves.

In January Myers had warned Cairo that, in his opinion, ELAS had long-term ambitions which went beyond immediate resistance to the Axis Powers, and he pointed out that there was ample evidence in EAM newspapers to show that coercion was being used to win over reluctant villagers to their cause. One newspaper had warned its readers that there would be 'no wheat until you join ELAS'. Another EAM paper threatened that, 'Anyone not joining EAM would be considered as a traitor to Greece.' Such threats were hardly

conducive to a free choice even without 'armed banditi' supporting the messages with menacing gestures and weapons.

Despite initial setbacks, Myers continued to negotiate with
the ELAS leaders, and after much argument and time-wasting
the first move towards an agreement was signed, in return for
which arms and supplies were to be delivered by Middle East
Command. The brigadier had shown admirable patience,
although Sarafis accused him of working for political ends
under the pretext of helping to organize the guerrillas. Nevertheless, at the time of Myers' departure, Sarafis's verdict was
that, 'He showed honest sincerity and was thought to be
friendly towards EAM.' In fact, Myers had no doubts about
the long-term aims of ELAS, but within the directive he had
been given, an agreement had been achieved between ELAS
on the one hand and EDES and EKKA on the other, with
BLOs and their signallers attached to the main groups
throughout the mountainous area of Greece. Bill Jordan's
opinion was that Eddie Myers, although not an effusive type of
man, was always fair and just. Not surprisingly, Zervas did not
share Myers' faith in ELAS's professed good intentions and
said so in these words: 'I believe I know what is good for
Greece. I believe what you are doing is wrong for my country.
However, I realize you are only obeying your orders.'

To confuse the picture of Greece under Axis rule in 1943,
SOE was receiving very different reports from Rufus Shepherd, a BLO who initially spoke little Greek and relied on an
Egyptian-Greek interpreter. (Myers did not know that Shepherd had been parachuted in by SOE to join ELAS in the
Mount Olympus area.) His signals contained glowing comments about the wonderful discipline of ELAS, in particular
stressing how well the *andartes* marched in columns during
night moves – not necessarily the best tactics for partisans to
adopt! His early telegrams were so full of praise for ELAS that
Bill Jordan commented on Shepherd's naïvety in these words:
'He had dropped into Communists who immediately fed him
with the Communist line, little realizing that he was swallowing
it. Swallow it he did and he became quite arrogant towards
Brigadier Myers.... He passed to Cairo the Communist tale
that Myers was not doing his job, that Zervas was a traitor.'

The second liaison officer to join an ELAS Group, Nick
Hammond, with knowledge of the Greek language, was able

to understand the movement's thoughts and policies more deeply than Shepherd could. The latter's optimism was not reflected in Hammond's reports to Myers, and at a conference held at the London School of Economics, organized by the Society for Modern Greek Studies, it was clear that Professor Hammond had not changed his opinions some thirty years later. (12/15 May 1978.)

It was some time before Myers was able to meet Rufus Shepherd and thrash out their differences. Once a lecturer in English at Cairo University, towards the end of the Occupation and before the Liberation of Greece, he visited Athens on several occasions, latterly living there to organize anti-sabotage operations. By a cruel twist of fate, Shepherd was killed by an ELAS mine in Athens during December 1944. After his death, one or two left-wing sources alleged that he had been shot by a sniper and produced a story from a witness who claimed to have seen 'a Britisher hiding behind a window with a gun'. With both protagonists wearing battle-dress at that time, from such a fleeting impression another fable was born!

After BLOs and their signallers had been attached to the majority of the main partisan groups, Myers was in a much better position to co-ordinate action, provided, of course, the ELAS commanders were prepared to participate. Although the total number of British and Allied agents, officers and signallers dropped into Greece did not exceed 200, the part they played and the influence they exerted was out of all proportion to that number in arranging arms and supplies for the partisans, especially during the period between May and July 1943, in organizing sabotage against a wide range of targets. For those who survived and subsequently returned to Greece in happier times, there has been the reward of being greeted as friends by people from all walks of life.

Having helped to arm a substantial number of the regular ELAS units, Myers was under pressure from Sarafis and his colleagues to start procuring weapons for their reservists, a request that was not granted – with good reason, perhaps. For a start, it had never been the intention of the GHQ Middle East Command to raise and equip a Greek army within the occupied country because, for sound military reasons, that would have risked a blood-bath: half-trained *andartes* could not have hoped to take on well-equipped German and Italian troops in open conflict, especially if they lacked the support of heavy weapons or help from the air. To have done this would have thrown away their ability to move and react as guerrillas – a lesson Nikos Zacharides was to learn in 1948/9 when he dared to take on the newly raised, American-equipped Greek Army by using conventional military tactics. Moreover, the task of delivering supplies by air had a low priority in the Middle East during the early summer months of 1943 – only one squadron could be spared. The full-time efforts of 148 Squadron RAF (Halifax aircraft) were employed in nightly missions whenever the moon was favourable, and every other night when there was no moon – which meant an average of twenty night sorties a month between April and August of that year. Greece was well down the list of Allied strategic priorities at that time, a truth that was hard to accept by men operating in the mountainous areas of that country.

After the war, it was alleged that Aris turned against the British, and Myers in particular, only when ELAS did not receive arms and supplies in the quantities they sought. Bill Jordan (later a Roman Catholic priest) strongly refuted that assertion: 'Aris was always anti-British.... Although I had great respect for Aris's intelligence and for his ability as a guerrilla leader, never, however, did he try to conceal his hatred for Britain or for our mission in Greece.' Jordan was one SOE officer who felt that it was wrong to arm too many *andartes*, maintaining that ELAS HQ's request for extensive arming of their men was for political rather than military reasons.

The most effective acts of sabotage during June and July were carried out by small groups under good leaders rather than by large formations of the 'Liberation Army' – which is what ELAS proclaimed itself to be. Although Sarafis' understanding of guerrilla warfare is open to serious doubt, it cannot be denied that he was an efficient staff officer, endowed with energy and enthusiasm which enabled him to carry out much-needed reorganization in a short time. Training schools for officers were opened, a wide-ranging network of telephonic communications was established, and ELAS formations began to be organized on the lines of a regular army. In time, ELAS enlisted the services of sixteen generals, thirty-four colonels and some 1,500 other officers of the pre-war Greek Army. As to whether the overall result was of benefit to ELAS, in their role as partisans, is open to dispute. Officers with Force 133 have stated that some of the Greek regular officers did not understand guerrilla warfare and were more interested in regaining their pre-war status as officers. Sarafis believed he was laying the foundation for a National Army in a Socialist state. His opponents, including such Republicans and Liberals as Papendreou and Psarros, were convinced that the weapon he was forging would be taken over by the KKE, and pointed out that six members of the EAM Committee of eight were hardline Communists. By autumn 1943 Papendreou's views, so much opposed to those held by Sarafis and his colleagues, had hardened, until the chances of a peaceful reconciliation between the opposing factions diminished as the war in Europe moved to its climax.

Why Greece should have suffered far more than any other occupied country in Europe, not only in the immediate aftermath of liberation but in the five years that followed, is a question that has exercised historians and commentators alike. Perhaps one major reason is that, more politically minded than any other European race, the Greeks loved a cause, and only a tiny spark was needed to set on fire a kindling forest. With an insatiable curiosity not only about his neighbour but everybody else in the street or village, the average Greek peasant was a great talker, ranging over the whole field of human activities. In the mountain villages especially, men embroidered common tales without being liars, and invented new ones which in turn became myths. All this made the Greek an unrivalled propagandist.*

---

* The past tense has been used by deliberate intent as the author has based his opinion, and that of others, on wartime experiences and those of the immediate post-war era. BBC journalist Kenneth Matthews has produced an example from C.M. Woodhouse regarding a judicial enquiry held in a village into the alleged murder of a country priest: voluble witnesses were describing the scene, including pools of blood, in great detail when the subject of their testimony, the priest himself, walked in as hale of body as he was no doubt blameless of soul. In a village near Kilkis in mid-1945, the author had a similar experience when his company was searching for hidden weapons. Once again, witnesses bewailed the brutal murder of a respected elder, only for the 'victim' to appear an hour or two later apparently in the best of health and spirits.

The Greeks in the mountains were hot-blooded, volatile, capable of extreme courage and absolute despair; although great patriots, they were also capable of disregarding fellow-countrymen to a degree not found in other nations. It is for this reason that, having fought the Germans and Italians during the Occupation briefly and spasmodically when led by audacious Greek and British commanders, with increasing passion they then fought each other; following that, they took on the British Army; and finally they fought a long-drawn-out, atrocious civil war. Caught up in a cause, thousands threw away their lives at a moment's notice: truly a Greek tragedy which continued to cast a black shadow over the nation years after the fighting had ended.

For a few weeks in mid-1943, the internecine struggle between ELAS and EDES virtually ceased. Using BLOs and their network of communications, Myers orchestrated 'Operation Animals', the code-name for an intensive period of guerrilla activity throughout the country. Prior to that, he had divided the mountains of Greece into four regions, each co-ordinated by a British lieutenant-colonel, with subordinate BLOs with radio links in each group. The purpose of 'Animals' was to deceive the Axis into thinking that an Allied landing in Greece was imminent, thus drawing reserves into the country and diverting attention from the real target, Sicily. Away from Athens, road and rail communications came under attack and were cut in dozens of places, one of the most successful being a raid led by Themi Marinos against a strong German force on the Arta-Agrininon road. Myers' security was so tight that even his field BLOs sensed and shared Greek hopes that liberation was imminent.

The deception worked because the Germans reacted strongly, moving two divisions into Greece especially to counter the threat, to meet what they anticipated would be a sea-borne invasion. With communications disrupted in many parts of Greece, expectations among the local people were high, too, so that, when the true purpose of the operation was revealed after the invasion of Sicily had been announced, the complete anti-climax engendered a deep sense of bitterness at the let-down, with yet another winter to be faced under the Axis. In addition, the acts of sabotage provoked a vicious response from the German troops, who burnt down villages and shot innocent hostages by the score. While 'Animals' probably helped the Allied war effort in the long-term, Greece suffered grievously immediately afterwards. Woodhouse commented, 'It was hard to deceive our allies as well as the enemy.'

The German troops brought in to bolster the Italians soon made their presence felt and the *andartes* found they could no longer carry out raids with impunity.

SOE (Cairo) had asked Myers if it was possible to repeat the Gorgopotamos attack, which prompted Denys Hanson's comment: 'Really, their lack of appreciation was something incredible.' Hanson knew that the Germans had taken over the responsibility for guarding the viaduct from their unreliable and, by now, disenchanted Italian allies. Gorgopotamos was no longer a feasible target but the nearby viaduct of Asopos was a possibility, provided *andarte* support was available to divert the attention of the guards, while the demolition party set the charges and blew up the bridge.

Initially Aris appeared to be enthusiastic and even set off on a preliminary reconnaissance with Myers, only to be recalled by his two colleagues, Sarafis and Tzimas. Sarafis was adamant that 'on military grounds it was impractical', Tzimas that it was too risky and would bring savage reprisals onto the heads of innocent people in the district. As an alternative target, Sarafis suggested the nearby Tirnavo tunnel, a few miles north of Lamia, an idea which did not appeal to Myers; as a professional engineer, he estimated that the damage caused could have short-term benefits only. Nevertheless, ELAS did carry out the raid against the tunnel and blocked it – for about a week, as Myers had forecast, it was a success in that German soldiers were trapped in a troop-train and as a result ELAS obtained a quantity of arms. Retribution followed: the Germans announced that they would shoot fifty Greeks for every German soldier killed. It was no idle threat: 118 Greeks, all members of EAM, were taken from the internment camp at Larissa and shot at the scene of the incident. Such savage reprisals inevitably discouraged too much subversive activity and indirectly led to inter-partisan strife.

Undeterred by the refusal of ELAS to co-operate, Myers decided that the Asopos viaduct operation would be carried

out by a small group of British officers, helped by two
escaped prisoners of war. Two officers who carried out the
first reconnaissance were the driving force behind one of the
most remarkable and hazardous acts of sabotage in occupied
Europe during the war. They were Captain Geoffrey Gordon-
Creed, the BLO with Psarros, and the tall, fair New
Zealander Donald Stott, who had already survived a series of
wartime adventures. After being wounded in Crete, he had
escaped from captivity as a POW to spend some seven
months at large in the Greek mountains before sailing a small
boat from Greece to Alexandria. Now he was back for an
even more eventful chapter in his short life. (He died when
the submarine in which he was travelling, on another SOE
assignment in the Far East, disappeared without trace in
1945.)

The Asopos viaduct was closely guarded by a German
garrison of about forty men, with six heavy machine-guns
and a variety of other weapons, while their surveillance at
night was assisted by a powerful roving searchlight. The only
possible approach was down a long rocky cleft, never more
than ten feet wide, sometimes as narrow as two. With the
explosives wrapped in waterproof covers, the first party
made their way beneath waterfalls and through deep pools.
They still had not reached the main gorge a day later, only to
find they had run out of rope necessary for negotiating
further waterfalls. Back they went to their base at Amatoli
and, after more rope had been dropped by parachute to
them, and the moonlight gained sufficient strength to enable
them to move during hours of darkness, they set off once
more.

Apart from Gordon-Creed and Stott, the party consisted of
three sapper officers, Wingate, Scott and McIntyre; a
Gorgopotamos veteran, Sergeant Michael Khuri, a Palesti-
nian Arab who had been awarded the Military Medal for that
exploit; two escaped British prisoners of war, Lance-
Corporals Chester Lockwood and Charlie Mutch; and finally
Greek interpreter George Karadjopoulos. On 16 June Stott,
Mutch and Khuri, using the extra rope, went the whole way
down the gorge in daylight to observe the viaduct. Once
there, they noticed that workmen were riveting and
concreting, with scaffolds surrounding both ends. Three

days later, Gordon-Creed, Scott and McIntyre arrived at the head of the gorge and, following another reconnaissance at dusk by Gordon-Creed and Stott, which took them to a point almost under the viaduct, the decision was made to attack that night.

Fortunately for the saboteurs, not only had the workmen cut gaps in the barbed wire at the foot of the main central span but conveniently they had left a ladder giving access through the scaffolding to a platform about thirty feet up, from which the main girders could be reached. The two sappers, Scott and McIntyre, ascended and pulled up the explosives after them. One German sentry who approached had to be coshed, his body toppling over the cliff, with the roaring torrent drowning the sound of his fall. Although there were German guards on the bridge, pacing to and fro directly above them, the two young officers prepared the charges with meticulous care beneath the bright light of the moon, drawing back at intervals whenever the German searchlight illuminated the bridge. Just after midnight everything was ready and, although on one occasion they were caught in the glare of the searchlight, the saboteurs were not noticed as they scrambled their hazardous way back up the gorge.

At 2.15 there was a short explosion which reverberated like loud thunder claps, and Stott, who had remained as an observer, saw the whole of the structure collapse, dragging down the spans at each end. A day later, completely unscathed, the tired men were back at base. Myers was to comment that, 'For sheer guts and determination to succeed, and pluck, there was no greater achievement.' Donald Stott was recommended for the VC by Myers but, as no shot had been fired throughout the whole operation, that award had to be changed to an immediate DSO. All other members were given richly deserved gallantry awards.

It was to take the Germans two months to repair the viaduct, and when the first train was crossing it, the pier collapsed, so that a further two months elapsed before the line was working properly. The Germans could not understand how the viaduct had been destroyed. The Wehrmacht High Command newspaper of 21 June reported that, 'During the night of 20/21 June, the Salonika-Athens

railway line was cut in six places by explosions in the
Katerini-Asopos region. The spans of the Asopos Bridge
have been destroyed. It is presumed that this sabotage was
carried out by Greek workers who have recently been
reinforcing the bridge under the supervision of German
engineers. The workers have been arrested. [Later reports
indicated that 40 were shot.] There was no passage of arms
with the detachment guarding the bridge.'

Strangely enough, this act of sabotage, unique in the annals
of the Second World War, because it was carried out by a
small band of British parachutists without any assistance
from the Resistance forces, one that completely blocked the
vital Salonika to Athens line for so long, was not mentioned
by Sarafis in his memoirs. Despite a firm refusal to assist and
commit ELAS to the operation, his reluctance to give any
praise or even to record such a major blow against the
Germans is difficult to understand. Having forecast that it
was bound to fail, it would have been generous of the ELAS
commander if, at least, he had acknowledged that a small
body of men, after risking all, had achieved so much by their
daring. Perhaps that is why Bill Jordan was to write that
Sarafis was 'still a rather neutral personality, in spite of the
high post he was holding'.

Having got everything going at full speed so that the
original SOE directive of arming, organizing and training
guerrilla groups had been amply justified, the brakes were
put on by SOE after the Sicily landings. For the BLOs,
the weeks that followed were a trying period. In his book,
Denys Hanson explained how much he enjoyed himself
during three weeks of maximum activity. But, unknown to
Hanson and other members of the mission, politics had
begun enmeshing the Resistance Movement not only in
Greece but in GHQ Cairo and London, and especially in the
FO.

Despite warning signals relayed back by Myers as soon as
his communications began working efficiently in January
1943, the FO continued to view EDES with more suspicion
than they did ELAS, chiefly because of Zervas' known
association with the exiled General Nikolas Plastiras, an
avowed opponent of the King. The FO's information about
life in occupied Greece was scanty, to say the least: the King's

unpopularity with the majority of his subjects was not appreciated, and a few more weeks were to pass before opinions in Whitehall began to change.

As to why the gist of the messages sent by Myers to SOE in Cairo were not relayed back to London, that is outside the scope of this book, except to state that evidence of the inter-departmental wrangling between SOE, the FO and at times the War Office can be seen in the relevant Foreign Office papers, now open for study. Unfortunately the equivalent SOE documents are either missing or will remain under wraps until after the turn of the century. For the moment, then, SOE's case against the FO has gone by default.

On many occasions SOE was caught in the cross-fire between the Foreign and War Offices. The FO distrusted SOE and considered that their meddling in Resistance movements inevitably involved them in politics, while the War Office tended to view SOE officers as amateurs, even though many were gifted (and a few eccentric) – some of their views on waging war were anathema to the more hide-bound regular officers. To complicate matters even further, and as already mentioned, came the series of telegrams originated by Rufus Shepherd from the ELAS lair near Mount Olympus, which contradicted views sent back first by Myers and later Woodhouse.

It is hardly surprising that Shepherd's glowing reports about ELAS caused confusion and negated the doubts expressed by Myers. When Sarafis had been held captive by ELAS, Myers sent messages advocating strong measures, even to the extent of breaking off relations with ELAS. At the same time, and unknown to Myers, Shepherd was sending such messages as: 'The EAM is an organization uniting all political opinions from Communist to Royalist. Each party has at least one member on the Central Committee.' Three weeks later he signalled, 'EAM leaders are very pro-British and fully understand need [for] our recognizing King.' Not surprisingly, Myers and Woodhouse were taken aback when these messages were relayed back to them by SOE, whereupon the indignant brigadier stressed the importance of bringing Shepherd into line, to adopt the same policy as that which the BMM was trying to carry out. It was

Woodhouse's opinion that Shepherd's views had been
derived from his conversations with Kostas Karayiorgis, the
political leader of EAM in Thessaly. Karayiorgis had not
admitted to Shepherd that he was a Communist. 'His
handling of Shepherd was extremely skilful and I am not
surprised in retrospect that Shepherd's telegrams read
convincingly at the time.'

Such conflicting reports only served to heighten the bitter
argument between the FO and SOE, with the diplomatic staff
querying the role of the officers in Greece and questioning
whether they should even be there at all without FO
approval. The desk officers in London continued to show a
reluctance to believe that EAM/ELAS posed the major threat
to British policy in Greece. The attacks by guerrilla leaders
on each other did not strike them as being highly significant,
and it was only when there was firm evidence of Communist
activity among the Greek armed forces in the Middle East
that attitudes changed. Such insurrections in March 1943 led
MI5 to report that, 'These mutinies have been organized by
members of the EAM who were sent out of Greece for that
purpose.' For the first time the FO began to appreciate that
great power had passed into the hands of the KKE.

While all this was taking place, for purely military reasons
the Chiefs of Staff and their planners in GHQ Cairo were
attracted by the possibility of developing the Greek
Resistance into a major force – hence 'Operation Animals'.
They wanted a countrywide operation, and that was clearly
impossible without ELAS. Myers, therefore, was caught
between two opposite viewpoints: having made out the case
that EAM was a distinct danger to British policy, he then had
to argue that ELAS was indispensable to British military
strategy, both arguments being perfectly valid, especially as
by April 1943 he had realized that ELAS was by far the
strongest force in Greece and that there was not the slightest
possibility of eliminating it. For sound operational reasons,
Myers patiently continued a dialogue with the ELAS GHQ
triumvirate, a dialogue that was later held against him, with
the charge that he had been too sympathetic to the ELAS
cause.

The only hold Myers had over Sarafis and his colleagues
was the ability to supply arms and gold sovereigns – or to

turn off the tap completely. During meetings held with the partisan leaders, starting at Liascovo when the joint GHQ was set up, Myers recalled that Zervas had been obstreperous and Sarafis childishly obstinate, making ridiculous speeches. Nevertheless, a little progress was made, and on 14 June yet another round of talks were set in motion until finally, on 4 July, an agreement was reached. The communiqué issued afterwards promised an amicable relationship and a peace, neither of which was to last for long. 'It is therefore now an accomplished fact that all Greek *andartes* and bands, irrespective of their political or other tendencies, have been welded into a united and co-ordinated instrument for the furtherance of the Allied struggle.'

Later Sarafis was to comment that, 'ELAS observed the agreement it has signed with complete sincerity', and in his opinion subsequent disagreements between EKKA and EDES on one side and ELAS on the other were always due to the ill-discipline of the non-ELAS *andartes*. During this period the ELAS commander continued to display great energy in touring the mountain villages, and there is little doubt that he had considerable organizational ability, a point conceded by Woodhouse, who wrote, 'Communications in the mountains, by wireless, courier and telephone, had never been so good before or since; even motor roads were mended and used by EAM-ELAS.'

Myers and his subordinates did not know of the reservations expressed by the FO about accepting Zervas as an ally. Firstly, he was alleged to have an unsavoury past, something that had never been divulged to Myers and Woodhouse during their pre-Harling briefings in Egypt. And secondly, Zervas and his political deputy Komninos Pyromaglou were closely associated with the Republican General Plastiras, a possible leader for a united Resistance Movement, whom SOE was keen to support. In contrast, the FO was '... strongly averse to any encouragement being given to policies which might prejudice the return of the King and the existing Greek Government, while SOE wanted to build up resistance regardless of the policies of the band they contacted' (General, later Lord, Wilson).

The King's projected return to Greece was to occupy the attention of diplomats in London and Cairo as well as being a major stumbling-block during negotiations between the BMM and the *andartes*. Early in the year, Myers had recommended most strongly that the King should promise a plebiscite to decide whether there should be a monarchy after the War was over. After considerable pressure, in a broadcast on 4 July King George promised that he would abide by the will of the people and that there would be elections within six months of his return. That guarantee was greeted with scepticism by EAM/ELAS, who maintained that 'Glucksburg' (a name they used as a reminder of the King's German origin) would have six months in the country in which to rig the elections. Even the professional politicians of other parties were wary and remained sitting firmly on the fence.

After 11 July, the nation-wide series of sabotage acts ended and in a matter of days the various factions once more snarled at each other with suspicious distrust. On 18 July EKKA was attacked again. Their leader, Colonel Psarros, was a fine officer, but in Myers' opinion the situation had become too difficult for a man who was 'a straightforward soldier, far too honest'. EKKA rarely boasted more than a thousand *andartes*, and after August their numbers dwindled. On more than one occasion, it was only the presence of a BLO that saved EKKA, as had happened in May, when the 5/42th Evzones had been surrounded and escaped death or captivity only because the British acted as arbiters. (Because of this Myers recommended that their strength be doubled and other agents were parachuted in to join the mission, including some Americans from OSS.)

When Myers suggested to GHQ Cairo that he should return by *caique* to Egypt for a full briefing and to report on the situation in occupied Greece, he was instructed to prepare a landing strip capable of use by a Liberator or Halifax. It was Denys Hanson who found a suitable plateau, near Neraidha, where he was occupying General Plastiras' house – the owner conveniently being in exile in southern France. The RAF had stipulated that, unless the projected site was at sea level, it would have to be some 1,700 yards long. The go-ahead was given Hanson who, having volunteered for the Harling operation only, by now was desperately keen to leave the country after his enforced stay.

He organized gangs of Greek civilians who worked in relays to prepare the strip. Precautions had to be taken against the occasional reconnaissance plane, German or Italian, and various subterfuges were employed with notable success. As it reached completion, fir-tree saplings were cut and stuck in the ground at irregular intervals and in groups, to camouflage their efforts; so successful was this that, when an RAF reconnaissance aircraft came over to check the landing site, the crew reported that far more work needed to be done – even their air-photo experts were fooled after developing the photographs! Perhaps even more remarkable was the fact that its construction failed to attract the attention of the Axis authorities: Hanson's theory was that, when talk reached unfriendly ears, the story was '... so embellished by the time the enemy heard it, it was too fantastic to believe'.

By now, Myers had completed almost a year in Greece. About two months before, Ambassador Leeper had arranged for Major David Wallace, a diplomat in peacetime, to parachute in, not only to offer Myers advice on political matters but to report back to Cairo, giving a fresh, independent view of the situation within the country. Wallace's reports were strongly antagonistic to ELAS and confirmed Myers' suspicions that their immediate aim was to liquidate EDES and EKKA. Unfortunately, Wallace's long enciphered reports to the Ambassador piled up in Cairo, and when Myers reached that city he was dismayed to learn that the Embassy was still very much in the dark – the reports had yet to be deciphered.

Years later, Thanasis Hajis, former Secretary of EAM, was to accuse Myers of having written Report 85/4 AS dated 12 August 1943 'to undermine the work of EAM and ELAS'. One of the statements alleged to have emanated from Myers was that British agents, '... have a right and duty to denounce the EAM/ELAS leaders to the Occupation authorities'.

In fact, on 12 August 1943 Myers was in Cairo, and for that reason alone there would have been no need for him to write such a report. Moreover, in the mountains of Greece all his reports were sent, in code, over the wireless. 'A blatant, inaccurate and malicious forgery' was Myers' denunciation of the letter, and it is of interest that Marion Sarafis has since reported her husband as saying that it could not be genuine:

'... though others might have written thus, it was not in character for Brigadier Eddie'. Documents purporting to support a particular faction's allegations required careful scrutiny – and still do!

A week before Myers' so-called report had been written, on 7 August, the long-awaited Dakota landed, to the unrestrained joy and intense interest of the local villagers who had worked so hard to prepare the strip. Just prior to its landing, Myers was presented with a thorny problem. Instead of two ELAS representatives only, George Siantos, Tzimas and Sarafis arrived, all expecting to go, plus a Socialist representative, making four passengers from the extreme Left as opposed to one representative each from EDES (Pyromaglou) and EKKA (Kartalis). Later Leeper was to comment: 'The arrival of the *andarte* was completely unexpected by the King and Tsouderos: I was taken aback to find that ELAS were represented by three Communist politicians and one fellow-traveller.' For such an unpromising beginning to the talks held in Cairo, Myers was to be blamed – and not forgiven either.

The early discussions did not go well, and the gulf between the Greek politicians in Egypt and the partisan leaders who had come from occupied Greece was never bridged, despite lengthy meetings. All the Resistance leaders insisted there should be a plebiscite before the King returned, and EAM made strong representations that they be given three key posts in the Government.

Myers was to find that many senior officers at GHQ Cairo and, indeed, the FO in London felt that he had been exaggerating the dangers of the Communist take-over in Greece, alleging that he had been 'too close to it for too long'. To EAM's demand that the King should virtually sign his own abdication, Reginald Leeper, supported by Churchill, Roosevelt and Jan Smuts, advised him not to act with haste, so that the delegates from Greece were informed that the matter was still under consideration. The almost total ignorance in Cairo about the true situation in Greece worried Myers considerably, a situation accentuated by the fact that not a single liaison officer had come back from Greece from the time the mission had gone to that country.

An interview with the King did not help the brigadier's

future. King George II, with a 'somewhat glassy smile', spoke English fluently with hardly a trace of a foreign accent. Myers told him bluntly that there would be civil war if he returned without a plebiscite being held first. The King reiterated that he must return at the head of his army and not shirk his constitutional duty to Greece. That conversation was yet another factor that added fuel to the Foreign Office's disaffection from Myers and his team of officers. A telegram sent to Winston Churchill by General Smuts makes that point all too clearly: 'There appears to be a strong suspicion that British Intelligence Agents who brought Greek patriots and other Party representatives to Cairo are anti-Royalist and that the patriot representatives even have Communist leanings.'

That suspicion, which was unproven to say the very least, was to cost Myers his job and David Wallace a reprimand. Sadly, in August 1944 David Wallace was killed in a skirmish, the fourth of five brothers to die during the war.

Bill Jordan was to make some acid comments about political interference with the work of the mission. 'Intervention in Greek politics by the British was something for which I had no stomach. It degraded our mission, which was a military one.' The New Zealander paid tribute to Myers' perseverance, patience and diplomacy, adding his opinion that it was '... unfair that Myers was made to suffer – he worked himself almost to dropping point'. In his place, Chris Woodhouse was told to act as commander of the Military Mission while Myers returned to London, where he had interviews with Churchill, Eden and certain Foreign Office officials. Here he was told that he ought not to have spoken out on political matters as he had – they were not his concern, to which he gave the heartfelt reply, 'How I wish they were not!' Churchill's emotional support for the Greek King was both obvious and understandable, stemming from the dark days of 1941 when the pro-British King George had played a big part in persuading his reluctant ministers in Athens to stand firm and accept British intervention in Greece. For such a reason Churchill continued to express the view that he wanted the King 'to have a fair deal'.

In London Myers learnt that, although General Maitland Wilson wanted him to return to the Middle East, political objections from the FO were so strong that reluctantly the

Commander-in-Chief had agreed to his dismissal. Zervas sent
a generous telegram thanking Myers for all his efforts,
ending with the promise that he was to always regard the soil
of Greece as his own. Myers' disappointment was increased
when news started trickling back from Greece that the fabric
of his eleven months' patient work had begun disintegrating:
differences between the partisan groups had developed into
an all-out civil war, something that many historians like to call
'the First Round'.

5 Divided Resistance – The First Round

> 'When tremendous dangers are involved, none can be
> blamed for looking to his own interest.'
>
> Thucydides

The realization that liberation was not to come during the winter of 1943/4 caused a deep resentment and acute distress throughout Greece. The incentive that had persisted throughout the nationwide sabotage campaign was no longer there and, as one BLO was to state, 'In no time whatever they were at each other's throats.' Another, Bill Jordan, felt that the decision to give arms and gold sovereigns to ELAS (payment was £1 a month for each *andarte*) had been a grave mistake: 'We backed the wrong horse – not only losing our money but we were getting kicked by the ungrateful nag.' But ELAS GHQ was not worried about being accused of ingratitude, especially when a heaven-sent opportunity came that allowed them to obtain arms in plenty, without having to rely on the British – who, they alleged with good reason, turned off the tap whenever their relationship with ELAS deteriorated.

Such an opportunity occurred when, following Mussolini's downfall, the Italians surrendered to the Allies in September 1943. In Greece the Germans acted swiftly, moving down more troops to fill the void created by the surrender of the Italians. For a day or two there was chaos in Athens, during which time many prisoners of war managed to escape from gaols left unguarded by Italian sentries. (In time, the Germans rounded up the majority of the fugitives, but one who remained at large was Frank Macaskie of *The Times* –

who reminded Jeanne Tsatsos of Lord Byron.) The Germans showed no mercy to the Italians, and so brutal was the treatment meted out that the average, hospitable Greek took pity on their erstwhile 'occupiers'. Jeanne Tsatsos agreed; 'How can the Germans so treat the Italians, their old allies? As for the true Greeks, their ancient humane tradition governs their conduct. They have forgotten humiliations they suffered from the Italians; they've opened their homes to them, they've hidden them....'

In the mountains, steps taken by Woodhouse to prevent the weapons of the Italian Pinero Division falling into the hands of ELAS proved unavailing. It was only due to the British that the divisional commander, General Adoles Infante, holder of the Distinguished Service Order, was smuggled across the border to Albania and thence to Italy, aided by Anthony Quayle, in peacetime to become a famous actor but at that time acting as liaison officer to the Albanian guerrillas.

Infante was fortunate compared with the majority of officers and men of his old division who remained behind, who were to suffer dearly. British attempts to keep the formation as an organized group or groups proved abortive, chiefly because ELAS moved quickly and broke the Italian division into manageable bands, removing all their arms and ammunition in the process. Thereafter different sources have tended to paint conflicting pictures of the treatment of the Italians meted out by ELAS. Sarafis, after commenting that, 'We could be free of worry about them', maintained that the Italians who were sent to work in the ELAS mountain villages were treated with fairness and fitted in well with the life of each community. Reports relayed back to SOE by BLOs with ELAS were quite different, stressing that unfortunate Italians were herded into remote concentration camps, there to be used as forced labour under inhuman conditions, with many dying as a result.

A most reliable witness from the British side was Philip Worrall, who parachuted in as a sabotage officer the day after the Italian armistice was signed. He was in the Pindus area from 14 September 1943 until December 1944 and was assigned by Chris Woodhouse as liaison officer to an Italian force of 7,000 who overnight had eluded the Germans, changed sides and marched up into the mountains, claiming – and getting – co-belligerent status. Woodhouse had handed this assignment over to Worrall with the words, 'They're all yours, Philip; there's no one else.'

In 1951 Philip Worrall wrote to *The Times* about the task that had faced him eight years before: 'Very soon I became their only champion after the Greeks had dispersed them, disarmed them and robbed them of most of their clothes. We were chased by the Germans and imprisoned by ELAS. The hard winter of 1943-4 reduced them to a starving, frost-bitten rabble of which nearly a thousand did not survive.'

Worrall himself had several narrow escapes. One example he has recounted was a day when things went wrong. He was sitting, just before lunch, in the Karditsa cake shop, when there was a shout in German, 'Stop!' Worrall ran, throwing himself head down in the back of an old lorry which took off at speed. When the Germans opened fire with rifles and mortars, he looked down to see he was lying on a dangerously insecure load of Italian hand-grenades. However, he got away and in the evening returned to Karditsa. But again luck was against him. At 9.30 p.m. after listening to the BBC Greek news broadcast over the town's amplifier (incredible in itself when it is remembered that this was occupied territory, 500 miles from the nearest Allied forces), there was another shout in German to stop. This time Worrall and his girl interpreter were given bicycles, on which they pedalled up the road to the mountains. As they left the road and were just about hidden, a German patrol swept past them. Despite such escapades, the daily buying and feeding arrangements for the Italians had to be organized, irrespective of the risks and dangers involved.

'Fifteen months later – and having personally spent 33,000 sovereigns on food which we had to buy and transport under the very noses of the Germans – the remainder and I left Volos in troopships....' The story of the evacuation from Volos will follow (on p. 180) when the events of 1944 are described.

Twenty-seven years later Philip Worrall was to receive the Order of the Crown of Italy for his outstanding service to those unfortunate Italian prisoners.

His factual account is at variance with Stefanos Sarafis' bland assurances that the Italians received fair, equitable treatment from ELAS. Sarafis' description is decidedly sketchy, and the reader is left with the firm impression that he chose to see no evil, hear no evil and write as little as possible about the more controversial incidents when compiling his memoirs after the war.

KKE, with its politico-military organizations of EAM and ELAS, was now riding on the crest of the wave and, with the recently acquired booty of some 12,000 small arms and a variety of support weapons, Aris in particular was eager to take on their much smaller rivals. Depending on the bias of the writer concerned, sources can be found to support the allegation that EDES began the inter-partisan civil war and vice versa. Be that as it may, no one can dispute that ELAS was the Goliath, with over 15,000 armed *andartes* and reputedly supported by 20,000 in reserve, against Zervas with fewer than 5,000 and Psarros with barely 1,000 in EKKA. Clashes between the groups began in October, and soon EDES was under severe pressure. In the struggle that followed, Bill Jordan was full of praise for Colonel Pantilides, an ex-regular officer with EDES, whose leadership was severely tested when ELAS moved towards the Akhelos river in the middle of October. Unfortunately at a critical moment Dr Houtas, who was Pantilides' military superior, changed the former colonel's plan and EDES suffered a severe reverse, which resulted in their being driven to the north-west in some disorder.

By this time, KKE Secretary-General George Siantos had joined ELAS GHQ in the mountains in order to tighten Communist control of the partisan forces. ELAS made it clear that no longer were they prepared for the resistance movement to be commanded or co-ordinated by the British; indeed, all they wanted the British to do was to provide liaison officers with communications so that Middle East Command could supply them with the necessary arms and supplies, at the right place and in the quantities they demanded. Sarafis continued to suspect the motives of the British in Greece, even alleging that any British officer who showed himself sympathetic to the Left Wing was recalled to Cairo and adding, in almost Marxist fashion, that, 'Most

British officers were serving City interests.' ELAS's relations with the British were now as cold as the winter; airdrops for their *andartes* rarely materialized, and if and when they did, few, if any, weapons were included with the consignment.

Increasing pressure on Zervas forced him back into an ever-dwindling conclave, and only the regular resupply of weapons and gold sovereigns, plus his own undoubted skill as a guerrilla leader, enabled his partisans to survive the buffeting they suffered at the end of 1943. With a civil war raging in most parts of the country, the only people who benefited were the Germans: for them the inter-guerrilla struggle truly was a gift from heaven. From their records, it is evident that they took full advantage of the situation and were not averse to letting slip information that one or other of the *andarte* groups had made contact with them. Much has been written about the alleged collaboration by EDES with the Germans during this period, and assuredly Zervas had an arrangement with the Germans which saved villages from destruction, as well as protecting his back, when he faced his fellow Greeks in ELAS. 'In the last analysis the evidence now available means what the particular author wants it to mean' (John O. Latrides), a sentiment which explains why writers holding different political views have been able to support their findings with documentary evidence.

That Zervas agreed to parley at moments of extreme peril between November 1943 and August in the following year cannot be disputed: not to have done so would have risked extinction and left his followers at the mercy of fellow Greeks, and, alas, little mercy would have been shown by Aris and some of his more ruthless subordinates.

General Hubert Lanz, whose XXII Mountain Corps had the task of first clearing and then occupying western Greece, confirmed that Zervas did make cease-fire arrangements with the forces under his command (Partisan Warfare in the Balkans', Army Group E War Diary).

ELAS also had parleys with the occupying forces at certain times, as Aris himself was to explain: 'Parleys were sound tactics … only pharmacists, notaries and milkmen never made truces, since they never made war.' Zervas' political deputy, Komninos Pyromaglou, described by Woodhouse as brave and scholarly, the intellectual inspiration of Zervas' forces, gave this interesting definition of collaboration: 'Contacts between the occupiers and guerrillas do not mean anything. What really matters is the co-operation in arms of the guerrilla units with the occupiers. This never happened.'

In order to survive, and not for material gain, EDES and EKKA were forced to make such contacts to cover their rear, a situation that never arose as far as the more powerful ELAS was concerned. The Germans wanted EDES to remain in being because it made their occupation easier, while the British gave their support to Zervas and his men, fearing that there would be nothing to prevent a Communist take-over once the German occupation forces had been ejected or forced to withdraw from Greece.

The safety of the military mission during the late autumn of 1943 was a matter of deep concern for Woodhouse, even though there was a deafening silence from his superiors in Cairo, apart from a message advising them to keep a low profile. Tom Barnes, the lieutenant-colonel in charge of Epirus, ran a gauntlet when the Germans launched assaults on both sides of the Pindus mountains. At one stage he was under fire from ELAS as well as the Germans.

After ELAS had crossed the River Akhelos to disperse the EDES unit under Dr Houtas, BLOs were forced to hide before eventually making their way to safety. One who did not survive was New Zealander Arthur Hubbard, a close friend and colleague of Bill Jordan. In the village of Triklinos, the hut in which they were working was attacked by armed ELAS *andartes*, and Hubbard was shot and wounded, later dying of his wounds. Jordan himself was maltreated and wrote, 'They were beside themselves, some actually frothing at the mouth. It was maniacal.' A fabricated story was spread around that the British had fired first, something that was not believed by the villagers themselves, who turned out in force to attend Hubbard's funeral. The ELAS leader of the group's offer to provide a burial party was turned down with disdain by Jordan. Later, when SOE told BLOs not to get involved and to 'sit on the fence and smile', his bitter reply was, 'I hope you heard me smiling as I buried Arthur Hubbard.'

To add to the misery of the First Round, from the month of October onwards the Germans moved against the mountainous strongholds of ELAS and inflicted hundreds of casualties. The savagery of these punitive raids was appalling. Brutal examples were made of the villages of Konnero and Ligiades, where innocent people were not only shot but shut up in cellars and burned alive. Even these atrocities were to be overshadowed when reprisals were effected on 13 December 1943 at Kalavryta in the Peloponnese: it is reported that about a thousand people were machine-gunned or burned to death during a reprisal expedition that lasted eight days. An estimated figure of those who perished at the hands of the Germans during the occupation has been put at 20,000, a figure only exceeded by the Bulgarians during their reign of terror in Macedonia and Thrace, where they were so brutal that some 25,000 terrified civilians fled from the towns of Drama and Kavalla to seek German protection in Salonika.

German records make one valid point in defence of the shooting of civilians: that the majority of *andarte* did not wear uniform and thus made it impossible to distinguish partisans from innocent people. That did not excuse the murder of children, women and old people. SOE officer John Mulgan summed it up in these words: 'The real heroes of the Greek War of Resistance were the common people of the hills. It was on them, with their bitter, uncomplaining endurance, that the German terror broke. They produced no traitors. We moved freely among them, guided by them into German-held villages by night without fear.'

Prosecution lawyers at the Nuremberg Military Tribunal trials of German war criminals summed up German atrocities in Greece with these words: 'In Greece there are a thousand Lidices – their names unknown and their inhabitants forgotten by a world too busy and too cynical to remember.... There is, for example, the village of the Peloponnese peninsula which was levelled to the ground in December 1943 during the notorious "Operation Kalavryta".'

One of the Resistance's unsung heroes was Edward Chapman, an unknown British soldier of the 3rd Royal Tank Regiment. Captured during spring 1941, Chapman made four escapes before joining first EES (a Royalist partisan group in Macedonia) and then an ELAS battalion under Kapetan Georgio. By that time Chapman was well known and liked by the Greeks, living in the Kilkis-Polykastron area under the name of Kariakis. He earned himself a high reputation in action but found the group's political officer, Petros, rabidly anti-British. Three times a day, lectures were delivered by Petros: 'the propaganda, particularly the anti-British part of it,' sickened Chapman, who was able to see that trouble lay ahead for his Greek friends.

In an attempt to crush Greek Resistance, the Germans introduced their notorious *'Wacht und Nebel'* ('Night and Fog') order, whereby hostages in large numbers were taken away from their homes, and relatives were told nothing about their fate. Despite these tactics, the Nazis never broke the spirit of the Greek people and 'never succeeded in dissuading them from fighting as guerrillas or supporting the Government forces'. Industrial sabotage, too, was carried out throughout the country: bombs and shells fired by Axis troops against the partisans were often duds, and a variety of go-slow tactics reduced industrial output to a meagre level.

Resistance was not confined to the mountainous areas of Greece. In Athens, the Apollo Group continued their sabotage of ships in Piraeus and other ports. In order to obtain information about the sailing of ships, that group had to have agents within the German organization, brave men and women who faced not only detection but in time to come the bitter accusation from fellow-countrymen that they had collaborated with the German masters.

One of the most famous Apollo agents was Yiannis Peltelis, who was in the classical mould of double agents. He organized, or helped to organize, the destruction of twenty-six large ships and many more smaller craft, as well as relaying back to the Allies vital intelligence about German movements by sea and air. Later Peltelis was accused of passing a significant number of gold sovereigns to EAM, and at Churchill's instigation he was taken before a court martial. As we are still witnessing today, once a secret service agent becomes a public figure, with a full-scale public investigation following, it is his colleagues who suffer. Seventy-one were rounded up by the Germans, of whom fifty-nine were executed. As a final bitter twist, Peltelis was cleared in August 1944 and given a DSO, a paltry reward for the humiliation and suffering the courageous man had been forced to endure.

Towards the end of 1943 Woodhouse, now confirmed as Head of the Allied Mission in place of Myers, noted that KKE had become more co-operative, because they had come to appreciate, first, that, despite their efforts, Zervas had survived and, secondly, that the end of the occupation was not yet at hand – or likely for months to come. The Germans were now in control of the major towns and cities throughout the land.

The 'First Round' had been inconclusive because, although Zervas had appeared to be on the verge of defeat, after the New Year he counter-attacked ELAS vigorously until, as a result of Woodhouse's patience and negotiations, an armistice was signed on 4 February 1944, thus bringing the four months' struggle to an end. By now the Foreign Office was keen to break off all relations with ELAS, but such a proposal was resisted by Middle East Command. With ELAS controlling about four-fifths of the country, and the safety of the BLOs assigned to them a factor that could not be disregarded, Woodhouse advocated direct liaison with ELAS GHQ – even though there was deep distrust on both sides, and in this he was supported by General Maitland Wilson.

Sarafis continued to press for the formation of a single liberation army under a Greek Commander-in-Chief – General Plastiras was once more suggested, which, of course, would have meant the end of EDES: 'Once forces amalgamated, his [Zervas'] men would cease to be a separate group' – a statement about which there can be no dispute. The ELAS Commander-in-Chief appreciated that the British were supporting Zervas in order to make EDES strong enough to combat ELAS, a situation that existed for a few weeks, and the ensuing stalemate helped to bring about the temporary truce.

Following lengthy discussions, at the end of February, the so-called Plaka (Bridge) Agreement was signed. ELAS and EDES were allotted their own areas, with a boundary running between them. In theory this should have relieved the tension but in practice the agreement did not work, with constant violations that led to a stream of accusations and counter-accusations as each side blamed the other with ever-increasing vituperation.

When writing his memoirs, Sarafis found it difficult to

avoid simplistic conclusions on many of the controversial
disagreements between ELAS and EDES, EKKA and the
British, an unfortunate trait which detracted from an
otherwise singular account of ELAS activities during the
occupation. A prime example occurred in Roumeli where,
during January 1944, Psarros, at the head of the 5/12th
Evzones, achieved some remarkable results against the Axis
forces, so much so that Jeanne Tsatsos' diary entry enthused,
'The relief and enthusiasm in Roumeli are tremendous.
Psarros is their adored hero.' Barely three months later that
gallant colonel was killed after being captured by an ELAS
unit. Sarafis, after lamenting the death of a close colleague
and friend for over twenty-five years, maintained that it had
been a tragic mistake: those EKKA who survived called it
murder. Aris had ordered the 2/21st Regiment ELAS to
march and deal with EKKA, only to countermand his earlier
instruction, but by that time the deed had been done. It was
to be the end of EKKA as an independent partisan force. A
weeping George Kartalis, Psarros' deputy, told Jeanne
Tsatsos: 'Yesterday the ELAS guerrillas killed Psarros and
more than 150 of the officers and men of the 5/42nd
Regiment. But why so much hate? Why all this evil? The war
will surely end and the Allies will win. But what will become
of Greece?'

That the death of Psarros was a personal shock to Sarafis
and to another of his colleagues, Colonel Bakirdzis, was
undoubtedly true, and deeply regretted. However, the end
result, the crushing defeat of EKKA, was something that
ELAS had been trying to bring about for months past. In
addition, the death of Psarros was to accelerate British
mistrust of ELAS, especially in Government circles. 'Later the
Central Committee of EAM admitted that it had been a
terrible mistake, which was probably true but no disciplinary
action was taken.' Those words were written by Woodhouse,
although he maintained that it still required some dramatic
events in the Middle East before the FO could be finally
convinced that EAM/ELAS presented a real threat to British
policy in Greece.

The events referred to by Woodhouse were political
mutinies in the Greek armed forces stationed in the Middle
East. Prior to those breaking out, the warm-hearted Liberal

Emmanuel Tsouderos had resigned as Prime Minister of the Greek Government-in-Exile: he had tried and failed to obtain King George's approval of the appointment of Archbishop Damaskinos as regent, a move that might well have won over some of the Liberal and Republican politicians. Such a suggestion had been made in 1943 by Eden but, after consulting Churchill, Roosevelt and others, the King stuck to his guns: a return to Greece at the head of his army, with the promise of a plebiscite within six months. Leeper's view, written a few months before, was: 'I find the King a bit of a problem. He is a very nice, honest and straightforward man but he is definitely a man without big ideas. He never seems to think in terms of the best future for his country.'

After a few days of political in-fighting, Tsouderos' successor was George Papendreou, another Liberal politician who arrived in Egypt during April after being smuggled out by the British. Having spent a period in Averoff Prison, he was free from any taint of collaboration, and was a splendid orator and had a fine presence. Papendreou being a little further to the left than the majority of his colleagues in the Government, the FO hoped he might influence EAM/ELAS into being represented in the Government – without allowing them too much influence unless they changed their tune. That such a hope was beyond the realm of possibility became abundantly clear when EAM set up the Political Committee of National Liberation (PEEA) as an alternative provisional Government at Viniani in the mountains of Greece. Such an act of open defiance only served to make the King even more reluctant to agree to the appointment of a regent, as well as leading to hard-line attitudes in London and Cairo.

The establishment of the PEEA, directly or indirectly, led to fresh trouble in the Greek armed forces in the Middle East. On 5 April all members of the Greek Government in Exile tendered their resignation, and shortly afterwards the British military authorities were forced to take a series of measures in order to prevent a wholesale mutiny of Greek naval and military units. At such a time Churchill sent one of his remarkable telegrams: 'First in priority, order and discipline should be maintained in the armed forces:

secondly, the safety of the King's person to be ensured; thirdly, every effort to be made to induce Tsouderos to hold office till the King returns and has had time to look round; fourthly, try to get Venizelos to remain with Tsouderos; fifthly, celebrate Easter Sunday in a manner pious and becoming.'

The mutinies came at an extremely awkward time for the British service commanders in the Middle East, because much-needed military formations had already been taken away from the Mediterranean theatre to participate in the invasion of north-west Europe. This point is important. One writer has alleged that the British stage-managed the mutinies, as a pretext before purging the EAM elements and then building up a pro-Royalist force. Records show that the FO, Middle East Command and SOE (Cairo) were all surprised by the mutinies and for the first time really began to treat EAM/ELAS with serious caution. Nevertheless, it cannot be denied that the final suppression of the mutinies enabled the British authorities to take full advantage of the outcome, to ensure that there would not be a repeat performance.

The insurrection in the Greek Navy took place shortly after the downfall of Tsouderos. On 8 April a general mutiny broke out at Alexandria. By this time Greek officers had completely lost control so that an invitation was made to the ships by loudspeaker to serve under direct British control, which meant British naval discipline too. It was made clear to the mutineers that political committees would have to be dispersed and they would have to obey their own officers, to which there was no immediate response. The situation continued tense for several days.

On 16 April the C-in-C Mediterranean, Admiral Sir John Cunningham, reported that in each of the ships a passive majority of the crew was being dominated by what appeared to be a small minority of hard-liners. He posed the question as to whether action should be taken against the mutineers by the Greeks or British, pointing out that the time had come to act, otherwise the stalemate would continue. After further discussion, it was agreed that action by the Greeks themselves was desirable, but on 17 April the Greek C-in-C, Rear-Admiral Alexandris, found that he was unable to screw his courage up to the point of taking action against the mutineers and resuming command of his own ships; accordingly, he was relieved in command that night by Admiral Cunningham and succeeded by Vice-Admiral Voulgaris. At first Voulgaris too prevaricated, until told that the British would be forced to take action if he refused to do so.

On 23 April, in the early hours of the morning, parties boarded the destroyer *Herax* and corvettes *Saktouris* and *Apoltolis* and, after some exchanges of machine-gun and small-arms fire, the three ships surrendered. Casualties were sustained on both sides, including the leader of the boarding party against the *Apoltolis*, Captain Ronssen. Meanwhile, at Port Said, the cruiser *Georgiois Averoff* still held out, and only after 200 men had been sent on 28 April to deal with her did the mutineers surrender to the Greek C-in-C. Thereafter there was a series of incidents which continued throughout May and June, the majority of which involved minor fracas without any blood being shed.

The Greek Navy had followed the example of their fellow-countrymen in the Mountain Brigade who had been training to go into action with the British Eighth Army fighting in Italy, having already won a high reputation at El Alamein: its arrival in Italy was eagerly awaited by General Alexander. Kenneth Matthews of the BBC, who had lived and worked in Greece before the war, wrote: 'There had been a time when Britain and Greece stood alone in the world against the common enemy, a moment of intensely shared peril and glory – how mad, how unbelievable they should turn their weapons against each other!' Kenneth Matthews was the one correspondent who was allowed to witness the subsequent trials – his name had gone into the hat with forty others. 'Fate, as well as choice, seemed to bind me to the fortunes of Greece.'

The mutineers in the Greek Brigade, who wanted a change of government, arrested the loyal officers in the middle of the night, shooting dead one who resisted, before confronting their brigade commander, General Pappas, with a demand for transfer of allegiance. Pappas had all but resolved the issue before the British moved in, for twenty-five of his officers who had taken part agreed to submit to discipline and asked for mercy. At the same time, Major-General Beaumont-Nesbitt arrived with an order from his superior, General Paget, telling Pappas that his men had one hour to surrender their weapons and board the British trucks. The Greeks were furious and trained their weapons and guns on the British. Thereafter British troops sealed off all roads to Cairo and Alexandria and threw a cordon around the camp. (To the average British soldier, 'The Greeks were simply a pack of foreigners who were making a nuisance of themselves.') In the event, the threat of force proved enough, although one British officer was hit and killed, the only casualty on either side.

After further investigation, the British authorities discovered that the mutinies had not been carried out by fanatics. Indeed, in some cases, from the commander downwards all members of a unit or sub-unit had declared in favour of the PEEA. Although one or two writers have alleged that the mutiny was permitted to develop for reasons of political expediency, there is no evidence whatever of such Machiavellian behaviour by Britain. On the contrary, with the Italian campaign suffering badly when more and more ships and military units were taken away, prior to the Normandy landing, the temporary loss of the Greek Navy and the Mountain Brigade was something that had not been bargained for – and which certainly upset the calculations of Field Marshal Alexander and his staff.

Sarafis was to declare that ELAS was not responsible for the mutinies, meaning by that statement that *agents provocateurs* had not been sent deliberately to stir up feelings. However, the establishment of the PEEA as an alternative government to the King's Cabinet in Exile was the signal for insurrection, and after Prime Minister Tsouderos had resigned a dangerous vacuum existed until Papendreou took over as Prime Minister. For a few weeks, the impending trial and punishment of the mutineers aroused the attention of the Press in Great Britain and the United States. A vigorous campaign was launched to stop any executions being carried out until, in the end, Prime Minister Papendreou commuted the death sentences on all these men. The Mountain Brigade was purged and reorganized, while of those who had mutinied well over half the original number were sent off to internment camps.

Papendreou's standing as Prime Minister was sorely tested at the conference held in the Lebanon on 17 May. To the surprise of many observers, EAM decided to send representatives to attend. In the opening speeches, the rival partisans slammed each other, and accusation and counter-accusation followed at a fast and furious rate; the word 'collaborator' was used so many times that it became meaningless. The tide of patriotic feeling was lost in the sands of political rivalries. As the conference progressed, however, Reginald Leeper noted that EAM became decidedly subdued, possibly because they had been accused of being responsible for the mutinies. Leeper himself did not attend the conference, installing himself in a hotel near Beirut, but all the delegates went to see him, and it was obvious that Papendreou could do nothing without British support.

Historians are still undecided as to why EAM decided to participate in the conference in the first place. One theory was that the EAM leaders were not confident about pushing through their policies to the bitter end; another was that, quite simply, they had not thought through the political situation and were content to await events fatalistically, rather than trying to fashion the future. Nevertheless, they did put forward some of their own proposals during 2½ days of emotional speeches and recriminatory remarks. In the end, they appeared to accept the Lebanon Charter, which included the all-important Article 5: 'On liberation, law and order to be restored in collaboration with Allied Forces to ensure the Greek people can make a sovereign decision on type and composition of their Government without being subject to moral or material pressures.' This clause was used to justify the controversial British military intervention a few months later.

For some time the EAM delegates were reluctant to sign and proposed several conditions on which the British were prepared to compromise, although Papendreou wanted to take a much tougher line. While they were wavering, the announcement was made that the British and Greek Governments, in the interests of national unity, had decided that no death sentences on the mutineers would be carried out.

So sign they did, but after returning to Greece Rousos, the chief EAM delegate, was virtually disowned by the Central Committee, whereupon his military colleague, Sarafis, threatened to resign. Sarafis alone was excused on the grounds that he was a soldier and the responsibility lay with the 'political delegates'. It was but one of several instances when KKE/EAM blew hot and then cold, adopting then abandoning policies, contradictions which were to contribute to their final defeat.

During the weeks immediately following the Lebanon Conference, EAM agonized as to whether they should join the National Government, with its Socialist members willing to do so, even though they were aware that it was always their Communist colleagues whose decisions were decisive. The flamboyant Aris summed up EAM's changes in policy with these colourful words: 'If you spit in the air, it lands in your face. If you spit on the ground, it gets caught in your beard.' The prevarication continued.

The refusal of EAM to ratify the Lebanon Agreement led to Churchill's minute on 6 August to Eden, after he had heard that EAM had declared that they would not serve under Papendreou as Prime Minister: 'Surely we should tell M. Papendreou he should continue as Prime Minister and defy them all. The behaviour of EAM is absolutely intolerable.... We cannot take a man up as we have done Papendreou and let him be thrown to the wolves at the first snarlings of the miserable Greek (Communist) banditi.... The case seems to me to have reached the following point: either we support Papendreou, if necessary with force as we have agreed, or we disinterest ourselves utterly in Greece.' It was a revealing minute, as it showed that Churchill had failed to realize how strong the EAM/ELAS movement was, certainly well beyond being 'miserable banditi'!

Churchill, however, had no intention of abandoning traditional British interest in Greece; on the contrary, in June he exchanged telegrams with President Roosevelt and Marshal Stalin on that subject. To the former, his cable read: 'We are an old ally of Greece. We had 40,000 casualties in trying to defend Greece against Hitler, not counting Crete ... not only did we lose the 40,000 men in helping Greece, but a vast mass of shipping, and warships; by denuding Cyrenaica to help Greece we also lost the whole of Wavell's conquest in Cyrenaica. These were heavy blows to us in those days.' Stalin refused to commit himself at that stage, although he was to do so later in the year, as will be recounted. What he did do was send a military mission to Greece.

The Allied Military Mission – the title changed after American officers had joined Woodhouse in September 1943 – knew nothing about the Soviet Mission until it arrived unannounced, under Colonel Popov. Prior to that, EAM/ELAS had been in radio communication with Tito's headquarters in Yugoslavia, a liaison that followed the visit by Tzimas to that country. It later transpired that members of the Soviet Military Mission were not impressed by what they saw of ELAS; one unconfirmed report was that, in their opinion, ELAS was 'just a rabble of armed men, not worth supporting'. It is possible that they were comparing ELAS with Tito's partisans, an unfair comparison as the circumstances were so different, but in the event the USSR lost interest in Greece and gave no material support to the Communists' cause thereafter. On the contrary, it was Russian pressure that eventually persuaded the KKE Central Committee to about-turn once more and send a telegram to the British Government, signed by EAM and KKE, signifying their belated agreement to join the National Government. For men like Aris it was a bitter moment, and only strict, rigid Party discipline drove the *kapetanios* to accept what they considered an act of weak appeasement.

As Head of the Allied Mission, twenty-seven-year-old 'Chris' Woodhouse had a most difficult task to perform during the summer of 1944, with pressure being put on him by the FO, as well as Leeper, to agree to a complete break with EAM/ELAS. At midsummer Woodhouse made a liaison visit first to Cairo and then to London, wondering to himself whether he might be travelling on a one-way ticket and find himself deposed, as Brigadier Eddie Myers had been before him. In London he met the Greek Ambassador to the British Government, and in conversation they found that each had been warned about the other being Left Wing! On 15 July Woodhouse was summoned by Winston Churchill, and after a long discussion the Prime Minister agreed to allow the mission to remain in Greece 'for the time being'. Woodhouse argued that members of the AMM were '... a valuable restraint on EAM and that it might be difficult and dangerous to get them out, but I feared that one day they would be taken as hostages and I asked for them to be reduced'.

With the war in Europe going well for the Allies in the late summer, pressure on the Germans to begin a withdrawal from Greece was growing. This did not stop their occupation forces continuing operations against the partisans, burning down villages and shooting hostages, who, more often than not, were innocent of any crime – apart from being Greek. Jeanne Tsatsos was to write in the autumn: 'The Germans are about to leave but yesterday again they shot twenty-five people.'

One major offensive, launched on 3 July 1944 under the codename 'Operation Steinadler', was designed to eradicate the ELAS Macedonian Division in the area of Pendalofon. Despite stringent security and with assault troops moving in from all sides, ELAS was not caught completely by surprise and its losses were not as great as the Germans had anticipated. After eleven days' intensive operations, the partisan losses were 455 confirmed dead, with a further 400 to 500 believed to have been killed or wounded. In addition, a total of nearly a thousand guerrillas were captured, together with seven British members of the AMM.

It has never been easy to assess the overall damage caused by the resistance movement before the Germans evacuated Greece. Ehrman, in his *Grand Strategy*, Volume VI, has this assessment: 'The guerrillas, aided by the Balkan Air Force, killed perhaps some 5,000 men, wounded and captured as many more, and destroyed or captured perhaps 100 locomotives and 500 vehicles, together with arms and ammunition.' Woodhouse assessed the German casualties as between 5,000 and 15,000, which is nearly in line with Ehrman's figures. He makes the point that German records show that ELAS' efforts did far more damage than was appreciated by the British Government at the time – so much depended, of course, on the attitude of the local partisan leader and the degree of co-operation that existed between him and the appointed BLO to that particular group.

That Stefanos Sarafis' claim about the damage and

casualties inflicted on the 'Occupiers' are greatly exaggerated cannot be disputed – British and German records do not support the inflated figures quoted in his memoirs.

On one point, members of Force 133 all seem to have the same opinion. Where KKE (Communist) influence was weak, then that particular group of ELAS *andartes* appears to have achieved far better results, when harassing the Germans, than those bands which were dominated by the political commissars.

In the end, however, it was not the resistance movement or the British armed forces that forced the Germans to pull out of Greece – it was the situation on the Eastern Front, where the Soviet Army was moving west towards the German homeland, forcing the Nazis to abandon the occupation of their European neighbours.

6 Liberation, with Dark Clouds Ahead

'Oh Liberty, what crimes are committed in your name!'

Attributed to Madame Roland; last words before her execution on 8 November 1793

After Woodhouse visited London in the summer of 1944, he was to write, 'I realized that, contrary to the Greeks' belief, Greece was not the centre of the world as seen from London. It was an interesting sideshow.' The sideshow was, however, soon to force itself more and more onto the world's stage until we find that Churchill's summer visit to Italy in July had as its main reason the impending Greek crisis. On 6 August the Prime Minister had minuted the CIGS that, 'Within a month or so we shall have to put 10,000 or 12,000 men into Athens.' He made it clear that, 'There is no question of trying to dominate Greece or going outside the immediate curtilage of Athens, but that is the centre of government and, with the approaches to it, must be made secure.... It is to be presumed that the Germans have gone or are streaking away to the north, and that the force landed at the Piraeus would be welcomed by the great majority of the population of Athens, including all the notables.'

The FO also recommended that there was a strong case for sending a British force in without delay, on the grounds that this would pre-empt EAM's taking over power, which, in the long term, would be a far easier situation to deal with than if a Communist regime were to be established. The devastation of Greece through famine, the ravages of the occupation and inter-partisan strife during the First Round also meant that it was vital that relief supplies be poured into the country as soon as possible. Because of poor and disrupted communications outside Athens, British armed forces would be needed to distribute food, medicine and other necessary commodities if another famine and widespread disease were to be averted. In London, Churchill and the FO saw the matter essentially as a political question, counting on the pro-British feelings of the mass of the Greek people, but understandably the Chiefs of Staff were deeply suspicious, looking at it as a campaign which might require up to 80,000 men – whom they did not have available. Churchill moved to reassure them in a message from Italy to the Foreign Secretary, despatched on 16 August: 'I strongly emphasize that the operation must be regarded as one of reinforced diplomacy and policy rather than an actual campaign, and that it is to be confined to Athens, with possibly a detachment at Salonika.' Although Churchill was clear about what the British Government should do, he was to find that Papendreou, in Rome, was deeply concerned that the wrong people in Greece had arms while his Government would have nothing, not even the support of an armed police force, after they landed.

It was on Churchill's advice that Papendreou moved his Government from Cairo's 'poisonous atmosphere of Greek intrigue' to Italy, and it was to there that General Maitland Wilson called Sarafis and Zervas (both now promoted to general) for a conference, held at Caserta on 26 September 1944. There a final agreement was not reached without much argument and deep reservations on both sides – Leeper was to acknowledge the important part played by Harold Macmillan in influencing those at the conference into agreeing to a compromise. For a start, the position of the Security Battalions gave rise to much heated discussion. When they were originally raised by the Germans as an anti-guerrilla force, many had flocked to join because their instincts for self-preservation from ELAS were stronger than their hatred of the Germans. In the eyes of EAM/ELAS, those who joined were traitors, hated collaborators, but Woodhouse was to maintain that the Security Battalions 'usually warned us about impending German operations'. At Caserta it was finally agreed that those units be treated as enemy forces after liberation had been achieved.

The Allied liberation plan, known as 'Operation Manna', was hurriedly prepared after the Caserta conference because it was anticipated that the Germans were on the point of leaving Greece. As part of the Caserta agreement, Lieutenant-General Ronald Scobie was appointed GOC Forces, which included all Greek formations: Significantly, both Sarafis and Zervas agreed to that apppointment while their separate spheres of influence were demarcated and approved. They also agreed that they would '... forbid units under their command to take the law into their own hands, and would place their guerrilla bands under Scobie'. The British had good reason to feel that an agreement had been reached which would enable the liberation of Greece to go smoothly.

American Ambassador Lincoln MacVeagh received the news of the signing with a degree of incredulity. 'All seems rosy, and the mere fact that Zervas and Sarafis could be got to sit down together and agree to anything, and with Wilson too, is amazing enough.' Events were to justify the long-serving Ambassador's gentle scepticism.

After Hitler decided to pull back his troops from Greece, assertions were made that the British had some sort of agreement with the Germans. Hermann Neubacher, the German plenipotentiary in the Balkans, was to maintain that the British '... did not effectively hinder the German withdrawal from Greece'. When the Germans began evacuating the islands in the Aegean, they were surprised that during August the tempo of British naval and air action diminished rather than increased. Prior to August the Germans had suffered significant losses, especially during the month of July. The welcome respite from harassment enabled them to evacuate their garrisons from most islands without too many problems and, as a consequence, rumours spread to the effect that British aircraft and ships held their fire during that period. In fact, from a study of 'Operations, Force 133, December 1943 to August 1944', it is evident that British restraint was due to lack of adequate forces at a time when there were heavy commitments elsewhere. Inevitably, there was a natural desire to conserve their limited resources, and in addition the weather was unusually bad during August 1944. Undoubtedly this affected both sides, and

General Korte, the Luftwaffe General in Greece, has confirmed that the evacuation from Crete was made under most difficult conditions '... and, because of the enemy action, only at night. The British did everything they could to prevent it. They even let submarines throw searchlight beams on the water about a kilometre in front of the islands in order to make the airplanes crash in the sea before they reached the island airfields.'

Although the number of German soldiers who reached the mainland safely in August and September was surprisingly high, from the available evidence, no firm conclusions can be made. Orders for the complete evacuation of the Aegean islands and the Dodecanese were issued on 14 September by Field Marshal Jodl. He also instructed Field Marshal von Weichs to take advantage of the inter-partisan civil war in Greece: 'Therefore you should, in collaboration with Ambassador Neubacher, extract all advantages for a withdrawal from the conflict between the two enemy groups, and on the other hand also foster the strife between the two groups after our departure as much as possible.' Neubacher himself elaborated on that theme when sending a similar message to the German Consul in Salonika, some two weeks later (30 September): 'There can be no question of our supporting one group or the other ... the point is not to save Greece from Bolshevism but exclusively to sharpen the Anglo-Russian conflict with all means.... Our political line is clear: in Greece we have to carry out a policy of destruction.'

Although it is clear that tentative feelers were put out by both British and Germans, in fact no deal was ever made. For a start, the two sides were not interested in the same kind of deal: the Germans wanted to get out of Greece to fight elsewhere, while the British wanted them to stay and surrender. With their own forces stretched to the very limit, the British did not consider that a successful German withdrawal would be very harmful to the long-term interests of the Western Allies.

The winkling-out of the small German garrisons which remained on some of the larger Greek islands was carried out by the Aegean Raiding Force, commanded by Brigadier D.J. Turnbull. With the British went the other Tzigantes brother, Khristopoulos, a heavily built man who had strong

Republican views which, in the 1935 revolution, he had
shared with such fellow regular officers as Sarafis. Tzigantes
was commanding the Sacred Squadron, which was composed, in the main, of ex-officers, most of whom were bitterly
anti-Communist. From island to island, they were greeted
with rapturous enthusiasm, with the only exception being
Levkas, known locally as 'the Red Island', where an ELAS
republic was established in the vacuum following the German
withdrawal.

Accompanying Turnbull's men was Richard Capell, the
Daily Telegraph correspondent, and in his book *Simionata* he
paints a vivid picture of the welcome they were given by the
islanders. He also reminds us that, prior to their liberation, a
succession of raids had been carried out by the SAS, SBS and
supporting units against the Axis-held islands.

One of the most daring cloak-and-dagger raids was that
which snatched German General Karl Krieper from Crete.
(Reported to be unpopular with his own officers, when news
of Krieper's kidnapping was announced, the immediate
reaction of his staff was to call for champagne! Whether the
courage and initiative shown by the two young British
officers, Patrick Leigh-Fermor and Stanley Moss, was worth
it in the long term can now be queried, but it was a fantastic
and audacious enterprise. Of far more importance, over 200
Cretans were executed in retribution, despite rumours on the
island that Krieper had deserted. It was difficult for the
Germans to believe that his disappearance was due to an
abduction until full details were known after the war, when
the story was to read like a James Bond thriller.

The best-known British name in the islands was Jellicoe:
Major, later temporary Lieutenant-Colonel, Earl Jellicoe was
to end the war with a DSO and MC and to win a high
reputation for the operations he led against the Axis on the
mainland and among the islands. In turn, Jellicoe paid a
generous tribute to his Greek colleague, Tsigantes, saying
that, 'He had been fighting longer and harder against the
Germans than any other Greeks.'

A special unit, the Raiding Support Regiment (RSR), had
been formed and equipped for these operations in the
Aegean waters and on the Greek mainland itself. One of its
members, Vic Goodall, recounts how they were trained to

fire enemy weapons: his troop had an Italian anti-tank weapon which could be stripped down into five parts to be carried on mules, while other troops in the unit used German 88mm mortars, 75mm pack howitzers and a variety of weapons. By dint of their particular skills and weapons, the Raiding Support Regiment was able to give much-needed assistance to the lightly armed *andartes*.

Later in the autumn, Goodall's troop landed in western occupied Greece, where they were to spend some six weeks. First they went to General Zervas' HQ, then, accompanied by some sixty mules and their owners, the RSR travelled by night and hid up during the day as they moved deep into ELAS territory. Goodall felt that it was a great credit to the muleteers that not one item of kit was lost over those six weeks. The Greek muleteers risked far more than their British allies, who were in uniform, because if they had been captured by the Germans, the punishment would have been death without any mercy being shown. When the journey through the mountains from east to west eventually ended, 'Many of us had wet eyes.' Goodall added that some of the ELAS partisans, who had marched and fought alongside the RSR in the mountains against the Germans, were to become their enemies on the streets of Athens, 'where we lost more men fighting the Greeks than we did against the Germans – what a sad time'.

Another member of the RSR was Alan Rose, serving with B Troop, which was equipped with 3 inch mortars. They landed at Parga on the west coast of Greece at the end of April 1944 before moving to their operating area in the Pindus mountains. After B Troop reached ELAS territory, Rose said that, 'Life seemed to go on much as usual, except for an undercurrent of threat, of pressure, an uncomfortable feeling that we, the British, were upsetting a plan, which counted fighting the Germans as very low on their list of priorities. By "their", I am, of course, referring to the political masters of that territory, the EAM.' Unlike Vic Goodall, Alan Rose did not remain in Athens to confront ELAS. Instead the fortunes of war took him to Yugoslavia, where other partisans were fighting the German occupation forces.

The Peloponnese was the first part of the mainland to be

evacuated by the Germans and, with the spectre of EAM/ELAS seizing power in the vacuum created, the British were stirred into action. They were right to act quickly, for Aris, surrounded by his bodyguard of black-bearded ruffians, was in the Peloponnese hunting down policemen and members of the Security Battalions, the so-called traitors, with People's Tribunals being established and brutal sentences being passed.

When the British decided to seize Araxos airfield in the north-west Peloponnese, from which German troops were already withdrawing, once more it was the swashbuckling Jellicoe of the SBS who was to lead the venture. Fifty-eight of his parachutists dropped to seize Araxos airfield unopposed and received a terrific welcome from overjoyed Greek civilians. When Jellicoe landed a day later, the situation was extremely complicated, especially in the port of Patras. A German garrison of under a thousand, supported by some 1,600 men of the local Security Battalion, waited uneasily while the port itself was entirely surrounded by ELAS *andartes*. Jellicoe switched his patrols in rapid succession to make the Germans believe that his tiny force was much bigger than it was, while, to his surprise, officers and men of the Security Battalion, desperately afraid they would be massacred by ELAS, surrendered to him at once and, having been disarmed, were led off to hastily contrived prison camps. By means of the SBS action, Patras was captured with the port still intact, and the tiny British force was given an enthusiastic welcome that almost amounted to adulation. Jellicoe detected an air of apprehension as well, which he explained: 'The reason was undoubtedly because I actually drove into Patras with Aris ... although we did not discover until later, ELAS had already carried out horrifying massacres at nearby Kalamata and Pyrgos, slaughtering Royalists, bourgeois, Security Battalion men, anyone who was obviously anti-Communist.'

By imposing a strict curfew, Jellicoe was able to curtail some of the slaughter but his action led to violent protests from Aris to General Wilson. Of Aris himself, Jellicoe was to write, 'Despite his considerable personal brutality, I found Aris a man of some charm.'

During this period the BLOs had been given an impossible

order, when instructed to influence ELAS to stop shedding blood, because they had no means of doing this until the first small body of British troops arrived in the Peloponnese. That certain Communist leaders were determined to take over the Peloponnese can be seen in the message, 'Win before Allies arrive' received by Aris from Zevgos – a 'rapturous type of Communist, exalted with a religious fervour' – who was a member of the Central Committee of both KKE and EAM. Fortunately for the non-Communist citizens, Jellicoe and his 'Bucket Force' did arrive in time but the margin was desperately close and hundreds perished before some sort of sanity prevailed.

R.A.L. Summers, then a member of L Squadron, knew nothing about the political undertones when he arrived – the enemy, as far as his squadron was concerned, was still the Germans. In his words: 'Patras became a bitter battle. We tried to penetrate the port and stop the demolitions. The Germans were being evacuated mainly by the port.... As usual the Germans covered their retreat very carefully but I think they would have got a shock when they found that the opposing numbers were really very small.' Summers confirms that the Security Battalion men in Patras were only too keen to surrender to the British rather than face the vengeance of fellow Greeks serving with ELAS. After meeting the Security Battalion at an RV, 'Everything became very matey. Batmen spread a white tablecloth and we all joined in a lavish picnic with the senior officers of the Greeks.... A promise had been made that the Security Battalion would be under our protection and we were to ensure that the ELAS guerrillas would not be allowed to murder them.'

One man who played a major role in curtailing the bloodshed was Panayiotis Kanellopoulos who, as previously stated, had escaped from Greece in 1942 to become Deputy Prime Minister in the Government in Exile. Kanellopoulos had come to the Peloponnese as a plenipotentiary from the Greek Government and, being a local man, born in Patras, he was trusted by the majority of the people and was to play no small part in persuading Aris to moderate his actions. When Brigadier George Davey, commanding Land Forces Adriatic, arrived, he was to find that the initiative taken by the first

British forces to land, supported by Kanellopoulos' influence locally, had combined to save the Peloponnese from complete anarchy and widespread killings – all under the pretext of punishing the so-called collaborators, many of whom were patriotic Greeks, albeit of the 'wrong' political persuasion.

Liberation moved first to Athens and then to the north. The Germans did not attempt to defend Athens, only holding the approaches to the city so that their evacuation could go as smoothly as possible. The small number of commandos, SBS and LRDG found that the hospitality of the Greeks slowed them up far more than German resistance did. In Summers' words: 'The villagers always seemed to know when we were to go through their villages. Tables were laid out with food and drink. At that time the Greeks were really very short of food but gave us everything they had; the roads were strewn with flowers. And one old woman shouted: 'You must take the flowers; they are all we have to give.'

On 12 October, in Athens, the swastika was taken down for the last time and a wreath was laid on the tomb of the Unknown Soldier before the last few Germans withdrew from the city. Jeanne Tsatsos closed her diary with words that were not meant to be ironic: 'Greece is once more our own, our very own.' Athenians came out in their thousands, laughing, cheering and crying with emotion; British soldiers were carried on the shoulders of the rejoicing crowds. The city was unscarred and, thanks to the brave initiative of a small group of ELAS guerrillas, the electric power station on the outskirts of Athens was not destroyed by the Germans before they withdrew. On the following day, a company of the 2nd Independent Parachute Brigade landed (in a strong wind which caused casualties) and secured the airfield at Megara just outside the city before moving into the capital, only to find that Jellicoe and about fifty-five men from the SBS were already installed in the best hotel, the Grande Bretagne. Twenty-four hours before, German officers had been sleeping in the same beds.

Amidst all the rejoicing, there were those who feared the situation could change very quickly. One who sounded a note of warning was the intrepid Frank Macaskie, who was staying, in hiding, with Archbishop Damaskinos when the Germans pulled out their rearguard from the city. Macaskie suspected that the 2nd ELAS Division had resolved to take over important buildings within Athens and might well have done so had the British troops not arrived on the heels of the departing Germans. An officer with Zervas, Colonel Nikolopoulos, reported to BLO Nick Hammond, a classical scholar whom Woodhouse rated one of the most level-headed of his subordinates, that EAM had plans for the massacre of 60,000 people in Athens during the first hours after liberation. As far as can be ascertained, that report was not confirmed and it is reasonable to assume that, even if there was such a plan, the figure of 60,000 was one of the gross exaggerations not uncommon in wartime Greece. On the other hand, there is little doubt that lists of collaborators and 'enemies of the state' had already been prepared, and that the vendettas that began in earnest during the first few days of December had been postponed only by the sudden arrival of the first British troops within Athens on or after 12 October.

'Pomp Force', a composite force comprising a battalion of paratroopers, some attached engineers and an RAF Regiment contingent, together with armoured cars and a battery of 75mm guns, adding up to about 950 men, moved up north under the command of Jellicoe. The intention was that they would harry the Germans until they left Greece, and after making good speed, despite widespread destruction of road and bridges by the Germans, they met up with the enemy south of Kozani. At dawn the British paratroops launched a full-scale attack, supported by heavy weapons manned by the SBS. With understandable sarcasm, Summers remembers that, 'We had also been joined by a few war correspondents, British and Americans. Provided they could be assured of their creature comforts, they were around us.' But there were others who did not join in as 'Pomp Force' attacked the German rearguard. ELAS *andartes* were waiting on the sidelines and, after the British had driven the Germans out of Kozani, the guerrillas decided it was time for them to appear. Within a few hours, the EAM news-sheet in Macedonia published a lurid account of 'the Battle of Kozani'. One colourful paragraph stated that, 'Our units shattered enemy resistance ... in this battle our *andartes* fought with unparalleled heroism and determination. After a

bitter five hours' fight Kozani was taken and the enemy is
now in retreat northwards.' Perhaps it was that report that
has led Thanasis Hajis to allege that, 'The British did not fire
a single shot against the Germans who were pulling out'
(*National Liberation Movement or Resistance*). Such versions
were certainly at odds with the accounts of the British
servicemen who took part in the battle. Their commander,
Earl Jellicoe, maintained that no help was received at all from
ELAS, '... although they did a spectacular charge into Kozani
after the Germans had gone'.

That was virtually the end of the occupation of Greece by
Germany. On 22 October the first SBS patrol of forty men
under Anders Lassan, a Dane destined to win a posthumous
VC later in the war, arrived at Salonika, in the belief that the
Germans had evacuated the city already. In fact, Lassan and
his men had arrived five days too early and had to hide,
powerless to act while the Germans blew up the dock
facilities. When Lassan's party was able to emerge from their
hiding-place, they were given a tremendous reception by the
people of Salonika. They were also astonished to find that
ELAS had moved its positions in and around the city and
were taking no action to attack the retreating Germans. By
being allowed to withdraw virtually unopposed, the German
occupiers ruthlessly and systematically stripped farms and
the Macedonian countryside of livestock, cattle and poultry.
Bridges, factories, road and rail communications and
urgently required machinery were destroyed, which left the
incoming British forces with a monumental problem, as the
Papendreou Government had no means by which they could
receive or distribute the UNRRA supplies that followed the
British Army into Greece.

There seems little doubt that KKE/EAM had anticipated a
much larger liberation army to arrive, although, with six
EAM members in Papendreou's Cabinet, it is strange that
they did not have some prior inkling of the actual size of
Scobie's force. The only fighting troops available consisted of
two brigades (the 2nd Parachute and the 23rd Armoured,
both in an infantry role), a few hundred British commandos
and a handful of Americans, with the Greek Mountain
Brigade due to arrive later, as was the Sacred Regiment
following its operations in the Aegean islands. By the end of

October, General Scobie's III Corps consisted of about 26,500 British troops and five squadrons of aircraft. This meant that the small liberation force could be stationed only in Athens, Piraeus, Salonika and one or two other towns, so that the rest of Greece remained under the control of the existing guerrilla factions – under the Caserta Agreement that had been anticipated.

The attitude of the Soviet Government towards British involvement in Greece was crucial during this period. Winston Churchill was to write a graphic account of his meeting with Stalin on 9 October in Moscow. His proposition was made to Stalin: 'Let us settle our affairs in the Balkans. Your armies are in Romania and Bulgaria.... So far as Britain and Russia are concerned, how would it do for you to have ninety per cent predominance in Romania, for us to have ninety per cent of the say in Greece, and go 50-50 about Yugoslavia?' Churchill added that, 'It was all settled in no more time than it takes to set down.' The KKE Central Committee in Greece, therefore, received no message of support from Moscow. Russian abstention had been obtained at a heavy price by Churchill and, as the Papendreou Government had no power to act independently, the immediate future of Greece lay in the hands of the British Government. As a consequence, it was not long before the growing disorder forced the Prime Minister, on 7 November, to write to Eden: 'In my opinion, having paid the price we have to Russia for freedom of action in Greece, we should not hesitate to use British troops to support the Royal Hellenic Government under Papendreou. This implies that British troops should certainly intervene to check acts of lawlessness.'

The formal arrival in Greece of Papendreou and General Scobie did not go as planned. A Guard of Honour was to be led by the commander of the 23rd Armoured Brigade (Brigadier H. Arkwright), consisting of a platoon from each of his two armoured regiments, and platoons from the Greek Sacred Squadron and ELAS *andartes*. Inevitably they had a wide variety of 'arms drill', so practices were held until, during a last-minute rehearsal, a large rowing boat was observed circling in a suspicious manner. Captain Hugh Lee, then Flag Lieutenant to Rear-Admiral J.M. Mansfield, explains what happened: 'The next day, it was intended that

a MTB would take General Scobie and the Admiral over to
the *Averoff* to pick up the Greek Government in Exile and
take them ashore. We hailed the only sailor visible in the
Averoff – a very stout gentleman – and asked where the Greek
Government was. He clearly spoke no English and ignored
us. We hung on as long as we could and then made off at
high speed for the harbour.

'We had gone half way when ahead of us we sighted a small
boat, gunwales practically awash, loaded with gentlemen in
trilby hats. It was, of course, the Greek Government, who had
not trusted the British or the arrangements and had set off
on their own. We just managed to get into the harbour before
them, scrambled up one side of the jetty as the Greek
Government, having taken a dangerous short cut, started
scrambling up the other side. General Scobie was just in time
to welcome them and, theoretically, hand the country over to
them.

'There were two Guards of Honour drawn up on the jetty,
one of Evzones and the other the most murderous brigands
imaginable. Bandoliers, beards, well-greased rifles, filthy
clothes – hardly uniform – and a very high level of aroma.
These were the guerrillas from the mountains who had been
fighting the Germans.

'After inspecting both Guards of Honour we embarked in
cars with the usual muddle of not knowing which car was
which and Papendreou was ushered into a leading car by the
Admiral. I climbed into the front of the car and just as we
were about to set off, a huge guerrilla opened the door and
squashed in beside me, wiping the greasy bulk of his rifle all
down my beautiful white trousers! We set off for Athens
along the road lined with people, all, what I thought
innocently, cheering like mad. They were, in fact, shouting
E-A-M, K-K-E, a real rent-a-crowd!'

Lieutenant-Colonel W. Byford-Jones, one of the earliest
arrivals in Athens, was to put into words what several others
have recalled. Having been told there was little or no food
and having heard stories about 'the starving Greeks',
Byford-Jones and his companions found that food was
readily available – at a price – including luxuries not seen in
war-time Britain. Hugh Lee has supported that statement:
'The locals we met were all on our side but they were mostly

middle-class and pretty well off, plenty of food on the Black
Market, when food was so scarce: but they had most to lose
from an ELAS victory.'

Outside the British Army, Ronald Scobie was little known;
now, as a comparatively junior general, he was about to face
'a trial of character and willpower such as no other Allied
Commander had to face in the Second World War' (Henry
Maule). Prior to going to Greece, Scobie had achieved several
distinctions: in his youth, he had played Rugby football,
being capped by Scotland; he was an experienced fighting
soldier – during the First World War as a brigade major –
and in the Second World War he commanded the Tobruk
garrison which stood firm against Rommel's attacks during
November 1941. Scobie had the reputation of being a
straight, honest man, a first-class leader who had little or no
interest in politics. Nevertheless, prior to his arrival in Athens
to take up the new assignment, he had done his best to find
out as much as he could about Greece.

It has been said that Scobie's very distinctions may have
been a handicap because, only too recognizably a British
officer and gentleman, he was put in a position where he had
to order the Greeks about on their own soil and, like some of
his subordinates in Greece at the time, he may have been
guilty of under-estimating their deep national pride. His
military achievements in both World Wars did not necessarily
mean that he understood guerrilla warfare or the mindless
violence that had been part of Greek history for so many
years. After his arrival as GOC in Greece, Scobie took great
pains to cultivate General Sarafis, inviting him to dinner in
the hope that they could establish a degree of rapport.
Although Sarafis respected him as a fellow regular officer, he
also knew that open collaboration could lead to his being
branded a lackey of the British, thus to join the long list of
Greeks accused of being collaborators with the Germans and
Italians.

After reaching Athens, Scobie was given a fantastic
welcome and for the few hours of euphoria would have
agreed with the 'You are lucky to be going to Greece'
introduction to the HMSO booklet, issued to all officers and
men prior to their joining him in that country. Because of the
booklet's optimism, the majority of British soldiers sailed

from Italy believing that for them the war was over and that, as part of the liberation force, their attitude towards the local people would be of more importance than their ability as fighting soldiers. The booklet went on to state that, 'The Greeks will respect you, you must respect them', words that were to be recalled and derided when ELAS fired at and pinned down British troops a few days later!

As to whether one of Scobie's ADCs had studied the pamphlet is doubtful because, when the young officer was asked why the *andarte* leaders were not participating in the celebratory procession, Woodhouse was shocked to hear his reply: 'The guerrilla leaders? What has it got to do with them?' For proud Greeks such an attitude could only be interpreted as insulting and a mockery of the resistance movement as a whole.

Early in October, when Brigadier John Hunt went to Athens to receive orders from General Scobie, he was given a vast area of responsibility for his brigade, which was to take him five days to reconnoitre, even in a cursory manner. During his travels, John Hunt was quick to appreciate that behind the smiles of welcome there was apprehension – and not everybody was smiling either. Thus he expressed grave concern at the huge area that had been given his brigade. Hunt said that despite all his responsibilities, Scobie, was a man of 'great serenity, tolerant, calm', adding that he held the GOC in considerable respect during that very difficult and critical period of the Greek Rebellion. Ronald Scobie advised Hunt to have a word with General Sarafis himself. At Thebes, where Sarafis was addressing a meeting, Hunt recollected seeing '... a lean, earnest, somewhat insignificant-looking person, humourless but with a burning fire within him as he harangued the crowd from a balcony overlooking the Town Square. Sarafis' appearance and character certainly contrasted strongly with his rival partisan leader, General Zervas.'

Despite that rather unfavourable impression, one that most British officers who met him shared, Sarafis did give Hunt some reassurance to allay his fears, so that when the 11th Brigade from the 4th Indian Division sailed across the Adriatic, the first units that arrived moved into their far-flung locations, stretching from the Pyrgos area in the south up to the troubled region north of the Gulf of Corinth, with detachments on the large islands of Zante and Cephalonia; and with the last battalion due to arrive (2/7th Gurkha Rifles) earmarked to go to Corfu and to Preveza on the mainland.

During November it was all too evident to those stationed away from Athens that the Papendreou Government had no writ outside the capital city. Communications had been badly, and in many areas totally, disrupted so that the work of relief was difficult to organize. And promises that a plebiscite, followed by elections, would be held in the near future meant little when the civil administration was on the verge of collapse and there were no electoral rolls. As a consequence, the air of optimism at Scobie's HQ did not reflect the opinions of the 'demi-gods of Force 133' (Richard Capell). These included John Mulgan, Tom Barnes (called 'Lord Tom'), Arthur Edmonds, Nick Hammond and Philip Worrall, among others – and, of course, Chris Woodhouse who, at the age of twenty-seven, with the temporary rank of colonel, found himself being lionized as 'the most famous soldier in Greece'. Based on their experiences with the partisans over the past few months, the officers of the Allied Military Mission, which included American officers of the OSS, were under no illusions that the struggle for power would be resolved by peaceful means alone.

Most American liaison officers, who were usually of Greek origin, soon saw through the EAM propaganda, unlike members of the US Press Corps whose reports increasingly adopted a stridently anti-British tone. It was not long before Scobie found himself under similar pressure from many of the British newspapermen in Athens, whose other target was Australian-born Reginald Leeper, the *bête noir* of the media. Accused of being 'stand-offish', in the eyes of the journalists Leeper was pro-monarchist, an unfair accusation because he was but carrying out the British Government's policy of supporting Papendreou's Provisional Administration, in which EAM was represented by six ministers.

During November the disorder increased and spread throughout the country, despite the Politburo of KKE passing a genuine resolution 'welcoming the brave children of Great Britain, our freedom-loving ally'. Although George

Siantos and a few of his colleagues still wanted to pursue power by political means rather than attempting a military *coup*, there were other KKE and EAM leaders who, on realizing that the British forces were thinly spread, organized for relief operations rather than a military occupation, felt that their opportunity had come to take over the country. Churchill recognized the threat and on 8 November sent a telegram to General Wilson in Italy, with a copy to Reginald Leeper in Athens: 'In view of increasing threat of Communist elements in Greece and indications that they plan to seize power by force, I hope that you will consider reinforcing our troops in Athens area by immediate despatch of the 3rd Brigade of 4th Indian Division or some other formation....'

This cable led to the eventual despatch of the complete 4th Indian Division from Italy, as well as the Greek Brigade which was to be at the heart of the controversy between Papendreou and his EAM colleagues. Their arrival on Greek soil meanwhile only served to increase the bitterness, while during the troubled days of November the British Army continued to perform wonders, helping with relief work and reconstruction, as well as showing a remarkable tolerance in the face of unforeseen issues. The vast majority of the officers and men had come to Greece expecting to be greeted as friends, and it was to take a little time before they realized that, amidst the cheering and the flowers, unfriendly elements viewed them as occupiers rather than liberators.

R. Waites, at that time an RAF wireless operator, together with eleven other colleagues arrived in Athens to take over military communications at the Cable & Wireless Telegraph Company. The only accommodation available was a floor containing eight rooms above a brothel. Waites recalls that, 'Nobody believes us when we say that nothing happened all the time we were there, but it is true, although the girls were very good at darning socks and general repairs to our uniforms, and on many occasions cooking for us.' For several days when off duty, Waites and his friends 'mixed with the ordinary Greek people.... I've never been anywhere as enjoyable as one of those Name-Day parties.'

But a few days later the atmosphere began to change: 'We still visited our Greek friends in the suburbs of Kipseli which

Part of the crowd in Constitution Square on 3 December 1944 before
the firing began

General Napoleon Zervas (minus his beard) returns from Corfu after
his defeat by ELAS, end of December 1944

Greek policemen accompany paratroopers along Duripidhou Street,
Athens, December 1944

Field Marshal Alexander and Rear-Admiral Turle (Senior Naval
Officer in Greece) visit Athens, 12 December 1944

Removing an ELAS roadblock by explosives – an airborne sapper
watched by Greek children

Pipers of the 6th Black Watch entertain civilian 'customers' at the
soup-kitchen, 2 January 1945

Wing-Commander James MP, talks to South African sapper, C. J.
Basson, after his release from ELAS custody, 27 January 1945

Archbishop Damaskinos, with Frank Macaskie, before his inauguration as Regent of Greece

King's Dragoon Guards' 'Thanksgiving Service', watched by civilians on Arios Pagos (near the Acropolis), January 1945

An enormous crowd in Athens celebrating the 'Second Round' victory, carrying posters of Churchill, as well as praising Scobie, 'The popular hero', 14 January 1945

George Bagnall, member of the TUC delegation, talks to paratroopers
in the ENSA Cinema in Athens, 28 January 1945

Four ELAS delegates signing the cease-fire. *Left to right*: Athinellis,
Partsalidis, Zevgos and Macridis. The cease-fire came into effect from
0001 hours on 15 January 1945

General Sarafis at the armistice negotiations held at Varkiza,
12 February 1945

we frequented during our off-duty periods, but we began to notice a little nervousness creeping in, there wasn't the hilarity that there used to be, and it seemed the conversations were guarded.... One of our very close friends, Nikos, told us there was trouble brewing between the political factions, Communists and Royalists, KKE and ELAS, but none of us knew anything about Greek politics and had been told not to interfere in any political activities.'

And so it was for the majority of the servicemen who landed in Greece before the Second Round began in earnest. The HMSO booklet had given that other reassuring message: 'The Greeks will respect you, you must respect the Greeks', and the scenes of great and genuine rejoicing only seemed to reinforce the booklet's message. However, it was not long before the more discerning of the British visitors began to realize that the Royalists believed the British had come to kill the red ELAS and that ELAS felt sure they were there to throw out the Royalists! Those sentiments were to be echoed in the 23rd Armoured Brigade's account of operations between the middle of October and 7 January 1945: 'ELAS, not believing that the British would intervene, did not change their attitude towards us in any way. This made it harder to indicate to them what our final reactions must be.' The writer was referring to the ELAS rank and file, large numbers of whom were unfortunate dupes, rather than to their leaders. George Siantos continued to believe that the key to absolute power lay in the main centre of population: 'He who rules Athens rules Greece.' The truth was that many of the Communist leaders felt the prize was there for the taking, and their preponderance of strength was to prove too great a temptation.

The question then has to be asked: did the British have to be caught up and embroiled in the conflict, or was there any alternative? In theory, it could be argued that it was not Britain's affair, that British soldiers should have stood aside, but having encouraged Papendreou from the very start – and knowing that he had nothing with which to meet lynching, murders and anarchy – it would have been quite impossible for the British Armed Forces to remain bystanders while a bloody civil war raged around them. Scobie was faced with a situation at the beginning of December 1944 which did not stem from a sudden move by either the British or ELAS: it came as the logical and direct result of Anglo-Greek relations which had been interwoven for so many years. For such a reason did Scobie receive Churchill's order to restore the situation 'without bloodshed if possible, with bloodshed if necessary'.

Following that order, General Scobie broadcast a solemn warning to the Greek nation: 'I am determined as far as lies within my power to make a success of the task assigned to me by my Government. I am convinced that in many parts of the country there is no freedom of speech, no freedom of the Press, and that terrorism and victimization still exist. I stand firm behind the present Constitutional Government until the Greek State can be established with a legally armed force and free elections can be held. I will protect you and your Government against any attempt to effect a *coup d'état* or act of violence which is unconstitutional.'

Those were brave words, especially in view of the disparity in numbers between the ELAS divisions and the small British force on Greek soil, many of whose members had been sent to help with the relief programme and to carry out administrative tasks; they were not trained or suitably armed to fight the ELAS divisions which were being moved into strategic positions around Athens, Salonika and Patras. In truth, the KKE Central Committee had decided that the moment to strike had come, appreciating that if they delayed much longer the British might be able to send in reinforcements for their III Corps – despite the fact they were badly needed in Italy, France and the Far East.

Athens was destined to be the battlefield for which two prominent members of the Central Committee, George Siantos and General Mandakas, had full responsibility. Mandakas had established a fine reputation as a guerrilla leader in Crete where, as a Republican, he had led the ELK (National Organization of Crete); as a result, Crete was one island where EAM/ELAS failed to get any sort of footing whatever. Now recently promoted from colonel to general, Mandakas had the 2nd (Attica), the 3rd (Peloponnese) and the 13th (Roumeli) Divisions under his command, a total fighting strength of about 18,000 armed men. Meanwhile, elsewhere in the country other ELAS divisions were moving to their battle stations. But surprisingly Sarafis and Aris, with a force of about 23,000 men, were to march against Zervas rather than besieging Athens. Politically, the desire to wipe out Zervas and EDES became an all-important factor, and in the long term it was to be one of the reasons for ELAS's defeat in the Second Round.

On 1 December, the six EAM members resigned from the Papendreou Cabinet, which meant that open conflict became inevitable. It was a war that was certainly not sought by the tiny British force or the vast majority of ELAS *andartes*, a war blundered into by mistake rather than design, Initially many *andartes* were to find it difficult to shoot at British soldiers who, traditionally, had been their friends and allies, not only in both world wars but years before in their country's struggle to achieve independence.

7 The Second Round
– A Near Thing

'Let the sword decide after stratagem has failed'
Arabic proverb

Even before 1 December, no one would have pretended that
Athens was a normal city. During the hours of daylight life
went on, with the Greeks smiling and polite not only to the
British but, apparently, to each other as well. After darkness
shooting began. Night after night it continued, without any
clashes or battles being fought – indeed, no one seemed to
know exactly what was happening. For the man in the hot
seat, Ronald Scobie, it was a period of ever-increasing
tension; with a dual politico-military role to undertake, he
had to deal with a multitude of problems. Even had there
been no dark clouds of civil war approaching, it was a
tremendous task to bring the ravaged land back to normal,
with inflation roaring out of control, while in many parts of
the country food was a commodity that few could boast as
being theirs. Greeks of all classes dearly needed peace – but
that was one thing they were not going to enjoy.

Prime Minister Papendreou, by now convinced that a civil
war was becoming inevitable, signed an official order
demobilizing all *andartes* by 10 December, making it clear that
any unauthorized to carry arms after that date would be
prosecuted. This message was put into leaflet form and
dropped by the Royal Air Force all over the country. EAM
countered by announcing that they would obey the order to
disarm with the provision that Scobie agreed to the Greek
Mountain Brigade's forming part of a division with ELAS.
Their suggestion would have meant that the Greek

Government would have lost control of their only loyal troops, because in a mixed division the officers and men would have been subjected to Communist propaganda – as had happened twice before in the Middle East.

Thereafter events moved quickly, especially after the KKE Central Committee decided to take their headquarters away from the city. Aris, too, was champing at the bit: 'A hundred per cent of the [ELAS] Army and seventy per cent of the people are eagerly awaiting the signal for action against the powers of darkness!' All that was required now was the spark to ignite the fire, for tension had been growing apace. Huge slogans painted in red supporting KKE, EAM and ELAS abounded; one officer recalls that he woke up to find that during the night large parts of the city had been literally painted red, as if a gigantic carnival was about to begin. The reaction of non-Communist Athenians made it all too evident that trouble was brewing on a major scale.

Scobie, the man with a host of pressures on his shoulders, was attacked by KKE's Zevgos, who inspired the Communist Press to rage against the general's message to the Greek people, accusing Scobie of having 'fallen victim to the dark intrigues and malicious suggestions of the Black Opposition'. Fortunately, Ronald Scobie was not a man to be rattled by malicious accusations. Captain Hugh Lee, then Flag Lieutenant to Admiral Jack Mansfield, remembers Scobie as being 'a very fine man – the epitome of a British general – calm, unruffled and confidence-inspiring'. This professional soldier, unskilled in politics, never wavered in his resolution to save Greece from what he now thought was certain, a Communist take-over which would have led to a bloodbath and anarchy.

When EAM asked for permission to hold a demonstration in Athens on 3 December, Papendreou yielded to their pressure and gave his assent. It was a Sunday morning, and Athens was bathed in bright sunshine as hundreds of excited people moved towards Constitution Square. The Greek police were there but not too many of them, while British troops had been told to adopt a low profile. Reginald Leeper was one who stayed away, but from his study in the 'Pink House', the Embassy, he had a good view of the long procession as it passed underneath his window. It was, he later reported, orderly, with the usual banners and marchers shouting EAM slogans as they passed. Athenians take more pleasure than most in street manifestations. Eye-witnesses, British and Greek, were astonished at the ability of the left-wing groups to assemble and handle such large numbers.

Suddenly there came the noise of an explosion, and a burst of automatic fire followed from Constitution Square itself – the sound of what Leeper described as 'the rattle of musketry'. Again, there are several versions of what happened, and varying opinions about who fired first. British servicemen who were near or on the spot tend to agree that there was one single shot, before all hell was let loose. They also confirm that the crowd was in a highly emotional state, screaming, chanting, raising clenched fists and, even before the first shot was fired, in a dangerous, frenzied state. III Corps' HQ nearby was guarded by armoured cars, and one of the drivers has stated that he had never experienced anything quite as terrifying as that crowd, whose emotions suddenly erupted like a huge fiery volcano. Shots were exchanged; the panic-stricken police decided to defend themselves and began firing on the unarmed crowd. Several demonstrators were killed and others arrested, with the police also suffering casualties.

Not only was it the signal for the Second Round to begin, it was also to herald a series of scathing articles attacking Scobie, Papendreou and the British Government, with *The Times* correspondent leading the critics among the newspapermen in Athens who told their readers that, 'The Fascist police had fired on an unarmed crowd.' Notable exceptions were *The New York Times* foreign correspondent, who had a Greek wife to tell him who was who and what was what, and two British journalists who consistently supported Scobie and Leeper, Richard Capell (*Daily Telegraph*) and Kenneth Matthews (BBC).

Parading the martyrs of Constitution Square in open coffins after lunch on 3 December, an angry mob surrounded the British Embassy, shrieking 'Death to Scobie! Death to Scobie!' From now on the general was to be the target of violent abuse or, alternatively, adulation amounting to hero-worship: as in Greek politics of that era, there was no happy medium in Athenians' emotions towards him.

At the end of that day General Scobie was to note in his diary, 'What I think happened is this. The so-called peaceful procession had thrown grenades outside the PM's house *en route* killing two *gendarmes*. On arriving near the entrance to the Square it was halted by a body of Greek police armed with carbines. I think, however, they were armed with blank ammunition. When the procession moved forward again, the police opened fire, possibly aiming over the heads of the marchers. The latter, however, soon came to grips and started to seize rifles off the police. At this point a Greek officer who had been sheltering nearby appeared with a tommy gun and loosed off into the crowd, probably causing the bulk of, if not all, the casualties.

Harold Macmillan was one who believed that the fatal shots were fired by a Communist *agent provocateur*; he did not think that the civil war had been precipitated by the so-called massacre in Constitution Square. In his opinion the ELAS rebellion was a result of a definite decision '... taken by the Communist leaders, Siantos and Ioannides, at least five days before'. A very different story appeared in *The Times*, written by journalist Geoffrey Hoare on 4 December. Hoare maintained that the police opened fire with rifles and tommy guns, with the crowd trying to escape the bullets while the police continued firing. 'The firing was wild and savage and continued sporadically for nearly an hour.... No British soldier played any part in the offence and the presence of our units served only to associate Britain with what is everywhere condemned as "Fascist action". That had done grievous injury to Anglo-Greek friendship.'

Why Hoare and others composed such hysterical reports is not clear but, as Ambassador Leeper was to write, 'Those typewriters gave the EAM a major victory that day.' Soon Leeper had to have the iron gates of the British Embassy locked, with a small guard taking up their stand facing a large crowd that became extremely hostile, carrying banners dipped in the blood of one of the Constitution Square victims, bearing the message: 'Death to Scobie!' As yet no British soldiers had been involved but it was only a matter of hours before the tiny force in Athens was under siege and struggling for survival.

A most important and difficult question to answer is: did

EAM/ELAS make a definite decision to take power by force,
with events in Athens being pre-planned, or did they lurch
into confrontation with the British by mistake? Those commentators who tend to take the latter viewpoint base their case
on the protestations of loyalty made by EAM to the British
during November. Moreover, there can be no doubt that EAM
did have a genuine, justifiable fear that, if they handed over all
their arms, members of the police, Security Battalions and
Mountain Brigade would wreak indiscriminate vengeance
upon them. It was not a question of whether EAM/ELAS
trusted Papendreou when he made promises to the contrary:
they doubted he had the means to ensure that such promises
could be enforced.

Evidence to support both sides of the argument can be
found in the vast bibliography that now covers the Greek Civil
War in all its aspects. We know, for example, that Ioannis
Ioannides, Organizing Secretary of the KKE Politbureau, has
stated: 'ELAS was to clash with the British if political
manœuvres failed.' He also said that ELAS servicemen were
ordered to re-enlist in veteran associations so they could
disrupt armed bodies and infiltrate those raised in their place.
In later years Ioannides spoke about the demonstration in
Constitution Square: 'We were proceeding with preme-
ditation to create a pretext so that the war should begin.' On
balance, it does appear as if the plan of campaign produced by
General Mandakas – which involved the movement of ELAS
formations to their battle stations before 3 December – shows
that military means had been decided on before the demonstration in Constitution Square. By so doing, ELAS gained the
initial advantage of surprise, as to the very end the optimistic
Papendreou was hopeful that the worst would not happen,
which helped delay any call for the immediate despatch of
reinforcements from Italy or elsewhere. Those few days
gained were to be of crucial importance – and very nearly fatal
as far as the non-Communists were concerned.

At first light on 6 December the frantic ringing of church
bells announced that the Second Round had started. Nevertheless, for a day or two a 'phoney war' atmosphere persisted,
because ELAS expended their fury on the police and the
much-hated Mountain Brigade but left British troops
unmolested in the same localities.

R. Waites again: 'We still had our duties to perform but as we had to walk from our billet to Cable & Wireless, a matter of about half a mile, we wondered if we would be able to get through all right.... All of us set off with not a little trepidation, but it was amazing. Gunfire stopped as we approached and started up again once we had passed. We couldn't believe it.'

R.A.L. Summers writes in a similar vein about this strange interlude: 'Our remaining patrols were ordered to put up a road block at Scaramanga and prevent any armed guerrillas from entering Athens with weapons. We took this in a very light-handed way as we were not in the least worried by the Greeks! They were "our friends". We had fought together. We had fought and they had watched and kept their powder dry ready for killing Greeks.... The lads were busy telling the Greeks to be good boys and hand in their weapons. One or two "incidents" took place with ELAS officers and officials who were not keen to comply.'

Group Captain S.M. Kettle RAF, then DAPM Athens, was 'trapped' with his Flight in the Ionion Palace Hotel in Patrassion Street, which had been taken over as an RAF Police HQ. Until 23 December they were unable to carry out their proper military police role but were involved in a series of adventures during the fighting. Kettle is another who believes that, 'The ELAS action was merely delayed while they got their forces into position and the decision was taken to attempt a *coup*, in spite of the relatively weak, and not necessarily hostile British presence.... Perhaps ELAS misjudged the possible determination of the British reaction in the light of Allied preoccupation with much more momentous events in Europe at that time.'

On 4 December a large body of heavily armed ELAS *andartes* seized the police headquarters in Piraeus. Other police stations in the port were also taken and, as the day went on, ELAS captured a further fifteen stations within Athens itself. In the face of such blatant provocation, General Scobie had no alternative but to order ELAS to desist, handing them an ultimatum to clear out of the Athens area by midnight 6 December. That Scobie had doubts as to whether this would be obeyed can be seen from the signal he sent to Field Marshal Alexander: 'ELAS outside Athens

shows signs of marching on city. Already some evidence
ELAS may offer armed resistance to British if we insist on
putting orders into complete effect.' Scobie obtained
immediate support from his military superior, Alexander, as
well as from the Prime Minister and Chiefs of Staff in
London.

That there was no bloodshed during an eyeball-to-eyeball
confrontation between the 6th Parachute Battalion and a
heavily armed ELAS formation of some 800 men, moving
from Thebes towards Athens, was due in no small measure to
the firm show of force displayed by the paratroopers under
their CO, Colonel Barlow. At the crucial moment, the
paratroopers fixed bayonets, and within seconds the *andartes*
began throwing down their guns. It was to be the last major
bloodless meeting between the British and their ELAS
opponents – the next day there was fighting near the British
Embassy which resulted in all the diplomatic staff's families
being brought into the building, there to remain for five
weeks. The precaution was justified within a matter of hours,
for ELAS snipers were 'encouraged' to shoot at the Embassy
and did so for many days thereafter. Nevertheless, during
this period British troops were specifically ordered not to fire
until fire had been directed at them, and there followed a
series of tragi-comic incidents while both sides edged their
way to all-out street fighting in Athens and Piraeus.

Up to the middle of December, the majority of British
servicemen who had arrived in Greece for the Liberation had
not been briefed about the possibility of serious trouble or
the complex political situation. The 2/7th Gurkha Rifles
Newsletter, written immediately after the event, sums this
up: 'To Greece, therefore, where the German Occupation
Forces were already being withdrawn, where we expected to
be greeted as liberators and to spend an easy, pleasant
interlude until Germany surrendered. I think we were almost
across the Adriatic before anyone mentioned the possibility
of trouble and we heard for the first time the term ELAS.'
The author of that newsletter, in a private letter to his
parents, went on in the same vein: 'Whoever said there would
be no trouble over here? It all seems so stupid and
unnecessary.... Violence has begun – the Communist factions
are using the arms originally given them by us to be used

against the Germans. They are attempting to intimidate the average Greek citizen into accepting their system of Government. At the moment things are pretty tense and all eyes are on the struggle which is taking place in Athens. Will ELAS or the British win?'

Peter Lepel Glass of the 6th Black Watch summed it up well: 'Our move was far too sudden and hurried for us to appreciate what was in store ... we knew little about the Greek people, their language or customs. Maps were non-existent.'

Before we see how the British so very nearly lost Athens, let us examine the situation in three other centres, Salonika, Patras and Volos.

When despatching units of the famous 4th Indian Division from Italy, Macedonia and Thrace received first priority, with the 7th Brigade drawing 'those stormy cockpits'. Feuds were a common feature of life for the polyglot people of that region, the most serious being the political issue of Macedonia itself, a more or less undefined territory lying partly in Greee, partly in Bulgaria and partly in Yugoslavia. An international Communist like Siantos, brought up and trained in the Stalinist doctrine, was prepared to accept the dismemberment of Macedonia, to cede areas to Greece's northern Communist neighbours, but it was a question that tore KKE apart. The hard-line Greek Communists could never live down an unpatriotic reputation of being prepared to hand over parts of Greek Macedonia to Bulgaria and Yugoslavia.

The last Bulgarian troops had left Macedonia and Thrace by 25 October, and as a result ELAS was in effective control of the greater part of northern Greece. Their forces were well equipped and efficiently led under the overall command of the recently promoted General Bakirdzis. He was an able soldier but, as one observer was to state following a conversation with him at this time, 'General Bakirdzis was already in that terrible position for an honest man – the moment when he begins to doubt the righteousness of his cause but dares not admit it to himself. Perhaps the General's suicide in 1946 was due to the fact that at last he had faced this realization.'

There is little doubt that Bakirdzis, politically a Liberal, still

hoped that the extreme Leftists were only a very small
minority and would not be able to take over the country. By
the general's side was his political commissar, Markos
Vapheiades, a name that was to be known throughout Greece
after the Second Round was over. A tobacco worker by trade,
originally Markos had never belonged to the Party hierarchy,
but he had served several terms of imprisonment for the
Communist cause. During their early days in Salonika, HQ's
7th Indian Brigade and 4th Indian Division found Markos an
unremarkable man, although when the rebellion spread he
developed and revealed an instinctive understanding of
guerrilla warfare. Although in the main he had been a
political soldier, he had played an active role in the fighting
and taken a keen interest in military operations generally.
Undoubtedly, too, he learnt much from Bakirdzis. It was
fortunate for the 4th Indian Division (under Major-General
A.W. Holworthy) and the 7th Indian Brigade that the ELAS
forces in Macedonia were controlled by two able men who
were unlikely to act without considering the consequences
first.

On arrival in Salonika, the 7th Indian Brigade sent
detachments to Kozani, Kilkis, Polyrios and Drama, as being
the most likely trouble spots, where it was anticipated that
ELAS would exact revenge against those they accused of
being collaborators. The troops' timely arrival forestalled
serious clashes but things turned nasty when the Indian
Division received orders to disarm ELAS forces and reform
the Salonika National Guard. Twenty-four hours after the
incident in Athens' Constitution Square, there was a
well-organized *coup* in Salonika. ELAS detachments took
over the main administrative buildings and evicted, without
ceremony, cowed, abject Government officials. As the tension
increased in the city, so too did the anti-British propaganda,
with highly organized crowds of farmworkers slavishly
repeating slogans, shouted at them through a microphone by
their 'cheer-leader'. The British, Indian and Gurkha troops
showed a remarkable self-discipline in fact of taunts and
deliberate attempts to provoke them; such restraint was wise,
as they were heavily outnumbered by well-armed ELAS
andartes surrounding the city.

The fact that no attack was launched was due in no small

measure to the British Consul in Salonika, the GOC 4th
Indian Division, Major-General Holworthy, and Brigadier
Lovett of the 7th Brigade, who took over command when the
general had to return to the UK for health reasons. A day or
two before, Scobie had noted that Holworthy seemed
depressed and pessimistic about the problems in Salonika.
Prior to his departure, Holworthy had helped to establish a
working relationship with the ELAS commander, General
Bakirdzis. Day by day, Bakirdzis resisted orders from ELAS
GHQ to attack the British, choosing instead to keep talking
and negotiate: 'Conferences between this astute soldier and
representatives of 4th Division became the order of the day.
For more than a month the uneasy peace hung on
tenterhooks from meeting to meeting.'

But good use was made of these conditions to smuggle out
to Athens hundreds of men who were on the ELAS vendetta
lists. The CRA, Brigadier C. Eastman, organized these
undercover operations with great skill and, as the days
passed, a few officers from ELAS headquarters, including
Bakirdzis's Chief of Staff, deserted, thereafter to be spirited
away to safety. Inevitably, this activity infuriated ELAS, and
intelligence reports were received indicating that there would
be a mammoth demonstration on 15 December, which would
be followed by an all-out attack on the 4th Indian Division
units. To meet this contingency, detachments from Kavalla
were recalled, but the weather had the final say – with 15
December came a fierce blizzard. There was no attack, and
the demonstration fizzled out when the crowds failed to
materialize or took refuge from the storm.

The writer of the Central India Horse Newsletter No. 18,
stationed in Salonika during this nerve-racking period, was
one of many servicemen who was upset by the anti-British
tone adopted by Geoffrey Hoare in his articles for *The Times*,
despatched from Athens. 'For the benefit of those of you who
may not be fully conversant with the aims, means and
organization of EAM, ELAS, KKE etc, and who will have
read a lot in the papers, including *The Times*, about our
interfering in Greek private affairs, I should like to say
straight away that, in the opinion of everyone who has been
here, there is no shadow of doubt that we have taken the
right and only possible line of action.' He went on to explain

why he thought this to be so: 'Their [ELAS'] atrocities have been and still are shocking, hostages being taken and murdered, families being robbed and impressed, no one daring to express their views. If you knock on a village door and go in, it is no unusual thing to find the occupants cowering in a corner, thinking that you are KKE. In fact, a complete reign of terror existed and in places still does. These bandits represent just what we've been fighting against for the last five years.'

After news about the incidents in Athens had broken, it was decided to concentrate the Salonika garrison in a compound, bordered by the sea on two sides of the perimeter. Quite a large proportion of the troops belonged to administrative units and included supply companies, a workshop, field park squadron and ordnance. These and many others crowded into a confined space to await events in Athens, wondering if General Bakirdzis could withstand the pressure from his superiors to stop negotiations and launch an attack against them.

Despite the tension, there were one or two informal, unplanned contacts between ELAS rank and file and their British counterparts. D. Parker, who was serving with the 4th Indian Division Signals, and a friend who spoke German, '... with a few ouzos under our belts, decided to smarten up the scruffy sentry, standing outside ELAS HQ on the seafront. My friend immediately started to berate the sentry in German until he called for an officer. When the officer came, he was in fact an Austrian.' To their surprise, the officer invited them inside to join his men for a drink. Parker commented: 'The place was packed full of unshaven, scruffy-looking characters, bristling with arms, drinking and filled with tobacco smoke. A villainous-looking fellow was thumping an old piano and another playing an accordion. They all crowded round as we went in and sat down at a table.... It was apparently quite a friendly chat, non-political, just about old times and swapping war experiences. After a while, we said it was time to get back to billets. The "band" then struck up a fairly good rendering of "It's a long way to Tipperary" and a not very tuneful version of "God Save the King". They all crowded round to shake our hands when we left, and the final accolade was a smart salute from the same sentry still on the door.'

That story, and others of a similar nature received from ex-servicemen, illustrates the love-hate relationship which often existed between many of the ELAS junior ranks and their British visitors, some of whom had been comrades-in-arms in the war against the Germans a few weeks before.

The situation in Patras was even more disturbing. The main body of the 11th Indian Brigade arrived on 22 November, and units were sent to various towns and villages in the Peloponnese and north of the Gulf of Corinth. Prior to the troops' arrival, officers had been reconnoitring the respective unit areas, one of whom was twenty-two-year-old J.R. Probyn of the 2/7th Gurkha Rifles. Setting off in a jeep, accompanied by an interpreter, a driver and a Gurkha orderly, Probyn reached a village in north-west Greece where, after consulting the local authorities, an amicable agreement was reached that the school building was best suited to be a billet for his company when it arrived. The locals were all smiles when he left. Next day, on returning to the village, Probyn found that ELAS had installed machine-guns behind sandbags in the houses that overlooked the school building, making it quite clear that the Gurkha soldiers would not be welcome. Probyn added that until that moment he knew nothing about Greek politics but, 'It became quite clear that the Communists were preparing for some sort of show-down.'

While his men moved into their allotted areas, Brigadier John Hunt had daily meetings with Colonel Tsikliteras, commanding the 3rd ELAS Division, and the 'sinister, bearded figure of his political Commissar, Kapitanos Akritis, who was all too evidently in effective charge of the party'. Although Hunt liked the grizzled little colonel – like Bakirdzis, Tsikliteras was wearing First World War ribbons, including the DSO – the daily conferences became more and more acrimonious until the crunch came during the night of 3/4 December, when ELAS surrounded 900 defenceless National Guardsmen and herded about 750 of them away to captivity in the mountains.

Furious at ELAS' 'treacherous trick', Hunt was keen to retaliate but three telegrams from HQ III Corps, the last dated 7 December, forbade him to break off relations with ELAS 'until you consider it necessary'; as for disarming them, he was told that no attempt was to be made, because, 'We are not in a position to enforce this at the moment.' To reinforce those signals, General Scobie even sent an Auster aircraft to take Hunt to Athens, where the GOC impressed on him 'the need to avoid getting involved in fighting, subject only to securing my own force'. Thereafter, all ranks of the 11th Brigade faced days and nights of provocation which taxed their patience to the limit – but their forbearance saved the lives of countless innocent civilians.

Orders were issued to the 2nd Camerons to concentrate on Patras, with one company returning from Pyrgos, some sixty miles from the town, a move that was effected without any trouble, and they brought back with them some anti-Communist families who knew what their fate would be after 'the Jocks' had left Pyrgos. Companies of the 2/7th Gurkha Rifles, originally earmarked for north-west Greece and Corfu, were diverted to Patras, where they remained until the New Year. The third battalion in the brigade, the 3/12th Royal Frontier Force Regiment, was about to be recalled from Epirus only to meet disaster when concentrating at the port of Missolonghi, where the name of Byron has long been remembered for his part in supporting the Greeks in their struggle to throw off Turkish rule in the nineteenth century. Following the ambush of one of the Frontier Force patrols and the capture of a party which went forward to negotiate their return, within the space of three days two landing craft were blown up by mines laid by ELAS in the entrance to the port, which they had laid a few days after the Royal Navy had swept the area. On the landing craft casualties were heavy, seventy being killed and over forty wounded, with some 200 vehicles and other battalion equipment lost.

After fighting with such distinction in the Italian campaign, it was a devastating blow to the 3/12th Frontier Force, and they suffered more casualties when two platoons were attacked at Krioneri. Hunt received permission from III Corps to withdraw the unit back to Patras immediately but was told that no shipping could be spared from Piraeus. A mini-Dunkirk situation inspired Captain Kalergis, the Naval Officer in Charge of Patras, to rustle up an assortment of *caiques* and small craft which brought the Indians back to safety – but without their vehicles. John Hunt was to write: 'It marked a very low point in our misfortunes, which continued to pile up.'

A few days later, on 23 December, the advance party of two officers and fifteen men from 171 Battery, 57th Light Anti-Aircraft Regiment, Royal Artillery, which had been sent to the island of Zante, were treacherously attacked after some double-dealing – the Zante Chief of Police was the chief culprit. Despite being completely surprised, the little force resisted until all their ammunition had been expended. Some of the party tried to escape, and would have done so if the *caique* they selected had been functioning properly. When the incident was over, four had been killed, six wounded and the rest taken into captivity, while ELAS were reported to have lost fifteen killed, with many more wounded.

Before Christmas 1944 the whole of the 11th Brigade had been concentrated within Patras, where they took up defensive positions, fully aware that the well-armed ELAS 3rd Division completely surrounded the town. British Intelligence had reported that there were also some 2,000 *andartes* inside the urban area, masquerading as civilians. 'Armed men in different and varying degrees of uniform swaggered around, some smiling arrogantly, others looking like sullen gypsies on the rampage', was the comment of one officer. There were incidents and the occasional attack on British and Indian soldiers because the situation in Patras was more precarious than in Salonika: 11th Brigade units could not be concentrated in one area, with the sea affording protection on the flanks. In order to test the nerve of his ELAS opponents, Brigadier Hunt ordered his units, in turn, to drive outside the town and carry out field training, but when one column was attacked, that had to be suspended as a matter of expediency. Thereafter it became a battle of nerves, of awaiting events in Athens, although the brigadier was able to evacuate most of the local Security Battalion, adding, 'I must admit to having derived pleasure at the fury of Kapitanos Akritis after he had seen the ship conveying the Security men, sailing westwards out of the Gulf.'

James Thomson, then second-in-command of the Queen's Own Camerons, recalls how terrified the local population were, with shopkeepers having to pay protection money, while the ELAS police, the OPLA, 'were as bad as the

Gestapo had been'. He also remembers that the Camerons' pipe band was a wonderful boost to morale for units in the brigade and for the local people who came from far and wide to watch and hear them. When the mass funeral was held of the 3/12th Frontier Force soldiers, and those of the attached battery of the 11th Field Regiment who had been killed at Missolonghi, it was transformed into a parade and, 'Thousands of people who had hidden behind the shutters for days came out and joined the procession.' John Hunt, too, remembers that day as one when the feelings, the true feelings, of the vast majority of the local people became evident: 'I wish I had kept the moving petition I was given, signed by fifty per cent of the male population, after addressing the public from a balcony at the Town Hall. My speech reassuring the people of continuing Allied support in those difficult days was greeted with fervent, almost frenzied, enthusiasm.'

Nevertheless, as New Year's Day 1945 approached, it was still obvious that the 11th Brigade was not strong enough to take on the 3rd ELAS Division in street fighting; even if it had tried to do so, hundreds of civilians would have been caught up in a confused struggle in a built-up area, and heavy casualties would have resulted.

On New Year's Day, in bitter cold, Brigadier John Hunt held a parade for the whole garrison during which he presented the ribbon of decorations won in Italy to various recipients (including the author). The parade was a gamble because the ELAS commanders could have been tempted to make a move while the bulk of the brigade was drilling with ceremonial weapons only, but it more than paid off, with the Greek population turning out in force to witness the spectacle. Later, ELAS prisoners captured by the Camerons stated that Patras was not attacked because their senior commanders had been much impressed by the parade, as well as by the night exercises the brigade had been carrying out. 1945, therefore, began in Patras without bloodshed, even though the 11th Brigade readily appreciated that a British defeat in Athens would lead to their being attacked by a force vastly superior in numbers and weapons.

The Royal Navy played an important part in a wide variety of operations during the liberation and later during the

Second Round, over and above transporting army personnel
and stores, as well as UNRRA supplies to Greece. Clearing
coastal channels and harbour entrances from mines proved a
mammoth task and one that cost ships and lives. Naval records
confirm that over 10,000 mines were swept by the Royal Navy
by 30 August 1945.

J. Leins was one of the crew on HMS *Larne*, the leader of the
5th Minesweeping Flotilla, which struck a mine on 15 October,
south of Piraeus. The *Larne* was beached at Paros and over the
following months was patched up before finally sailing and
going into dry dock at Malta. During the time spent at Paros,
Leins was one of the skeleton crew accommodated in King
George's summer palace. He has written: 'Having spent five
months with the Greek people immediately after the German
Occupation, I can tell you that at all times we were met with the
greatest friendliness and hospitality. In spite of shortages and
a worthless currency one was invited into their homes and
offered their frugal diet of dark bread, fish and wine.'

During the first few days of December, destroyers and other
smaller warships were sent, at one time or other, to Kavalla,
Kalamata, Volos, Mitylene, Syra and other ports to show the
flag, and in most cases the mere arrival of a British warship led
to a temporary improvement in the local situation. It was due
to the close support afforded by the Navy that on 16 December
the Frontier Force Rifles and attached troops were evacuated
from Krioneri after being attacked without provocation in the
Missolonghi area. 16 December was also the day on which
III Corps issued orders for garrisons to be evacuated from
Volos, Kavalla, Kalamata, Preveza, Levkas, the north shore of
the Gulf of Corinth and the Ionian islands. In the main, these
evacuations went smoothly but there were problems at Volos,
the third port in Greece, where a fragile peace just held.

Major Robert Henderson, 2nd Royal Sikhs, was OC of about
600 British and Indian troops, only a third of whom were
infantry, with the remainder being military liaison staffs,
movement and transportation units and other ancillary services. Their object in coming to Volos was to bring and
distribute badly needed supplies and relief stores for the
people of the Plain of Thessaly, a large number of whom were
reported to be on the verge of starvation.

As Henderson was to put it, 'Initially matters were quiet in

Volos: the chief reason being that the Communist parties of EAM and KKE, reinforced with more than 3,000 armed ELAS, were in complete control of the town.' To add to his problems, there were never fewer than 4,000 Italian ex-POWs in the town, between whom and ELAS there was no love lost. Philip Worrall, with the Italians, had the task not only of ensuring that those 4,000 men were moved to safety but also of calling forward another 6,000 who had been hiding in the hills. Although relief supplies had arrived for the allegedly starving people of Thessaly, daily strikes of the dock labourers, organized by EAM and KKE, held up the unloading of stores, while mass demonstrations intimidated the local people into passively accepting the situation rather than helping the British.

The commander of the local ELAS brigade, Peliorides, bore the name of the mountain which rises immediately behind Volos to a height of 5,000 feet. Peliorides began to throw his weight around, and it was only the timely arrival on 9 December of HMTS *Musketeer*, commanded by Commander (later Rear-Admiral) Ralph Fisher that gave the small garrison much-needed support and added to their potential fire-power, in the event of hostilities breaking out.

On 16 December Henderson, like all the other commanders of outlying detachments, received a signal which told him he was to evacuate forthwith. Withdrawal from parts of the town began as he concentrated his men into one area while awaiting the arrival of ships to evacuate the whole force. An anxious, nerve-tingling forty-eight hours followed: stores, ammunition and equipment had to be manhandled onto lighters and taken out to ships forced to lie outside the harbour for fear of fouling the wreckage which lay at random inside. Initially Peliorides refused to allow any more Italians to leave Volos but, after being told that he would have the task of feeding and administering some 6,000 of the ex-POWs, reluctantly he agreed to let them go.

One stage of the evacuation which Henderson remembers well was when LST 602 (US Navy) appeared on the horizon: 'A naval officer went aboard her, took over the helm and brought her straight in. A large crowd had collected round the far side of the harbour on the sea-front, because so large a ship had not been seen to enter Volos harbour for five years. They were not to know of the shallow draught of an LST and were amazed as she nosed her way unhesitatingly between the wreckage.... The "Stars and Stripes" broke from her main mast – a gasp went up from the crowd and we, too, were delighted, because in our imagination Peliorides would be on the telephone already to his HQ asking whether he was to take on the United States as well!'

It appears that the only people who were sorry there was no fighting were the GIs on LST 602, who were reported as being most reluctant to leave without making use of their ship's fourteen Bofors guns. A few hours later, an ultimatum arrived from Peliorides demanding that all British troops be clear of Volos by 1600 hours – he actually wrote 'by the fourth hour today', which Henderson deliberately took to mean the afternoon. Loading continued throughout the day until at 15.58, two minutes before the deadline, Henderson embarked on HMS *Unst*, a minesweeper. As the convoy steamed out of the Gulf of Volos, his final thoughts were: 'How the Germans would laugh when they heard of our evacuation.... For years we had supplied arms to these partisans, for years German convoys had run the gauntlet along the roads of Greece in fear of them. Now they had turned on us. So this was rehabilitation!'

The support that was given by HMS *Musketeer* in a number of ways, including communications, was beyond praise, while for his part Commander Fisher stressed in his report that the arrival of the American LST undoubtedly saved the day. As a final postscript to the evacuation at Volos, Philip Worrall went aboard HMTS *Banfora*, together with excited and relieved Italians. On 19 December his diary entry read: 'Marvellous food. Italians, of course, in chaos. Had thought I was finished with Italians but am made practically ship's adjutant with a broadcasting system; a lot of work.' Within two months the 5th Indian Brigade returned to Volos, and only from that day on did the people of Thessaly begin to benefit from the relief programme, which had been brought to a sudden end by ELAS in mid-December.

A final evacuation was carried out by the Navy immediately after Christmas. The EDES partisans under General Zervas were attacked by vastly superior numbers of ELAS under Sarafis and Aris. Why ELAS split their army to send two of their best divisions, under their top commanders, against EDES is difficult to understand, even with the benefit of hindsight. The personality of Sarafis might have had some part in it. He was 'a man of few words and a resentment that ferments slowly' (Byford-Jones) and made no secret of his detestation of Zervas – although his colleague, Aris, grudgingly admired the EDES leader. In his memoirs, Sarafis skates over the selection of Zervas as a priority target by baldly stating that it was a curious decision by 'the Central Committee', but he does not say that he, as ELAS C-in-C, made any strong representations against their decision. Be that as it may, within two weeks from the time the first attack was launched on 18 December, EDES *andartes* were scattered to the wind. It was reported that Zervas and his men had little stomach for the fight.

What were the reasons for Zervas' poor showing in the fight against ELAS after liberation? His partisans were better trained even if fewer in number. His excuse was that he had handed over large quantities of ammunition as required by Scobie and was reluctant to pit Greek against Greek – although that was something that had never worried him before! However, unlike ELAS, EDES had never planned to retain a large fighting force after the Germans departed, and because the partisans of ELAS looked as if they were going to be the victors after liberation, many EDES changed their allegiance. Zervas may also have realized that the British would defeat ELAS eventually, so that there was nothing to gain from a bloody fight against superior forces.

It was left to the Royal Navy to evacuate those EDES who had not deserted or changed sides. Between 28 and 30 December, when Preveza fell to ELAS, some 6,500 EDES partisans, over 3,000 refugees and 1,000 prisoners of war (mostly Italians), together with large quantities of stores, mules and vehicles, were taken off to safety by the Royal Navy. It was to mark the end of EDES and Zervas' career as a leader of partisans in the Second World War.

There were contrasting reactions to the defeat of Zervas. In Bill Jordan's opinion, 'Zervas was the greatest Greek of his rank I met in my fifteen months in the country.... A skilful mountain fighter, had Zervas not been so dogged in his resistance to the KKE's efforts to wipe him out, Greece would probably have been under Communist control from the moment the Germans withdrew, and today would be another country behind the Iron Curtain.' Many Greek commentators and historians do not accept that last statement, maintaining that, if the Communists had taken over the country, Socialist Greece would have emerged on the lines of Yugoslavia under Marshal Tito, rather than as a Moscow-dominated country like East Germany. The arguments for and against that hypothesis are intricate and would require a detailed study well outside the scope of this book.

In contrast to Bill Jordan, there was open glee in the Athens Press Room at Zervas' defeat, with some newspapermen describing the EDES leader as one of King George's chief lackeys, conveniently forgetting that he had long been a supporter of the staunchly Republican General Plastiras. Zervas was a patriot and was glad to accept the King's return – but only if the Greek people expressed such a wish in a plebiscite held in the country, and one that was free from coercion. A short period of relative stability did allow such a plebiscite to be held in 1946, even though intimidation by extremists on both sides was not to disappear from Greece for a long time to come.

'Among those who dislike oppression are many who like to oppress' (Napoleon): such a maxim seems wholly apt when applied to Greece during this era, which witnessed so much heroism and self-sacrifice, cruelty and terrorization, tragedy and suffering: countless acts of oppression were perpetrated in the name of freedom, with the innocent being the chief victims.

The joy of being 'liberated' was short-lived for a variety of reasons, and the passing years have done little to clarify the issues, chiefly because there has been a plethora of conflicting evidence, much of which is biased to a degree that makes it suspect.

8 The Second Round
– Victory of a Sort

'Blood cannot be washed out with blood'
                                   Persian proverb

While the British forces struggled to keep the little of Athens they held, the contents of a top-secret message from Churchill to Scobie, leaked to American columnist Drew Pearson was to spark off a chorus of indignation, not only in the USA but in a stormy House of Commons debate, with angry Labour members jumping up and down with indignation. The sentence that stirred up such a heated controversy was, 'Do not, however, hesitate to act as if you were in a conquered city where a local rebellion is in progress.' Churchill later admitted that the whole telegram was somewhat strident in tone, stressing that his intention had been to reassure Scobie of his support in whatever well-conceived action the GOC might decide to take.

Until substantial reinforcements arrived – about which there was no definite information in early December – Scobie's options were limited to holding on to what he could in Athens and Piraeus, where ELAS action was escalating hour by hour. Orders were issued to the 23rd Armoured Brigade (Brigadier R.H.B. Arkwright) to clear central Athens, with the 2nd Parachute Brigade (Brigadier C. Pritchard) given the task of taking over the northern sector of the city; the Greek Mountain Brigade was ordered to establish itself in the south and attempt to clear the Piraeus area. The capture of police stations had not presented ELAS with much of a problem, chiefly because the defenders were

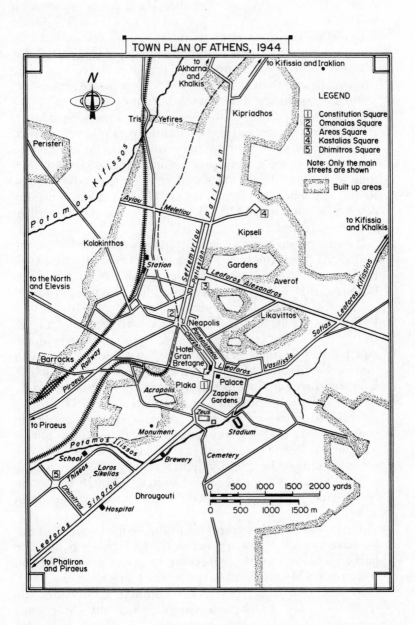

TOWN PLAN OF ATHENS, 1944

LEGEND

1 Constitution Square
2 Omonaias Square
3 Areos Square
4 Kastalias Square
5 Dhimitros Square

Note: Only the main streets are shown

Built up areas

forced to watch their wives and children being paraded in front of the buildings they occupied, while men with loud-hailers called on the policemen to surrender. When they did so, the marked men among them were led off to a summary execution, often after varying degrees of torture.

Scobie's forces were under so much pressure that they controlled less than a square mile of built-up area – or, putting it against a London background, it was as if the British Government was confined to Parliament, Buckingham Palace and the residential part of Chelsea only. To add to a variety of military problems, Scobie had to contend with Americans proclaiming their neutrality at a time when their British allies were struggling to hold Athens. Reginald Leeper was adamant that, 'Their blatant neutrality acted as a tonic to ELAS and was made abundant use of in their propaganda.'

Ex-servicemen correspondents have confirmed that the attitude of most Americans enraged them at the time and still rankles some forty years later. Lieutenant (later Lieutenant-Colonel), R.H.A. Cockburn commanding the recce troop of A Squadron, 4th Reconnaissance Regiment (4th British Division), recalls that during the Athens fighting all US troops had large 'Stars and Stripes' sewn on their uniform and painted on their vehicles. Cockburn had a brush with them at Elevsis airfield which the Americans were running. A US major drove up in a jeep and informed him that he would have to leave as the airfield was 'neutral territory'. The young British subaltern was quick to retort: 'I have three 37mm cannon, three .50 Brownings, six .30 Brownings, plus a section of 3-inch mortars under command. Therefore if you wish me to move before first light tomorrow, you are willing to try!' That was the end of the matter, although Cockburn recalls that a protest was made to Ambassador Leeper in Athens.

There was notable exceptions to the neutral Americans, as we have seen at Volos when the US LST charged into the harbour, bristling with aggression, to save the small British force from a bloody fight and possibly a costly reverse.

Another anecdote from R.A.L. Summers illustrates the frustration felt by British troops when the Americans appeared to support the opposition: 'The Americans were not at war with ELAS and we were not too pleased to have to let them through our road blocks to fraternize. One party tried to come in from the wrong side after a riotous night out with ELAS. They did not have the password and suffered some casualties from our patrol. This incident was rather hushed up.'

At a time when the ELAS guerrillas had surrounded and compressed the British troops into tight perimeters, EAM continued a skilful propaganda campaign which influenced several British and American war correspondents into accusing the British Government of trying to put King George back on his throne against the democratic wishes of the Greek people. 'Democracy' – like 'collaborator' – was a word bandied around until it became almost meaningless. The reports sent back to the British Press by some of the journalists rarely reflected the opinions of the average British soldier, who did not like the methods chosen by ELAS *andartes* to silence and often liquidate their opponents. One Essex Regiment soldier summed it up: 'Too much like Nazism for me, sir.' And that remark reflected the views of the majority of British and Indian Army soldiers, a point that Churchill was to make most forcibly at the end of the month: 'Our own troops have no illusions. General Alexander had previously sent me a censorship report on their letters home. I was so struck by what I read that I had it printed and circulated to the War Cabinet. It completely disposed of the lies spread in Communist circles that their sympathies were with ELAS.'

If Geoffrey Hoare of *The Times* and Aneurin Bevan MP thought the 'other ranks' would automatically support the left wing in Greece, they were soon to be disillusioned. HQ 23rd Armoured Brigade's report on the operation contained this scathing criticism: 'It is certain that many thousand men learnt how much both public men and publications are in general to be trusted, and acquired a sense of contempt which could not have been gained from a lifetime's ordinary study of debates.'

Instead of venting their wrath on the police and storming Averoff prison so they could get their hands on ex-Prime Ministers Rallis and General Tsolakoglou, as well as other alleged collaborators awaiting trial, ELAS would have been far better advised to have attacked the RAF-held airfield at Kalamaki. As a consequence, there remained a life-line to III Corps from the world outside Greece, and it was at Kalamaki that Field-Marshal Alexander arrived unexpectedly on 11 December. While Churchill's dramatic appearance in Athens on Christmas Day boosted the morale of soldiers and civilians alike, as well as transforming the political situation, it can be stated with equal force that Alexander's visit saved Scobie and his men from defeat because, by seeing for himself, the Commander-in-Chief was able to take immediate steps to bring in badly needed reinforcements.

By 11 December, HQ 23rd Armoured Brigade had been forced to organize convoys with escorts along the Phaliron-Athens road because movement along the highway during daylight hours proved hazardous. The normal drill was for armoured cars to patrol the road after dark, engage known ELAS posts and then, when all appeared quiet, escort a long column of vehicles through to their destination. Alexander's unexpected appearance at Kalamaki caught everyone by surprise because the signal warning them of his arrival had not been received. When the duty officer dashed off to organize an escort, Alexander phoned Scobie's HQ and, in his words, 'ELAS obligingly put the call through to III Corps HQ.' There were two Staghounds available, 'the Athens Taxi Service', but as the tired crew had disappeared for a short rest and a morning cup of tea, the brigade duty officer was forced to detail two batmen to man the guns, a role neither had played before. When told to test the turret and gun, one batman-gunner promptly let off thirty rounds of .30 Browning – which proved that the gun worked, if nothing else!

The Staghounds set off at a spanking pace, with Alexander in the gunner's seat in the first car and Harold Macmillan in the one that followed. It was against his vehicle that ELAS directed their fire, with bullets pinging against the armoured plating. They arrived unscathed at Corps HQ where the Field Marshal was greeted not by a Guard of Honour but by a corpse being carried out of the building, the victim of shelling a few minutes earlier – '... probably the most impromptu reception ever received by a Field Marshal of the British Army'.

That experience was to drive home to the distinguished visitors the obvious fact that Scobie's force was in a precarious situation, hemmed in to little more than a square half mile of Athens, with their supply port, Piraeus, also under direct siege. Later the Field Marshal called on the British Ambassador, besieged with his staff and their families within the confines of the British Embassy, and briefed him in a sombre but realistic fashion: 'You are in a grave situation. Your sea port is cut off, your airport can only be reached by tank or armoured car, you are outnumbered, your dumps are surrounded and you have three days' ammunition. I can put that right in time but it may take a fortnight. It will need two fighting divisions to come from Italy. The heavy stuff will have to be landed on the open beaches of Phaliron and December is not the best month for that.'

That Alexander was able to divert two infantry divisions from Italy was due to a lull in the winter campaign there, and to speed up help the War Cabinet gave him a free hand to take all necessary military measures forthwith. Orders were issued for the 4th British Division to be flown to Greece immediately, and the arrival of its units during the second half of December was to be a vital factor in stemming the ELAS onslaught. Alexander's instructions to Scobie were to hold on to what he had, to ensure that Kalamaki airport remained securely held and, when sufficient reinforcements had arrived, '... having linked up securely both ends of the dumbbell, to institute the necessary operation to clear the whole of Athens and Piraeus'. A joint telegram from Alexander and Macmillan pressed the British Government to agree, as a matter of urgency, to the appointment of Archbishop Damaskinos as regent, a proposal that was vetoed by the King for a few more days to come.

Ronald Scobie's demeanour during those days of crisis earned him unstinted praise from everybody who worked for or alongside him. The non-Communist citizens of Athens were won over by his air of confidence and by the fact that nothing seemed to daunt him. He was what they expected a British officer to be like: good-looking, well dressed and seemingly imperturbable to danger. It was not long before admiring crowds would gather and shout 'Scompie! Scompie!' as he walked from the Hotel Grande Bretagne to nearby Corps HQ, completely oblivious of the sniper fire that often made it an interesting journey. His multifarious duties, however, influenced Alexander into sending in Major-General J.H.L. ('Ginger') Hawkesworth from Italy to take over as military commander, with the rank of Lieutenant-General.

That eminently sensible decision has been misunderstood by some, including, it appeared, Chris Woodhouse. In one of his books, Woodhouse gave his opinion that Scobie almost lost Athens and accused him of being pessimistic, even defeatist; he cites the fact that Scobie had contingency plans made for a possible withdrawal from Athens to Phaliron. Woodhouse was also under the impression that Scobie was sacked as military commander by Alexander and thus did not deserve the adulation given him after the Second Round was over as 'the hero who saved Greece'. That statement by Woodhouse is not supported by Scobie's subordinates at the time. In any such emergency, it would have been normal military practice for the senior commander to instruct his staff to draw up a contingency plan for an evacuation from Athens – in case the worst happened. Lord Hunt has confirmed that he was instructed to do the same in relation to Patras. Moreover, there appears to be no evidence to support the allegation that Scobie was sacked as military commander by Alexander. If the general had been sacked, surely he would have made an entry in his private diary? He kept a day-by-day account in that diary to which Henry Maule had access when researching and writing *Scobie, Hero of Greece*. The truth was that General 'Ginger' Hawkesworth was selected with a specific military role to perform, because, in due course, he was to command over 50,000 men, while Ronald Scobie continued to be responsible for the British Military Mission as well as the overall political situation in Greece. Hawkesworth had a wealth of experience as a commander on active service, and Alexander's 'I'll send the best general from Italy' was no idle promise.

Although the right decisions had now been taken by the senior commanders, reinforcements could not appear in any significant numbers in the twinkling of an eye, so that those fighting in Athens and Piraeus had to hold on, as best they could, to what they had. There were to be one or two serious setbacks.

The Infantry Barracks which housed the 23rd Armoured

Brigade rear HQ and signal squadron, as well as the main supply depot for Athens, and which contained the gun lines, was heavily mortared in the early hours of 13 December. After blowing a large hole in the barrack wall, a force of about a thousand ELAS streamed through the gap to destroy the telephone exchange, shooting all the operators but one. In the confused fighting that followed, the guerrillas killed twenty and wounded forty of the defenders before withdrawing with over a hundred British prisoners. However, ELAS also lost over thirty killed, with forty prisoners left in British hands, and though they had struck a severe blow, fortunately they failed to locate or destroy the field guns which had been their main objective. The British prisoners were marched away to the first of the so-called POW camps north of Marathon, over thirty miles from Athens, where they were held in the most primitive of conditions. So appalling was their treatment that, not surprisingly, ELAS steadfastly refused to allow Red Cross officials to visit the prisoners at that or any other location.

Following Alexander's momentous visit, the struggle for the heart of Athens intensified. The British units found that holding on to their own positions was much easier than trying to clear buildings or streets because, as soon as they attempted to do so, ELAS melted away, only to return after darkness, numbers of them dressed in civilian clothes and with women and children walking ahead of or alongside them. Another tactic was to freewheel tram cars full of explosive and connected to a time fuse, and direct the vehicles against armoured cars, tanks and British posts. These mobile Molotov cocktails proved far less lethal than ELAS anticipated, chiefly because the time fuses were so unreliable.

The importance of the port of Piraeus to the British had been appreciated by Mandakas from the very start. His intention was to hold the harbour under siege until Athens was in Communist hands and the Greek Government had been forced to submit to their demands. From 4 December onwards, the Combined Naval HQ, located in the Greek Naval College, was under attack, and only the timely appearance on 7 December of a Royal Marine detachment from HMS *Orion*, flagship of Rear-Admiral Jack Mansfield of the 15th Cruiser Squadron, helped stop the aggressors overrunning the defences. Nevertheless, the main wireless and cable transmitters were put out of action and the road to Athens was completely blocked. The speedy arrival of reinforcements became one of crucial importance because ELAS guns were raking the area at will.

As an example of speed into action, the 2/5th Royal Leicester Regiment (46th British Division), which was resting in Italy on 4 December, was flown from Bari to Phaliron Airport on 7 December in sixteen USAF Dakotas and went into action in Piraeus from 9 December onwards, when they established a defensive ring around the Naval College before attempting to push back the ring of ELAS snipers and bomb squads from the surrounding buildings. Other units of the 139th Brigade also arrived to ensure that Phaliron was kept open, as well as sending the 16th Durham Light Infantry to help defend the Combined Naval Headquarters. A much stronger force, however, was needed to drive ELAS out of the harbour area, and the 5th Indian Brigade, originally earmarked to deploy in the Aegean, was diverted to help in the task of ejecting ELAS and opening the harbour once more.

Major Denis Beckett of 1/4th Essex (later to become a major-general) recalls how difficult the task was when his unit began operating in Piraeus: 'The guerrillas had the enormous advantage of knowing the town, and only a few wore any kind of uniform, so could always mingle with the ordinary civilians if forced into a tight corner. Still, they were sometimes tough fighters, and attempts to enter buildings without heavy fire support almost always drew showers of grenades upon the attackers.' Denis Beckett also commented on ELAS' attitude to the Red Cross, which was '... a bit peculiar, to say the least. When some tanks returned fire on a hospital from which enemy snipers had been active, a small group of guerrillas appeared on the balcony and, in an attitude of magnificent defiance, hurled home-made bombs at our armour with small Red Cross flags attached to them. But less amusing was the morning after we had broken up an enemy attack to find among the dead the body of a nurse. She was fully armed and carrying ammunition.... The guerrillas were not above using women and small children to carry fresh supplies of ammunition for them. The problems of the soldiers trying to fight with care for the innocent became terrific.'

It was about this time that RAMC personnel were ordered to carry arms (something that had never been necessary in the Second World War), an edict necessitated by the fact that ELAS openly rejected the Geneva Convention.

Superior discipline, greater experience and heavier fire power eventually won but it was to take two days of heavy fighting before the men of the 1/4th Essex sealed off the Kallipoli Peninsula to a depth of 1,200 yards, from where the whole of the 5th Brigade (under Brigadier P.J. Saunders-Jacob) was able to launch an operation to clear the eastern side of the docks.

Despite many American war correspondents and UNRRA officials flying the flag of neutrality ashore, at sea there appeared to be more co-operation between the two wartime allies, and it was an American landing craft that ferried ashore the 1/9th Gurkha Rifles (5th Indian Brigade) at 0400 hours on 11 December. A few hours later, the third Battalion of the brigade, the 3/10th Baluch Regiment, joined their Gurkha comrades in 'beating' the built-up area. The last-minute change of destination – Piraeus, instead of the Aegean islands – meant that neither battalion had any real briefing about the political situation, but they were warned they would probably go 'straight into action' (John Hudson, CO 1/9 GR).

With the Gurkhas were three troops of 1st Field Regiment RA, without their guns and ready to fight on their feet as infantrymen. When they were in Italy, F.C. Dunn, then a staff sergeant, was one of the NCOs who attended a week's infantry training run by 'our old friends of Cassino, the 1/9th Gurkha Rifles.... We were learning something from experts and we enjoyed it.... The lessons we learnt stood us in good stead in the days which lay ahead.' With so little time for any detailed briefing, it was not surprising that one or two soldiers were under the impression that, 'It was to be our job to help to restore the monarchy', a statement that echoed accusations made by EAM/ELAS about the British decision to intervene in 1944. On occasions such an impression was given to the troops by Greek civilians who helped them with

information about ELAS. By that time, they were terrified of
the Communists and, with their countrymen so bitterly
divided, had come to the conclusion that the British must be
supporting the other extreme, the right wing and, in particular, the Royalists. After all, they argued, it had been traditional for Great Britain to support the King of the Hellenes in
the past, against Republicans as well as foreign foes, the most
recent of whom were the Germans and Italians.

In peace and war, the Gurkha and his *kukri* have been
inseparable but, with KKE and EAM spreading horror stories
about Indian and Gurkha troops, it was decided that the 9th
Gurkhas should not use their *kukris* in close quarter fighting.
George Challis, who was adjutant at the time, commented: 'As
far as *kukris* were concerned, the order caused great offence,
for it meant that we could not offer full protection to our men
under attack. It was agreed that Nelson rather than the War
Office should be our guide if difficulties arose!'

Before the main attack against the ELAS stronghold, Lofos
Castello, a fortified pimple overlooking the harbour, the
intervening area had to be cleared by the 5th Brigade's infantry units, supported by Sherman tanks. By this time the 5th
Brigade – like the 23rd Armoured Brigade and the 2nd
Parachute Brigade before them – had learnt that ELAS
andartes were not bound by the accepted conventions of warfare: they ignored Red Cross and white flags and wore British
battledress and police uniforms, often using women and children to carry arms and ammunition. F.C. Dunn recalls one such
incident; 'Then suddenly a grenade exploded in an alleyway,
followed by a scream. We reached the scene just as two
[Gurkha] riflemen were dragging one of their comrades to
safety. He was badly wounded in the legs and lower parts of his
body. A very enraged VCO [Viceroy Commissioned Officer]
shouted a warning to us. What had happened was a young boy
had run out of a doorway shouting a form of greeting in
broken English; without warning he rolled an Italian grenade
towards the unsuspecting Gurkha soldier and it exploded at
his feet. After that we trusted no one we happened to meet
during those street-clearing operations. Geneva Conventions
meant nothing to the ELAS.'

There were countless innocent victims, too. An entry in the
1st Field Regiment's war diary gives one illustration: 'Greek

children playing with old mortar bomb. 2 killed and 3 wounded.' A laconic afternote was: 'Quiet day.'

A platoon of the 11th KRRC, the battalion having been withdrawn from its mission of mercy in the hinterland of Trikkala and Larissa, had an experience in Athens similar to the one recounted by F.C. Dunn: 'Lieutenant B.E.D. Collier ordered a rifleman to fire at a young woman approaching his house with a tray of food and wine. The rifleman obeyed and then begged not to be given such an order again. He quickly changed his view when the German stick grenade in her right hand was pointed out to him.' By that time the 11th KRRC had no illusions about ELAS, having lost two platoons in an ambush in the Volos area.

In the early hours of 16 December, 1/9 GR, supported by the composite 'infantry company' from the 1st Field Regiment, began a steady approach towards Lofos Castella, an advance which remained silent until parachute flares soared high above the advancing troops. Contact was made with ELAS at 0140 hours but the narrow streets made progress difficult and slow, so that it was not until 1000 hours that the summit was taken. It was an important gain, because from Lofos Castella the southern suburbs of Athens came under direct observation.

Not all the problems that held up the British forces were caused by ELAS: the district swarmed with hungry vociferous refugees, whose numbers swelled as the partisans were driven back. The refugees had to be fed, and in turn units organized improvised soup kitchens. John Peacock, OC B Company 1/9 GR, remembers that, 'At the start it was a soup ladle of beans once a day to a crowd of pushing and shoving women.' From such a humble beginning grew the Brigade Clearing Centre which eventually served 22,000 meals a day to more than 10,000 hungry civilians.

Brigadier Adam Block of the 139th Brigade commanded Block Force's operations to open the road from Athens to Piraeus. He decided to use armour to blast a way down the road and, without any British casualties, opposition was brushed aside, with some partisans firing at the armoured columns ineffectually while others waved in a friendly manner. Their subdued behaviour was to prove, once again, that a sizeable proportion of the ELAS rank and file had been recruited against their will; many were bewildered by events, which was not surprising because, prior to 3 December, EAM leaflets and newspapers had been telling them, and the world, that their glorious cause had the full support of the vast majority of the Greek people and that British troops would stand aside as neutral, and not intervene. Instead, they were attacked by tanks and rocket-firing RAF Beaufighters which strafed strongpoints so that, even with their vast superiority in numbers, the *andarte* gunmen in Athens were beginning to lose heart – although they achieved two major successes, when they stormed Averoff Prison and captured the RAF Administrative HQ at Kifissia.

It is highly probable that the timing of the attack on the Averoff Prison was dictated by the fact that General Mandakas had realized that victory was slipping away from his grasp. If EAM/ELAS were to get their hands on the two quisling ex-Prime Ministers, John Rallis and George Tsolakoglou, and on other alleged collaborators, time was not on their side. Averoff Prison was guarded by gunners from the 64th Light Battery RA and about 150 men from the Greek Brigade when, on 18 December, an ELAS force of about a thousand created great confusion by setting the west block of the prison alight, while keeping the whole building under a heavy fusilade of small-arms fire and grenades. With the flames threatening to engulf the prisoners in their cells, the British commander had no option but to order that the doors be opened, whereupon the prisoners were told to escape from the building and make their way to a rendezvous. With the fire and battle raging about them, chaos reigned, and it was almost inevitable that fewer than half the prisoners made their way to the rendezvous, to be taken into custody again. John Rallis was missing for some time but was eventually recaptured by men from the KRRC and imprisoned once more – later he committed suicide in prison. The scenes around Averoff were reported as being horrifying, with a howling mob of ELAS guerrillas and bloodthirsty women indulging in an orgy of torture and slaughter of the prisoners unable to escape. Regrettably, too, during those moments of frenzy captured British soldiers were brutally murdered.

Nine miles out of Athens the British suffered another most

damaging reverse when the old Luftwaffe HQ at Kifissia, now occupied by the RAF, was surrounded and, in the early hours of 18 December, attacked, with mortar bombs exploding and machine-guns sweeping the buildings. The partisans used Italian 75s, and the RAF's four Bofors guns were soon under heavy attack. During the first day no significant intrusions occurred, although Scobie noted in his diary that he was worried about Air Commodore Geoffrey Tuttle and his men: 'Geoffrey Tuttle's party at Kifissia attacked. I've tried to get him to evacuate this detachment to a safer location but he had been confident it would be all right. Position now serious. Armoured cars could not get out owing to road blocks. A force with tanks is to move out at first light.'

Demands to surrender were sent in to the defenders, all of which were refused. Some of the airmen recognized their ex-girlfriends, who were now leading ELAS squads, armed to the teeth and distinctly hostile. Next day the besieged force was heartened when Spitfires and Beaufighters strafed ELAS groups, but supplies and especially all types of ammunition were badly needed. An airdrop carried out by Wellingtons proved abortive when the direction of the wind changed and the parachutes landed among the partisans' positions. When darkness fell, heavy fighting resumed, with ELAS infiltrating at several points, and a desperate struggle ensued as confusion mounted. Ammunition was running out when there was a thunderous explosion at the west end of the Hotel Cecil, which enabled the attackers to pour in. Some of them were prodding captured RAF prisoners ahead of them as a shield, behind which they moved forward, secure in the knowledge that the British would not fire on their own men. Eventually, when a general cease-fire was sounded, for the first time in the history of the Royal Air Force an entire headquarters had been captured. The British dead and wounded were left while ELAS took away over 250 prisoners for an ordeal none of them has ever forgotten. Next day relief columns reached Kifissia, engaged those ELAS who had remained and inflicted considerable casualties.

It had been a disaster which stirred Churchill's anger. The surrender of about 700 officers and airmen at Kifissia was something he could not forget – or forgive. On 2 January

1945 he wrote to the Chief of Staff's Committee: 'They had, I believe, two platoons of infantry to defend them. There appears to be a bad arrangement between the Military and the Air. In a matter like this the Military [Command] should have recalled this party instead of letting them linger on, with the inhabitants, on a precarious footing. I fear the sufferings of the prisoners may have been very severe.... I wish particularly to know how many of these men had rifles and what training they had in rifle fire. One airman told the Field Marshal, while we were together at one of the advance posts, that they were only allowed five rounds for practice per annum. Everybody – I repeat, everybody – who wears the King's uniform should be capable of fighting if it be only with a pistol or a tommy-gun.'

Although ELAS had won two battles, they were losing the war, and in desperation they began to take more and more hostages. Men, women, rich and poor, young and old, were driven like cattle over rough country tracks and through snow-swept passes. Many of the captives, who could not keep up, were shot or bayoneted to death. To the thousand or so British prisoners were added some 20,000 Greek civilians who had been abducted, the majority of them middle-class Athenians accused of being collaborators or having lived too well during the Occupation. The harrowing tales of suffering and the cold-blooded cruelty shown by the more fanatical members of ELAS, especially the dreaded OPLA, caused waves of revulsion throughout the country.

What caused such a breakdown of sanity? Was it a combination of the inhuman example shown by members of the Axis Occupation Forces, accentuated by pressures of war and famine, helplessness and an atmosphere of total unrest which persisted for so long? Such questions were asked by Greeks and British alike, the latter often in complete bewilderment, after having received truly generous hospitality at the hands of people from different walks of life. In the words of Bill Jordan: 'No one could live with the Greek people as we did and come away without a deep and abiding love of them.' 'Amen to that!' would chorus hundreds of Allied soldiers, from Britain, America, the Indian Empire and the Dominions of Australia and New Zealand.

To the question as to why the atrocities happened, a reply

given by many Greeks was: 'The atrocities must have been carried out by Bulgarians, men Greek in speech but black in soul.' An early refusal to face grim facts squarely gradually weakened when violence continued unabated until the shocked nation began to realize that bloodless *coups* – which had often taken place in Greek history – were things of the past. Richard Capell's words had a prophetic significance: 'Greeks feel their politics so intensely that they ruin themselves thereby' and especially when a vicious circle of vendettas spiralled until nearly every family in the land had suffered the loss of a dear one as a result of the hatred between the opposing factions.

The plight of some of the hostages was alleviated, to a certain extent, when food supplies were dropped to the moving columns by RAF planes. That was but one of the important tasks the RAF had to perform during the Second Round. Their close support was crucial during the struggle for Athens and Piraeus, and especially when the 2nd Parachute Brigade was fighting on the south slopes of the Acropolis, when care had to be taken not to inflict unnecessary casualties among the innocent civilian population. Officially, individual buildings were selected as targets for the RAF planes rather than complete blocks or streets, which meant extremely close co-operation with the Army. However, R.M. Honey of the Black Watch did not witness target-strafing when, from the Acropolis, 'We watched the RAF flying over and machine-gunning the streets of the centre of the town. It seemed unnecessary.' Moreover, complete accuracy was never possible, so that, inevitably, near-misses were described by ELAS as 'indiscriminate bombing'. (It still happens today, viz. the American raid on Libya and Israel's actions against terrorist camps in the Lebanon.)

By 17 December the RAF had increased its strength from three to eight squadrons, with Wellingtons, Beaufighters and Spitfires predominating. By the time the Second Round had ended in a truce, over 1,600 sorties had been flown for the loss of three aircraft, and all this in addition to the transportation of units flown in from Italy as urgently needed reinforcements. The RAF did not receive any assistance from the four Greek squadrons because Papendreou specifically requested that they should not be used in operations against ELAS.

While political manœuvring continued unabated during the fighting, KKE and EAM pleaded with their fighters to 'hang on a little longer', promising that, 'An Anglo-US-Russian Commission is to investigate the problem.' In the end, the USSR made no moves whatever, and although initially the American public supported EAM and the Left Wing, gradually they changed their views as news of hostage-taking and atrocities leaked out. Moreover, Churchill was able to promise Roosevelt that the British had no intention of putting King George back on his throne against the wishes of the Greek people.

Accusations against 'Scompie, the Black Fascist' continued to be made by EAM propagandists, as a prelude to their Central Committee's truce feelers. On 16 December they proposed terms for a truce. One condition was that the Greek Mountain Brigade should be withdrawn from Athens, all *gendarmerie* disarmed and British troops not interfere in Greek internal affairs. Such a request was quite impossible: had it been granted, ELAS would have been left in complete control of Athens – so the terms were rejected out of hand by Scobie.

By now, some politicians in London had begun to accept as true the despatches sent home by Geoffrey Hoare of *The Times*, as well as EAM propaganda which claimed to give an accurate picture of affairs in Greece. Attacks on the Government, made in the House of Commons by left-wing politicians, angered British troops in Greece, bewildered their Indian comrades and caused wry amusement among British officers serving with the three Gurkha battalions, especially when their men were singled out in Parliament by Aneurin Bevan. In a stormy debate, the fiery Welsh MP told the Commons that the Greeks objected to being '... dragooned by Gurkha troops as the Spaniards did being dragooned by Moors. The reason Gurkhas are used in Athens is that they are politically backward.' A storm of protests from Conservatives was unleashed by his remarks, accusing him of colour prejudice. Meanwhile, the unruffled Gurkhas continued soldiering in their normal efficient manner, despite KKE propagandists grasping the opportunity afforded them by Bevan and his fellow-travellers to spread rumours that they were 'kept in cages and let out at night, in all their bestial frenzy'. Later those lies were put to rest when Indian and Gurkha troops helped to rehabilitate Macedonia, where a warm relationship had been established by the time the 4th Indian Division left Greece for India. 'Gurkhas and Greeks, poor in worldly goods but both races tough and proud, the truest of comrades when danger threatens, had become great friends. So much for the prophesy of Aneurin Bevan.'

On 20 December Ronald Scobie warned the citizens of Athens that an all-out offensive to clear ELAS out of the city was about to begin, and as Christmas approached, the guerrillas were forced to withdraw from certain areas, despite the fact that Mandakas continued to send in more reinforcements. The atmosphere was ripe for political pressure to be put on KKE and EAM in an effort to persuade them to seek a truce, and the arrival of General Nicolas Plastiras from his long exile in Cannes was to speed up such a process. Aged about sixty, Plastiras had led an active political and revolutionary life, which had included a short period as dictator of Greece in March 1933, before being forced to run for his life, with a sentence of death passed on him in his absence. Although Plastiras' attitude towards EAM/ELAS was uncompromising – dubbing them mutineers – he appealed to them '... to abandon immediately the fratricidal rebellion and withdraw to your homes ... to prevent a conflict with the heroic soldiers who are our great friend and ally, Great Britain, whose assistance in the liberation of our Nation and our People evokes the eternal gratitude of the Fatherland'.

His appeal, which was a mixture of blatant sentimentality and fervent patriotism, led to Prophyrogenis from the EAM Committee seeking a meeting with General Plastiras, following which tentative feelers were put out by ELAS to Scobie, indicating a desire for peace and a withdrawal, but again including conditions which made it impossible for the general, or Papendreou, to accept. Meanwhile, Alexander had sent a telegram to Churchill expressing the fear that his forces were 'not strong enough to go beyond Athens/Piraeus and undertake operations on the Greek mainland'. Churchill's response was quick: 'There is no question of our embarking in any military operations away from the Athens-Piraeus area. We must however have a military foundation whereon a Greek Government of some kind or other can function.'

In the same telegram, Churchill indicated that he was not convinced that Archbishop Damaskinos would be a strong, impartial regent, expressing fears that he might '... quite conceivably make himself into a dictator supported by the left wing'. Churchill had not met the giant Archbishop and he could only rely on Foreign Office reports on His Beatitude, some of which were garbled. However, the restless Prime Minister could rarely resist a challenge, so that: 'Two days later I resolved to go and see for myself.' Having spoilt Mr Eden's Christmas by the proposal, he took him along as well.

For security reasons, Leeper, Scobie and the Greek Government knew nothing about Churchill's impending visit, apart from a signal which mentioned the imminent arrival of 'an important envoy' and referred to a telegram sent by Field Marshal Alexander – which had not reached Athens. It was only after Alexander himself arrived that the secret was out, and at 3 p.m. on Christmas Day Churchill, dressed in RAF uniform, flew into a heavily guarded Kalamaki Airport in an American Skymaster made available by Roosevelt. After he reached the Embassy, he took great delight in choosing the most sniper-proof area of the building in which to lunch. The visit was the highspot of Churchill's war, and it was also to be one of his most successful political initiatives. Even *The Times* was to say later that the Prime Minister's visit was 'one of real courage and statesmanship'. Prior to Churchill's arrival, Harold Macmillan and the Ambassador had been considering whether they should summon a conference of all the political leaders, which EAM/ELAS would be invited to attend. This proposal was agreed by Churchill and Eden, on condition that Archbishop Damaskinos was invited to take the chair so that, once the conference was under way, the British could withdraw, leaving it to the Greeks 'to fight it out'.

It was vital that Churchill and the Archbishop got on well, and from the telegram sent on Boxing Day, back to Deputy Prime Minister Attlee, it is clear that Churchill had been won over by Damaskinos: 'He impressed me with a good deal of confidence. He is a magnificent figure, and he immediately accepted the proposal of being chairman of the conference.'

When Churchill heard that the Archbishop's staff had the habit of deterring visitors with the announcement that 'His Beatitude is at prayer', he was both delighted and impressed, wishing that it was a manœuvre he himself could employ at 10 Downing Street.

The news that Churchill and Eden had arrived in Athens was a complete surprise to the people of the city. As one reporter wrote, it must have been the first time that anything important had happened in Athens without someone somewhere learning of it prematurely. His presence had a remarkable effect on the morale of soldiers and civilians alike. Smiles appeared as the magic of Churchill's name spread everywhere. There was a new air of confidence – except among the ELAS leaders, who well knew that the British Prime Minister described them as 'bands of gangsters, murder gangs' and accused them of establishing a reign of terror under the plea of purging collaborators.

An attempt to blow up the Hotel Grande Bretagne, by putting dynamite in the sewers beneath the building, was foiled by the vigilance of three British soldiers who had spent part of their Christmas patrolling the sewers of Athens. That they had done so was due to the fact that rumours had been circulating that ELAS might use such a method, and as a consequence sewers were periodically inspected by patrols. Churchill was not staying at that hotel, so it is likely that the terrorists' main target was General Ronald Scobie, who noted in his diary: 'Had this been set off it would have been the end of some of the newspapermen (amongst others) who had been so critical of our efforts on behalf of freedom for the Greek people.' Typically, the imperturbable Scobie made no mention of his own narrow escape.

On the evening of Boxing Day, the conference opened in the Greek Foreign Office. There was no electricity or power in the city, and it was left to a few hurricane lamps to cast a dim light on the scene. American Ambassador MacVeagh, the French Minister and the Soviet Military Representative had all been invited as Allied observers. Apart from the Archbishop, the Greek delegates were Papendreou, Sophoulos (Liberal Party), General Plastiras, Kafandris (Progressive Party) and Maxmious (Popular Party). They awaited the arrival of the three ELAS delegates in a bitterly cold room, while outside could be heard the continuing sounds of battle. An armoured car had been sent by General Scobie to collect the ELAS delegates, but it was only after the Archbishop and Churchill had both spoken that they arrived. They were George Siantos, Secretary of the KKE; Partsalides, Secretary of EAM, and General Mandakas, second in command to Sarafis and the military commander whose aim was to take over Athens.

The preliminary speeches, which included statements by Churchill, Damaskinos, Papendreou and Field Marshal Alexander, all stressed the need to find a peaceful solution as quickly as possible. More in sorrow than anger, Alexander said: 'It is with pain that I find my soldiers fighting in Greece, a country towards which we have never had any but the friendliest feelings of sympathy, admiration and affection. I and my soldiers have only one enemy – the Germans. But by force of circumstances we find ourselves compelled to come to the aid of the Greek people, our friends.

The statements were heard in silence by the three Communist leaders until Partsalides, reported as having a smooth manner and charming voice, acted as spokesman for his colleagues. After echoing the hopes of the other speakers that the outcome would be successful, he paid tribute to Churchill: 'I am expressing the feelings of the Greek people on behalf of EAM for the efforts of the Prime Minister of our great ally, England. Despite the fact we find ourselves face to face with exceptionally tragic circumstances, I feel that these clashes between the Greek people, and between them and British troops, will not shake the traditional relations of the Greek people with the British people.... We thank Mr Churchill once again for taking the initiative.'

Thereupon the British delegates, together with the Allied representatives, left the room while the Archbishop presided over a conference that lasted until nearly 10 p.m., when it was adjourned, to be resumed the following day. The one and only subject which all the delegates, irrespective of party or persuasion, agreed upon was that the Archbishop should be asked to become regent. Consequently it was left to Churchill, on his return in Britain, to persuade the stubborn King George II to accept the situation, and in a subsequent telegram to President Roosevelt (30 December 1944) he reported success: 'Anthony and I sat up with the King of

Greece till 4.30 this morning at the end of which time His Majesty agreed to the following announcement: "We, George II, King of the Hellenes, having deeply considered the terrible situation into which our well-loved people have fallen through circumstances alike unprecedented and uncontrollable, and being ourselves resolved not to return to Greece unless summoned by a free and fair expression of the national will, and having full confidence in your loyalty and devotion, do now by this declaration appoint you, Archbishop Damaskinos, to be our Regent during this period of emergency...." '

That message allowed the Archbishop to proceed with forming a new Government, which he did under the premiership of Plastiras, Papendreou having placed the resignation of the previous Government at the Regent's disposal. On one important issue, therefore, Churchill's visit had been successful.

At the all-Greek conference, EAM had said they would agree to disarm, with certain conditions which were akin to victors' terms and which included:

(a) Forty to fifty per cent of the Cabinet posts in the Government.

(b) The important Ministries of Interior and Justice as well as the Under-Secretariats of War and Foreign Affairs to be given to EAM.

(c) Complete disbandment of the *gendarmerie*, the Mountain Brigade, the Sacred Squadron and all new battalions of the National Guard.

(d) A plebiscite to be held on the first Sunday in February, followed by elections for a Constituent Assembly in April 1945.

Such terms were manifestly unacceptable, and indeed the plebiscite and elections were totally impossible as there were no valid electoral rolls in the country at that time.

Churchill and Eden returned to Britain while the war in Greece continued.

Inevitably, both factions took the opportunity to try to extract maximum propaganda value from Churchill's visit for their own cause. EAM boasted over their public-address systems that they had compelled the British Prime Minister to come to Greece and talk peace, a view shared by some of the

Press, who felt that Churchill was about to do a deal in order to extricate the British forces for use in another theatre of the war. They were wrong, as Churchill made clear at a Press conference before he left Athens, when he reaffirmed his belief that, 'There would have been a massacre in the city if we had not intervened with our troops.' He reminded the journalists that Sarafis had signed the Caserta Agreement in September and had not kept his promises. Richard Capell summed up the British position as explained by Churchill: 'What is not possible is that we should throw away all that in this cruel month we have stood for – honour, pledged word, the protection of an imperilled society.'

While the situation had changed, for the better politically, the southern part of Athens had still to be cleared, and the 4th British Division was redeployed to do this. H.B. Mackenzie Johnston, at the time adjutant of the 6th Battalion, the Black Watch which was pushing its way up the main road, remembers that they had a lot of trouble at their battalion headquarters, on Lofos Sikelias, from a sniper who was quick to fire at anyone who emerged from the building. Information was difficult to obtain but, 'We got unexpected and welcome help from a delightful rogue of a Greek who turned up saying he had been a pilot in the Royal Greek Air Force. We nicknamed him Shufti George, and for about ten days he acted as our plain-clothed spy, moving about at night and bringing us back details of where the ELAS were.'

John Clarke, in the same battalion and a staff sergeant, arrived one or two days later as he had been with the rear party in Taranto. The advance party of the battalion had already left for Palestine, where the unit expected to enjoy three months respite from war. 'We were angry that our rest period had been taken away from us, and it must be said that in Athens the fighting conditions were strange to us, and sometimes an embarrassment because we were unable to identify the enemy. Here we were, having sorted out the 1st German Para in Forlí and elsewhere, unable to progress against irregulars.' OC B Company, Peter Lepel-Glass, nearby had a narrow escape: 'From that friendly wave in a doorway, a sniper would suddenly open up from under his legs. On one occasion I was shot at in this way from about ten yards. Luckily my assailant missed.'

MacKenzie-Johnston and Clarke remember Christmas – 'a festival the Jocks don't celebrate, nor did they in 1944'. The ex-adjutant recalls 'a vicious little bit of aggression by ELAS, using mortars etc from which we suffered a few casualties, but we beat it off'. John Clarke's recollections are more vivid: 'The ELAS attacked, blowing down a wall with a poll charge; A Company platoon was ready for them and when we fixed bayonets and charged to the sound of the pipes, they ran. I don't know what caused the retreat, the bayonet or the pipes.'

Another member of the same battalion, Dr Brian Pownall (the RMO), recalls what a problem it was to evacuate the wounded when ELAS did not respect the Red Cross flag. He was also asked to see and report on a small ELAS hospital unit set up in a school building nearby. 'There were about thirty wounded in beds, some looked ill and by the smell most had infected wounds. Their look of malign hostility was very dramatic. One felt if one went too near they might spit in your eye or produce a knife from under the blankets. It was my first glimpse of the deep hatred and passion the civil war produced.'

Christmas was also a hectic one for those who were trying to complete the clearance of Piraeus. The gunners of the 1st Field Regiment, fighting as infantry alongside their Gurkha comrades, had their first fatal casualty of the Greek Civil War when a lance-bombadier was shot in the face and died later in the day. F. C. Dunn recalls that, 'Christmas 1944 was anything but a festive one. We did have a bottle of beer or two and some tinned turkey and plum duff. We were warned to be on the look-out, and no celebrating was allowed as ELAS weren't far away, over in the factories. We later had our full Christmas dinner some time in February – I remember it well as I'm afraid we all got blind drunk!'

5 Brigade units were extremely busy on 24 and 25 December, when they closed in on the final ELAS strongholds. On Christmas afternoon, two companies of the 1/4th Essex, supported by tanks, assaulted the Papastratos cigarette factory, the last defences held by ELAS at the top of the inner harbour, and following its capture a cordon was drawn across the southern Athenian suburbs. A great boost to morale was the visit of Winston Churchill and Field Marshal Alexander on Boxing Day, when the distinguished

visitors were briefed on what had happened and told that only one suburb, Evvyenia, where ELAS had been maintaining a siege of a battery from the 57th Light Anti-Aircraft Regiment, remained to be cleared.

Their story was a little epic on its own, which started at 1800 hours on 19 December, when information was received that an old woman had muttered to A Troop's sentry: 'Tonight ELAS, pom, pom, pom.' At the same time all women and children were seen evacuating the houses in the neighbourhood. That warning was heeded and the post took immediate steps to repel all boarders by building up their reserve stocks of arms and ammunition. It was not a normal role for LAA gunners to play but the 169th Battery were right on their toes when the partisans began their noisy assault. The 57th LAA history describes it in these words: 'ELAS appeared to be attacking in considerable force from every side but every gunflash seen was met by hundreds of rounds. It was quite impossible to stop 169. They were very angry and, as one bombardier afterwards said, "We learnt AA the hard way, now we'll learn this ---- infantry the hard way", and by God they did. The fire power coming out of the laboratory must have been terrific.' The battle continued hour after hour until ELAS turned a 75mm gun onto the building, which caused several casualties. They even produced a captured Piat mortar to open up at the British from close range but that dangerous weapon was silenced by some accurate fire from a bren. Further attacks were put in on the laboratory, occupied by A Troop, who, '... also lost their tempers and gave back a hail of everything they had.... ELAS again failed to sustain their efforts and no infiltration was attempted. And so ended a most exciting night, which resulted in a victory for 169 Battery and a safe landing for the whole of 5 Brigade the following night.' Indeed, the gunners had done well.

Thus ended 'the regrettable Piraeus operations in which hundreds of fanatical misguided Greeks fell in shedding the blood of those who had come to liberate them' (9th Gurkha Rifles History). The casualties suffered during this phase of the fighting by the 3/10th Baluch Regiment and the 1/9th Gurkha Rifles were approximately the same – ten killed and about sixty wounded in each of the battalions. In comparison, those suffered by the 2nd Parachute and 23rd Armoured Brigade in Athens were higher, as their totals included prisoners marched away by ELAS to a harrowing ordeal in captivity.

On 30 December, with the 2/5th Leicesters leading the advance, Block Force moved along the highway to the city and removed road blocks at Leoforos Salmaminos, an operation that proceeded like clockwork. The vigorous leadership shown by Brigadier Adam Block during the three weeks' operations, carried out by units from three different brigades under his overall command, had been most impressive.

For two hours only each day the local people were allowed to leave their homes and cellars; at all other times the curfew was imposed with a rigorous severity, as the order given the British troops was to shoot on sight anyone in the streets. Without such a curfew, street-clearing would have been impossible, '... but inevitably in a country where timelessness is a way of life, regrettably many innocent Greeks were killed as a result' (Lepel-Glass of the Black Watch).

By the time Churchill left Athens, the situation in certain parts of the city had improved but the industrial area west of Constitution Square continued to be defended with obstinacy by ELAS. Only after the *andartes* had been driven out did crowds of pathetic people, who had hidden in cellars and holes for days without food and water, emerge, seeking missing members of their families and crying out for food.

In Athens, as in Piraeus, battalion soup kitchens were set up for the starving, under-nourished people. At Droughouti, a working-class area, the Black Watch established their centre, with two pipers to entertain the crowd and a section of military police to help maintain control. On the first day, people poured in, until it was estimated that between 25,000 and 30,000 had been served with a hot meal, meagre offering though it was. Cries of '*Zito Churchill! Zito Hellas! Zito Scobie!*' rent the air here and at similar soup kitchens established by other units elsewhere.

In the welter of denouncements and denials about atrocities that have continued over the years, it is prudent, perhaps, for a British author not to become too involved in such matters, following the example of Kenneth Matthews, who wrote: 'I had learnt to be wary about atrocities' – and for such a reason he did not want to see any bodies. Other servicemen, who did see mutilated bodies brought out of deep wells and pits, were convinced that there were a number of savage sadists in the ELAS ranks, whose crimes appeared to be in imitation of, and even surpassing, the worst German atrocities during the Occupation. 'If there had been any doubt before our arrival of the righteousness of our cause, there was none now against this cruel, uncouth Communist enemy' (Peter Lepel-Glass).

As news of the corpses spread, there was an intense, growing hatred of the extreme left wing in Athens and sadly and inevitably innumerable young men began taking up arms in order to seek and exact revenge. In such a manner were the seeds of 'a white backlash' sown, despite the British doing their best to restrain tempers by pointing out that further acts of vengeance against ELAS could only aggravate the situation, making reconciliation and rehabilitation doubly difficult.

On 29 December the Greek Mountain Brigade, together with British troops operating in the area west and south-west of the Great Stadium, began a fierce offensive. The Greeks were fighting in Kaiseriani, the Communists' 'little Stalingrad', supported by armour from the 46th Royal Tank Regiment. Fierce fighting ensued, with many *andartes* showing fanatical resistance, even when they were facing tanks with nothing but rifles and pistols. The strategically important Ardhittos Hill was eventually captured by 11 KRRC, but only after a fierce battle. Suddenly, quite unexpectedly, a glimmer of victory brightened the dark horizon, and almost dramatically ELAS broke, streaming away into the surrounding hills, so that resistance was over in southern Athens. All that remained was to clear the north of the city, and for this the HLI, 50th Royal Tank Regiment, and two National Guard battalions moved into the congested and difficult built-up area, with the KRRC coming to join the battle later.

Truce feelers, put out by ELAS GHQ, still failed to recognize Scobie's conditions – that they should make a complete withdrawal from Attica, albeit retaining arms, while those who remained in Athens should be disarmed immediately. Politically, too, the EAM Central Committee continued to make demands: up to half the posts in any future Government and the disbandment of the Mountain Brigade and National Guard units – in line with their previous terms. Nevertheless, despite the KKE Central Committee's sending for Aris, in a desperate attempt to stiffen ELAS morale in Attica, the end was in sight. In spite of Aris's drastic measures – which included the summary execution of any men who refused to fight or attempted to desert – there was nothing ELAS could do to stop the advances made by the 12th and 28th Brigades and 'ARK Force'.

Even then there were to be a few reverses. For example, a troop of C Squadron, 4th Recce Regiment was ambushed in a gorge when heading the advance north-east from Athens, resulting in the leading and rear armoured cars being knocked out, thus trapping the remainder. Faced with an impossible situation, the troop leader surrendered, following which he and his men were marched through the snow to Lamia, approximately 120 miles away, in bitter weather and minus their boots, which ELAS took for themselves. All the British survived but were in a very bad way by the time they were handed over, after an armistice had been signed in the New Year.

At a simple ceremony on New Year's Day Archbishop Damaskinos took the oath as Regent of Greece. Thereafter he began interviews with a view to choosing members of the new Cabinet. His one aim, as he told his confidants, was to remove EAM's fears of monarchist intrigues and to try to break away completely from the immediate political past. Although he appreciated that he would have the support of the British military authorities, nevertheless General Scobie's powers were restricted to military affairs, so that immediate responsibility for bringing the Greek tragedy to an end now lay with the Archbishop. To this end he issued an appeal to the whole nation, pleading for 'the restoration of normality, putting aside all differences and hatreds and co-operating sincerely for the nation's sake'.

During the afternoon of New Year's Day a small delegation of the EAM Central Committee, headed by Zevgos (until 2 December, Minister of Agriculture) came to see General

Scobie at his GHQ. The representatives still did not bring any confirmation of the acceptance by EAM/ELAS of Scobie's conditions for a truce, which he had laid down during December. When discussing the future of the Greek Mountain Brigade and the National Guard, Ronald Scobie reaffirmed his readiness to return the brigade to barracks immediately after the terms of the truce had been carried out but pointed out that the future organization of regular Greek national forces was a matter for the new Government to decide, not his responsibility. The Regent sent a message to the delegation supporting General Scobie's statement and made a final appeal to the delegates to end hostilities as soon as possible, and to make terms with the new Government, headed by General Plastiras, which was wholly Republican and moderately left wing, with only one member of the Papendreou Government remaining in the administration.

By 10 January the British had cleared Attica and taken Thebes; after reaching open country, there was little ELAS could do to stop them. Victory had been achieved after five weeks fighting which left a badly damaged, scarred Athens, a city that had not suffered at all during the war. On 6 January General Scobie raised once more the question of hostages taken by ELAS, by now in the region of a thousand British and an estimated 15-20,000 civilians. Again Zevgos and Partsalides came to see Scobie, and on 11 January, at 10.30 p.m., a truce was arranged, to come into effect three days later. By that time, central and southern Greece had been freed up to a line running west from Volos. The Communist representatives agreed that British and ELAS prisoners of war would be released, on a one-for-one basis, but they still refused to return the Greek civilian hostages who were being held under harrowing conditions.

The Second Round had drawn in some 75,000 British forces from Italy and elsewhere, which highlighted Alexander's statement on Boxing Day to the EAM delegates: 'Instead of my having to pour British troops into Athens, you should be pouring Greek brigades into Italy to march against the common foe.'

The Commander-in-Chief's final warm tribute to his men was well deserved: 'I owe it to the fighting men of the three Services that, in spite of the aggravating circumstances and in spite of the scenes they witnessed, which were calculated to inflame them against their adversaries, they never failed to display a spirit of understanding, moderation and chivalry, and above all to do their duty.'

In the six weeks fighting, total British casualties came to 237 killed and just over 2,100 wounded. Some of them had died in the hands of ELAS, victims of exposure to the cruel winter or shot when they were unable to keep up with the marching columns of hostages while they were being driven away from Athens into the mountains.

As soon as news of the truce spread, ELAS discipline and morale crumbled in some units and disintegrated in others. In the military sense, its leaders did comply with the truce terms, which meant a complete withdrawal from the Salonika area, from the north Peloponnese, Attica, Boeotia, Phthoitis, part of Thessaly and the islands.

Salonika remained tense but relatively peaceful throughout the fighting in Athens, following which General Hawksworth visited the city and in a no-nonsense manner gave the ELAS commander, Bakirdzis, four days in which to withdraw his forces or face the consequences. That message was promulgated by leaflets dropped by the RAF, reinforced by a show of force with the arrival of Sherman tanks. Despite the defeat in Athens, EAM propagandists continued to attack the Indian Army units in Salonika in newspapers and leaflets. Gordon Richardson (commanding 1/2 GR) kept a newspaper extract from *Laiki Phoni* which alleged that, 'After all the raping of the heroic women of Athens by black-faced Zulus, after all the macabre meals off the brains of Greek children made by the dwarfs of Tanganyika, dressed as British soldiers, Greece will live and glitter, Mr Churchill.' Richardson gave full marks to the translator for his or her imaginative prose!

While still keeping a low profile, the 4th Indian Division's officers and men in Salonika watched the withdrawal of ELAS from the city centre. 'ELAS marched out in a military body but we witnessed one brutal incident. A girl from a balcony window shouted a Royalist slogan. Immediately a group of soldiers broke ranks, dashed into the house and threw the girl into the street, killing her instantly.' The same incident was witnessed by D. Parker, except that his opinion of the 'military body' was that it consisted of 'a long column of miserable-looking men, carts, donkeys and what have you, crawling past us.'

When units of the 4th Indian Division began moving out from Salonika to supervise the ELAS withdrawal, they entered a long association with towns and villages in Thrace and Macedonia, one that was to last for some officers and men until early 1946. It is strange, therefore, to find the Sarafis memoirs alleging that the sympathy shown by Indian officers towards the ELAS cause 'led to the 4th Indian Division's being hastily withdrawn from Greece'. On the contrary, in the context of the Second World War, a tour of over eighteen months in one country was a long one, and especially so for a formation like the 4th Indian Division which had begun its overseas travels back in 1939. When they sailed from Greece, their reputation was high, and deservedly so: 'They neither robbed nor raped nor flogged – unusual soldiers indeed. The hearts of the Greek peasants warmed to them and they sought to show their feelings to British, Indians and Gurkhas in many ways – by shy courtesies, by simple gifts, by timely warnings: a garland, a sheet, a flask of ouzo – small tributes meaning much.'

One journalist was to write that the oddest thing about the Revolution (Second Round) was the peace at Salonika and Patras. Perhaps he was unaware that before the end of 1944 there had been grievous casualties at Missolonghi and Krioneri and on the island of Zante, all in the neighbourhood of Patras. That there was no full-scale attack against the British Army garrisons in both centres was due, in some part, to the personalities of the ELAS commanders, Bakirdzis and Tsikliteras. Both were veteran regular officers, decorated by the British in the First World War, and although ardent Republicans, they hesitated before risking their men's lives merely at the prompting of the Communist Central Committee. Nevertheless, after the New Year the situation in Patras continued to worry Scobie, and he considered a proposal that the Force should be evacuated by sea, only to reject it, as can be seen in a diary entry – 'I did not agree to the suggestion.'

The fact that a full-scale evacuation was being seriously considered had been brought about by ELAS' moving up guns, ready to fire against the 11th Brigade, while quantities of explosives had been found in the sewers of Patras. Rumours of impending attacks, which came from intelligence as well as civilian sources, placed a big strain on all ranks, and the occasional incident did not reduce tension. At a dance held at Brigade HQ, organized by the British 'other ranks', a 36 grenade was thrown onto the dance floor by a person unknown, killing one and wounding six British soldiers. The adjutant of 2/7 GR reported in the unit War Diary that it was 'a dirty trick on somebody's part'. Now, forty years on, such an incident would almost pass unnoticed in Northern Ireland!

The dramatic arrival of HMS *Ajax* and escorting destroyers on 4 January lifted the morale of the 11th Brigade and brought broad smiles to the faces of the vast majority of the townspeople who had begun to lose heart. Arriving after dusk, *Ajax* played its searchlight onto ELAS columns ostensibly moving towards Patras. At the same time, Beaufighters carried out a series of noise mock-dive attacks. The period of bluff and counter-bluff had ended, of turning the other cheek while *andartes* swaggered about, hoping to provoke an incident which could have sparked off a riot or even worse, full-scale fighting within the confines of Patras. Five days later, on 9 January, the 139th Brigade, two squadrons of 50 RTR and a new Greek National Guard battalion sailed into Patras: 'It was a glorious, a stirring sight for us, if not for our opponents. The tables were turned and our quiet brigadier became a commander who meant business' wrote a 2/7 GR subaltern, not realizing at the time that overall command in the area had passed to Brigadier Adam Block.

For John Hunt it was a tremendous moment but also a bitter one '… despite a typically generous and appreciative personal message from General Scobie. I had planned this moment of the break-out, which would release our pent-up energies and avenge the insults and injuries we had endured all these past months. It was hard to have the leadership and the initiative taken from me at that time. Admiral Mansfield, who, with his ships' companies, had been a marvellous source of encouragement to me and my sorely tried soldiers ashore, was furious. He had a penchant for writing doggerel verse and promptly composed a poem full of bitter sarcasm, of which it is perhaps as well I remember only the appalling pun "Block blocks Hunt's elevation to peer".' In the end, the outcome at Patras was a happy one – and years later, John Hunt did become a peer.

Brigadier Adam Block was a type of commander different from Hunt, 'a man of little finesse and no nonsense'. Despite the bitter protests of Colonel Tsikliteras, he ordered the ELAS commander to get his disguised *andartes* out of the town and move away from their positions surrounding the enclave by first light on the following morning. Before dawn next day, the British struck, with the Camerons driving straight for Kalavryta, a village in which the Germans had murdered many hostages in cold blood during the Occupation. The Camerons reached Kalavryta in three days and scattered the *andartes*, even though defiance continued in a few outlying villages.

The 2/7th Gurkha Rifles were given a special role by their brigadier, that of making a rapid night march over difficult country to bypass the ELAS HQ in the wine factory at Klaus. In Hunt's words: 'Those swift silent little men did a most effective job; on a small scale it was the story of the Goums on the Garigliano all over again.' It was not a bloodless victory for the Gurkhas, especially for their C Company. 'Those Greeks had courage but fortunately for us their leadership was poor, many of their weapons were antiquated and ammunition was in short supply. Gradually we assumed control, disarmed many, captured scores of sullen and dejected men' (War Diary figures, thirty-two killed, thirty-five wounded and sixty-one captured). But for C Company the battle was not over, because 7 Platoon, on its own in an exposed position, was soon under heavy pressure from all sides. 'Gurkha and Greek fought with courage until neither side had any ammunition left. At such a crucial moment another platoon from C Company arrived to drive off the Greeks, and to find that 7 Platoon had already used *kukris* when the Greeks charged the position. Naik [Corporal] Chaturdhoj, about 5'0½" in height, had killed five ELAS soldiers with his *kukri*, leading a counter-attack at a time when the battle appeared to be lost. One Gurkha soldier was killed and another badly wounded but the story of the battle was soon to be known all over the

Peloponnese. The Gurkha and his *kukri* became a legend overnight.'

Late in the afternoon of 11 January, Brigadier John Hunt rode on a tank into the wine factory at Klaus, captured by the Gurkhas, and 'drank a toast to our success'.

Members of EAM/ELAS Central Committee now began to ask General Scobie to bring the fighting to an end before their military defeat turned into a rout. No longer did Sarafis and Zevgos find him ready to compromise. Brigadier Hugh Mainwaring, his Chief of Staff, wrote that the GOC was no longer prepared to put up any more with double-dealing and prevarication. Mainwaring singled out Sarafis as being 'an absolute four-letter-word shifty man'. However, it was Zevgos, the ex-schoolmaster, who kept harping back to the Communist ideology rather than facing the stark fact that ELAS had been defeated. The original truce had not specified that ELAS must release civilian hostages, an omission which angered the new Prime Minister, General Plastiras, and distressed the Regent. A storm of protests led to the British revoking the truce until hostages taken by ELAS had been 'effectively safeguarded or released'. Rehabilitation and relief work began in earnest, and within a short time just over a million people had received emergency issues of different sorts of food through Military Liaison and the Swedish-Swiss Joint Relief Commission.

While it is tempting to avoid a further mention of the mutilated corpses found in the suburbs of Athens at Peristeri, it must be remembered that the discovery was to have serious repercussions in Britain, raising doubts about 'the freedom fighters', ELAS. Sir Walter Citrine, leading a TUC Delegation whose primary purpose in visiting Greece was to advise and help re-build the trade union movement, inadvertently came face to face with the horrors at Peristeri at a time when shudders of horror swept through Athens and the Greek nation.

ELAS apologists have maintained that a handful of OPLA fanatics might have been responsible for some of the mutilated corpses found. Another writer, Dominic Eudes, has gone much further, alleging that Peristeri was an example of 'Red atrocities, manufactured by the Greek Police', thus conveniently forgetting how extremely difficult, if not impossible, it would have been to organize such a macabre operation, especially in a city like Athens where well-kept secrets were like precious stones of the utmost rarity. Moreover, such an operation would have involved an organizing ability well beyond anything shown up to that moment by the Greek Government or the police, following the liberation. Reluctant observer Kenneth Matthews described the scene of horror: 'If ever there was a scene straight from Hell, this was it. The bodies were being exhumed from a series of parallel trenches in which the diggers were still working. The weeping Greek families found it difficult to believe that these had been done by their own people.'

Later, at a Press conference, Siantos was to deny that either EAM or ELAS had ever given directions that hostages should be killed or ill-treated – if executions had taken place, they had been carried out by irresponsible people, not organized by EAM. But, he admitted, 'In such a war, it was natural for such events to take place.' Capell's comment was that, 'Greeks do not lack generosity towards a fallen foreign foe. They reserve their bitter animosity for fellow Greeks.' When Siantos faced questioning by journalists, he struck Capell as being 'powerful, tragic and sinister, like a monk in a Spanish picture of the seventeenth century, untouched by the events of the world. Like your Stalin, your Hitler, he believed what he said with something like a martyr's infatuation.' Kenneth Matthews' impression of Siantos was a little different: 'The man who had worked in the shadows was a shrunken figure, complexion like cracked varnish, and evasive of speech and manner.' Between 1943 and 1949 EAM/ELAS did not produce a leader of such stature as Yugoslavia's Marshal Tito, whose powerful personality was instrumental in establishing a Communist regime not subservient to Stalin – as Russia was to find out after the war was over.

Of the many missions that were to descend on Greece during the next four months, the one headed by Sir Walter Citrine was the most effective. The delegation arrived in Athens on 22 January, well aware that there was much confusion in the UK about the role played by the British Government and the use of the Army in Athens and elsewhere, with support for EAM being strong in certain circles. After Citrine had reported on the atrocities he and his delegates had seen in Athens, much of the sympathy for ELAS dissipated, and this, coupled with a variety of stories recounted by released British hostages, meant that the British Government's policy in Greece was reaffirmed by a massive majority in the Commons – despite one or two fervent speeches by Bevan and a small group of left-wing politicians.

Scobie agreed to allow Citrine and his delegation of four to go wherever they wanted and, although officially they had come to advise on Greek trade union matters, it was quite obvious that they would be probing into the British role, as well as looking for possible abuses by the Army, and the other two Services, during the Second Round. Citrine was to find that even in Greek Trade Union matters there was open disunity; it mirrored the divisions that split the country, politically and in just about all aspects of life. During their period of power in Athens, ELAS had made a conscious effort to liquidate all the trade unionists who were brave enough to disagree publicly with their politics, either by blatant intimidation or, in a few cases, by singling them out for execution. The pendulum had swung, Communist power had declined by the time Citrine arrived in Athens, and non-Communist trade union members who had adopted a low profile – especially when accused of being 'collaborators' – now came out into the open, hitting back in a bitter war of words far removed from the annual debates in the UK's Trades Union Congress. It was at Scobie's request that Citrine and his colleagues visited the mass graves, and the next day the general made a diary entry as follows: 'Citrine rang up to say that he had visited the mass grave, had been physically sick twice and was going to bed!' The news of the trade union delegation's discomfiture spread among the troops who by this time had become disillusioned by the criticism heaped on them by left-wing MPs in the Commons, aided and abetted by certain members of the British and American Press.

Of more significance, however, was the meeting Citrine's delegation had in an Athens cinema with British troops without any officers being present, most of the audience being men of the 2nd Parachute Brigade. In response to a

TUC official, Ernest Bell's, saying it was all rather wrong, and did they, as British troops, believe that their intervention was necessary, speaker after speaker made it abundantly clear what they thought of ELAS and their so-called democratic methods. Sir Walter Citrine and his delegation, completely unprepared for such a response, returned to the UK in a very different frame of mind, there to issue a report which included this statement: 'We were impressed with the universal opinion of the British troops that, had they not been ordered into action against ELAS, there would have been a wholesale massacre in Athens. We are firmly of the opinion that, when the full history of the struggle has been written, people of our country will be proud of the courage, cheerfulness, restraint and steadfast behaviour of our troops in Greece in circumstances of the greatest difficulty.'

Citrine's report, under the title 'What we saw in Greece', signalled the end of public argument in the UK, with Aneurin Bevan and other left-wing supporters being forced to refrain from further irresponsible accusations. Dominic Eudes' allegation that Citrine came to Greece at Churchill's instigation, with a view to supporting his policy, displays a total ignorance of the relationship between British Government and trade unions in the UK. Such a proposal, if ever made by any British Prime Minister, would be met with scorn, as well as inviting open opposition.

Serious negotiations between the Greek Government under Plastiras and EAM/ELAS began on 2 February at Varkiza, a large seaside resort some twenty miles from Athens, and the talks were to last for ten days. The presence of Harold Macmillan and Reginald Leeper softened the hard-line approach originally adopted by Plastiras. The Greek Prime Minister was angered by the attitude of the Communist delegates, Siantos, Partsalides and Sarafis – who was representing the ELAS guerrillas – because they did not appear to regard themselves as having been beaten. After protracted negotiations, it was due to British influence and sense of fair play (a weakness in this situation, perhaps) that the rebels received a peace that was, by Greek standards, tolerant and even generous.

At a Press conference afterwards, John Sofianopoulos, Minister for Foreign Affairs and the Press, read the agreement and, after one phase, 'EAM and the KKE Party', had been altered to read 'EAM', the delegates signed and peace was formally proclaimed. Siantos then tried to justify the Second Round, maintaining that they had tried to give practical effect to the Lebanon Charter, which meant the purging of all collaborators and Fascist elements from the Civil Service. He accused the opposite side of trying to restore and rebuild the old regime, and then explained how the war had started. The demonstration in Constitution Square on 3 December was '... peaceful and completely unarmed. It was this demonstration that the Papendreou Government attacked with rifle fire. We suffered no fewer than a hundred dead and wounded.... This is how the conflict began.'

In answering other questions, Siantos said the fact that the British Army was in conflict with ELAS was the result of 'an unfortunate misunderstanding which we hope will be forgotten'. Once more he denied that either EAM or ELAS had given directions that hostages should be ill-treated or killed and that, if any such incident had taken place, it had been committed by irresponsible people. In such a war, it was natural for events like that to take place – and he was certain that on the other side there had been even more. Richard Capell, who was in the audience, wrote that Siantos was 'unmoved in his fanaticism'; the outcome, in his opinion, smacked of appeasement which became obvious when Siantos declared that, 'We are very pleased and satisfied with the agreement.'

Under another clause, the ELAS army was required to hand in the bulk of its weapons and, in obedience to their leaders' orders, supplemented by a series of searches co-ordinated and often conducted by the British Army, most of the total laid down – 41,500 rifles, over 200 machine-guns and various mortars and artillery pieces – were taken into custody. Several ex-servicemen who took part in search operations in various parts of Greece have written to state that a large number of weapons handed over voluntarily were 'clapped out' and of ancient Italian vintage. Occasionally caches of more serviceable weapons were found, usually as a result of a tip-off from previously intimidated villagers.

There was an air of euphoria following the Varkiza
agreement which persisted for a few days. The Greek
Government had won the Second Round, thanks to the
British, but regrettably they were unable to see that the terms
of the treaty were strictly enforced by their own side. Bitter
memories of the excesses carried out by OPLA and other
fanatics could not be forgotten or forgiven and, almost
inevitably, encouraged the extremists on the right to begin
taking the law into their own hands. As this became more
prevalent, ELAS' desire to hold on to as many weapons as
possible, for their own security, was natural and understandable. A major problem was that firebrands like Aris had
other motives for retaining as many arms as possible, because
for them the war was not over. Scobie feared, and with good
reason, that ELAS diehards would lie low and make
preparations for another rising. The general later stated that
if he had been given a week or two more, there was little
doubt that he could have destroyed the hard core completely.
However, just prior to Varkiza there were strong political
reasons for peace to be restored as quickly as possible in
Greece: mounting American pressure, increasing Russian
suspicion and the necessity for Alexander to use the
maximum military effort during the last phases of the
campaign in Italy – all these factors helped to speed up the
peace talks and the final agreement at Varkiza. The KKE was
still allowed to operate and function openly in Greece, with
Communist newspapers, including the notorious *Rizospastis*
(organ of the KKE), which were not subject to any sort of
censorship whatever.

On 15 February Winston Churchill, who had been
persuaded by Damaskinos to return from Yalta via Athens,
arrived in the city. Prior to his arrival, the Regent had said:
'He will see on which side the people stand.' It was a
momentous occasion and obviously touched the Prime
Minister deeply. The scenes of jubilation made a lasting
impression on him: 'A vast mob held back by a thin line of
kilted Greek soldiers; crowds screaming with enthusiasm in
the very streets where hundreds of men had died in the
Christmas days when I had last seen the city.' That evening a
crowd of about 50,000 people gathered in Constitution
Square. When that well-known voice spoke, the voice that

had become a signal of hope to so many millions in Occupied Europe, there were tears of joy and emotion in the eyes of thousands.

Winston Churchill struck the right note from the beginning: 'Your Beautitude, soldiers and citizens of Athens and of Greece. These are great days; these are the days when the dawn is bright; these are days when the darkness rolls away.' He then expressed his pride in the part the British Army had taken 'in protecting this immortal city from violence and anarchy'. He ended with an appeal: 'Let none fail in his duty to his country. Let none fail to rise to the occasion of these splendid days. Let the Greek nation stand first in every heart, first in the thoughts of every man and woman.... From the bottom of my heart I hope that Greece will take her proper part in the ranks of nations that have suffered so terribly in this war. Let right prevail. Let party hatreds die. Let there be unity. Let there be resolute comradeship. Greece for ever! Greece for all!'

Alas, the party hatreds would not die, and there was to be no unity during the dark months that lay ahead of the divided country. For KKE a battle had been lost, but it was not the end of the war. They had survived to prepare for another day of reckoning which could be averted only if both sides proved capable of restraining the extremists. Unfortunately for warmhearted, volatile, hot-blooded men, the path of moderation held little appeal because, to most of them, it smacked of weakness and abject appeasement.

9 Reconciliation Impossible

'Hatred is a feeling which leads to the extinction of values.'

Jose Ortego Gasse

During January 1945 the British Army began to experience its second welcome in four months, warm and sincere in several parts of the land, deeply uneasy in others. Those who went south via Corinth into the Peloponnese found Royalist slogans everywhere, which were, in some part, a reaction to the EAM regime that had so dominated the lives of the people there for weeks past. The smiling faces that greeted British patrols often changed after their departure when armed members of ELAS reappeared to make threats and anti-British speeches. The problem that faced army commanders at all levels was to establish the truth when so many tales were reported to them by one side or the other, often unduly exaggerated.

Dr Brian Pownall, RMO Black Watch, while under canvas between Thebes and Levadia during the second half of January, described the population as hostile, especially when searches for arms were being carried out. A platoon from A Company was ambushed in the hills, and in the skirmish there were fatal casualties as well as some men being taken prisoner. John Clarke, a staff sergeant with D Company, went to the scene of the ambush. 'We found the bodies of some of our lads, stripped and mutilated. One was a friend, David Smith, a signaller, whose set had been taken. He'd obviously put up a fight. One officer and twenty-three ORs were taken prisoner, stripped and forced-marched even though most were wounded. This happened somewhere near Levadia, where the National Guard were treating the locals brutally. Eventually, with the help of Colonel Valentine RAMC and after the truce was ratified, we managed to rescue our lads.'

Like other ex-servicemen, Dr Pownall was under the impression that, in this area, 'Anyone who co-operated with the British Army would be dealt with later.' The adjutant of the Black Watch, MacKenzie-Johnston, agreed with that assessment. 'The situation tended to be tense, with the populations of these places by no means enthusiastic about us.'

Not many miles away, B.C.H. Harris, at that time a lance-corporal in 2 DCLI, remembers that the town of Chalkis '... was teeming with ELAS, and we saw strapping Greek women walking around with bandoliers slung over their shoulders and carrying rifles.' Harris also recalls that a platoon of his company took a wrong turning in a ravine, only to find themselves in an ELAS camp and surrounded by armed men. 'After a few hours, they were released after a bit of joking.... At that time anything was possible in Greece!' (The truce had been signed a day or two before the incident.)

The truce did not end the general mistrust between ELAS and their British opponents, as a story recounted by R.M. Honey, commanding Support Company 6th Black Watch, illustrates well. While searching for hostages taken by ELAS in the Larissa area, Honey found an attractive young lady, badly wounded in the breast, who was being held prisoner in the local doctor's house. Later, accompanied by the RMO, he made another visit and found the girl's wound was suppurating: urgent hospital treatment was required if she was to survive. After a delay of a day or two, the local ELAS leaders finally agreed to her removal on condition that it was effected by a small, unarmed party. Not unnaturally, the battalion CO suspected that ELAS would use the occasion either to demonstrate or as a pretext for violence, but if the girl's life was to be saved, the risk had to be taken. Let R.M. Honey complete the story in his own words:

'It was arranged that the battalion MO, a driver, a medical orderly and I would do the removal in a tracked carrier. 25-pounders would be trained on the village during the operation, and in the event of trouble erupting they would open fire without further ado. We would fend for ourselves in the confusion. At the appointed hour we drove up the hill into the village. The two or three streets and the square were crowded with hundreds of men and some women, armed and festooned with bandoliers. They were dressed mostly in ragged civilian clothes or cast-off uniforms. They were dirty and unshaven. There was a total silence. Nobody spoke. They just stood and looked. Over the cobbles we slithered up a steep slope to the house in our tracked vehicle.

It was uncanny. I feared that the carrier would slide into the close-packed watchers, cause a panic, violence would erupt and the guns in the valley would open fire. The driver strained every nerve and with skill avoided such a mishap. We went into the house, put the girl on a stretcher and placed her in the carrier. I bowed to the ELAS commander and said, "At least we might save one life." He agreed. Otherwise nobody said a word. The carrier inched its way down and out of the village, the girl was taken to an army hospital.'

There was an aftermath when some months later Honey was contacted by a young man who said that the girl had asked him to say she was recovering and, in time, hoped to be completely fit. The man added that she wished she could meet Honey in order to thank him, but unfortunately the battalion moved, so it proved impossible to arrange such a meeting.

If the reception given British troops (and Indians and Gurkhas) varied from the rapturous to a polite interest – depending on the political viewpoint of the villagers or townspeople concerned – that often afforded the National Guard was blatantly hostile. MacKenzie-Johnston recalls that, 'They would cheer us where they would stone the Greek National Guard. However, this was perhaps only fair when they were not sure whether ELAS had gone for good.' He was right. In many parts of central Greece, ELAS had not gone far or for good; instead, in the shadows, they awaited events, still making their presence felt by nocturnal visits or by open threats in the Communist newspapers, which continued to be published without any censorship restrictions whatever in Athens, Salonika and such smaller towns as Volos.

At the same time, extremists on the right began to make

their presence felt, and this gave rise to concern on the part of British officers and soldiers serving in Greece during this momentous period, several of whom were upset by what they saw and heard. R.H.A. Cockburn was adamant when writing: 'It must be stated, however, that, particularly in areas where atrocities had been committed by ELAS, short shrift was given to prisoners [in this case the Greek Sacred Squadron] and some were undoubtedly shot.' The Greek practice of beating prisoners as a deterrent and to obtain information was abhorrent to the British Army and has been commented on by ex-servicemen correspondents.

The fault did not lie at the top of the Government, where the Regent tried to restrain anti-Communist feelings: 'Taking justice into one's own hands will in no case be suffered in a capitalist state where law rules, into which we are now planning to organize Greece with the help of all Greeks. None of those arrested will be detained unless they are charged with acts for which there is no provision in the penal law. Courts of three members have been set up composed of career judges and appointed by the Supreme Court....' His declared intention was sincere: the courts were set up, and justice of a sort was dispensed, but the serious problem remained of how to obtain unbiased evidence that was akin to the truth, given without fear or favour. Few Greek documents were trustworthy, and all had to be subjected to the most rigorous scrutiny, which was time-consuming and not always possible or practicable. The judiciary could not cope, and the numbers in custody, awaiting trial, increased dramatically during 1945 – which, naturally, led to justifiable complaints by Siantos and his colleagues.

The British, of whatever rank, had to be continually on their guard, careful not to say anything that could be misinterpreted, or anything that might be construed as support of the Left against Right, or the reverse. Hospitality generously offered had to be weighed in case there was an ulterior motive, and again that was difficult when British troops arrived in a village where, although poverty appeared to abound, there was always ouzo from grape skins, retsina and dancing in the open air – the cheerfulness of spirit, the Greek *kephi*, has no accurate translation in English (so I am told!).

When my company was up in the mountains, near the

border with Yugoslavia, in late 1945, suspicion about the attitude of the reformed National Guard made my colonel decide that mixed patrols of Gurkhas and Greeks were the only way to curb the excesses being carried out in the name of justice, freedom and the Allies. I wrote the account of village hospitality that follows: 'A considerable improvement resulted and the scowls of villagers became smiles when they saw the Gurkhas.... Later, the whole village, under a starry clear sky, came over to our temporary billet and a spontaneous party began. Arms linked, men, women, Gurkha, Greek, irrespective of race or sex, we all went round in a huge circle led by a giant bearded Greek who chanted away in a tuneful manner.... The dance went on seemingly for ever. I thought, if only time could stop, this would be as good a moment as any. Peace, laughter, songs, all men brothers ... years later I can recall this evening with a vivid clarity.'

In those dark days, and Greece being Greece, it is more than possible that several of those dancing that night were biding their time, harbouring revenge in their hearts, and that later, when the pendulum swung towards the Communists in northern Macedonia, that village would once more be divided in bitterness. It was not to be long before the various non-Communist factions were being lumped together under the single title 'Nationalists', a distinction easy to make even though the majority of Greek Communists remained as nationalist in their attitude to their country and its disputed frontiers as did their political opponents.

As the weeks passed, the role of British Army units changed from searching for arms and disarming the more intransigent of ELAS to direct assistance to villagers who had suffered terrible hardships, from the retreating Germans as well as at the hands of their fellow Greeks. Red Cross parcels in bulk were flown into Greece, and it became a mammoth task to distribute them to the villagers; during that bitter winter, roads and communications generally were so bad that armoured cars and tracked carriers has to be used to reach bleak little hamlets or isolated houses. Despite the cold and poverty, Greek hospitality invariably prevailed: 'Having accepted, even snatched, the food parcels from us, they would still invite us in for a glass of wine or ouzo and some thick cheese. Many had helped British or Commonwealth prisoners, often at great danger to their own lives and loved ones, and they proudly produced photos or addresses of the hunted men they had befriended.'

Several correspondents had similar recollections when distributing UNRRA supplies in remote parts of mountainous Greece. 'My main memories are of incredible hospitality, during which the villagers must have slaughtered and fed to us (and themselves) much more food than we brought, and frequent potions of ouzo and wine.... There was more interest in our days-old newspapers than in our food, while we were expected to be able to discuss the political situation on which we had had next to no briefing.... Perhaps we were too naïve and apolitical!' (Henry MacKenzie-Johnston)

Distributing UNRRA food did not always mean that it was used by the recipients for the purpose intended. A 4th Indian Division observer recalls that a girl was found feeding her pigs with a mixture of US dried milk and packet soups because, she stated, it was cheaper than proper pig food. Regrettably, too, other items were resold on the black market; in any society there will be those prepared to profit at the expense of their less fortunate neighbours.

Volos, from which Major Henderson's force had been evacuated before Christmas, renewed its acquaintance with 4th Indian Division when the 5th Brigade moved into the area in mid-January. The port remained strongly left-wing in sympathy, and searches for arms soon discovered several caches, much to the chagrin of ELAS, who apparently hoped the newcomers would overlook such a precaution. 1/9 GR reported that their three-month stay in Volos alternated between periods of quiet and intervals of tension in which the still truculent Communists endeavoured to recover prestige by whipping up agitation locally. The Volos EAM newspaper *Anayennis* continued with its scurrilous abuse of Mr Churchill, and when this drew no response, alleged or real atrocities against ELAS prisoners of war were played up in huge headlines with a wealth of gruesome detail.

'When the British ignored the insults, delegations began to pester Brigadier Saunders-Jacob with a host of complaints, often fortified by the most impudent falsehoods. The Greeks talked and talked: British officers listened and listened. Towards the end of January fatigue set in and wronged parties grew less plentiful. A newly recruited battalion of the National Guard arrived in time to save the situation. In a trice, the alleged abominations of the British, Indians and Gurkhas were forgotten, and a spate of venom directed against the Greek soldiers who sided with law and order.' (4th Indian Division's *The Tiger Triumphs*.)

In addition to the maintenance of law and order, the duties of British Army units included the collection of arms and the training of the Greek National Guard. This latter task required careful supervision and unwearying vigilance as the majority of recruits were Royalists, bitter enemies of left-wing supporters. One officer in 1/9 GR wrote: 'In ELAS areas they are inclined to discover disturbances, in Royalist areas they condone them.' However, there were few open clashes as spring approached.

On 26 April, 1/9 GR did have one bout of fighting when a young officer, Lieutenant Dodds, and two platoons from C Company, supported by a detachment of National Guardsmen, closed in on Kali Vrisi, an isolated village high up in the hills, with the mission of arresting wanted Communists. A group of ELAS resisted, whereupon a fire fight broke out during which the Communists lost nine killed and eight were taken into custody.

That incident apart, patrolling tended to become fairly routine, especially when the more notorious ELAS leaders either went into hiding or were forced to flee over the frontier into Yugoslavia or Bulgaria. That so many 'wanted' men escaped was sometimes due to information about impending searches, by British and Government troops, being leaked deliberately – and on other occasions due to the inability of Greek villagers to keep a secret for long!

Another problem facing the British Army was that, when members of ELAS were apprehended and thrown into gaol, thereafter no charges against the detainees were brought for months on end. D.H. Cox, who was Town Major of Kozani, remembers a notorious member of KKE who had been arrested in his presence. Weeks later Cox saw the same man when he was inspecting the gaol; he was told that the prisoner had still not been charged with any offence. Cox's final comment was: 'Outside our supervision, I think there was little to choose between the questionable actions of either side.' Clearly, it was impossible for the thinly spread British forces to control or restrain the exuberance of the National Guard.

Because few could speak Greek fluently, British officers and NCOs were forced to rely on the services of interpreters. Some of these were exceptionally brave, fair-minded men but others found it difficult to resist the temptation to interpret and produce the answer they felt would please the British. 'The Greeks have a genius for divining what they think the foreigner wishes to hear and telling him it, regardless of the true facts,' wrote a British observer who knew the Greeks well and admired them greatly. Without doubt, a handful of interpreters were swayed by their right-wing sympathies, so that the inability of the vast majority of British troops to speak more than a few words of Greek was a distinct disadvantage in their difficult role of trying to hold the ring between two bitterly opposed factions.

All that can be claimed on the British troops' behalf is that they did their best, and although mistakes were made – and injustices resulted, often without their knowledge, in the main the average soldier had a genuine sympathy for the Greek people, especially in the villages, where they felt that the majority of the peasants were innocent victims of events. One aspect of the Greek character that the British found difficult to understand, and at times stomach, was their cruelty to each other and to animals. An emaciated donkey being thrashed by an unrepentant owner would rouse British soldiers to open anger.

The British Government's desire to keep Greece within its sphere of influence had been achieved at a comparatively heavy cost, but Varkiza did not resolve the country's problems. General Plastiras proved to be no politician, a man hasty in judgement and impetuous, by training and temperament unsuited to resolve the mammoth tasks that faced his Government. To make his task more difficult, in effect the British were saying: 'We will provide financial aid and advisers and help to raise and train your National Guard, but it is your country – get on with it.' Unfortunately successive Greek Governments – there were four during

1945 – were quite incapable of dealing with roaring inflation and its many side-effects and, with the electoral roll still in a chaotic state, were unable to comply with British pressure that an early election be held, followed by a plebiscite to decide the King's future.

Despite British protests, the numbers going into prison remained higher than the numbers being released; the judiciary were swamped, and inevitably this added fuel to the fire as far as Siantos and his colleagues were concerned. On more than one occasion, they visited Leeper to complain, accusing their own Government of fostering terrorism and carrying out illegal arrests. At the same time, the discovery of arms dumps and fresh graves of hostages served to stoke up the bitterness and encouraged the 'Monarcho-Fascist terrorists', such as the infamous 'X' under the right-wing extremist Grivas, to take the law into their own hands – especially if there were no British troops in a particular area.

In the end, it did not matter who was Prime Minister, Plastiras or Admiral Voulgaris (who succeeded to the bed of nails in April), because circumstances were against them: their Government had no resources, no power over the judiciary, so that death sentences were passed on ELAS prisoners rather than against known collaborators of the Axis Occupation period. As a retired Greek colonel was to state: 'Prisoners go in as ordinary people and come out as Communists.' There were too many men with bitter memories for true reconciliation to begin, let alone thrive.

In the midst of the continued political unrest, warm tribute must be paid to the reconstruction work carried out by the Royal Engineers, who generally helped to get communications going where none had existed in the hinterland. For example, the 4th Indian Division Engineers in Macedonia built and repaired forty-four bridges, often in conditions that were extremely difficult during a most severe winter. There was scarcely a bridge site which had not been mined by the Germans, and possible construction sites nearby were also suspect. As the warmer weather came, anti-malaria precautions had to be strictly observed, which prevented working parties camping close to some sites. Finally, and especially in the case of the 4th Indian Divisional Engineers, the sappers had been trained and employed continuously in an operational role during the war; now, for the first time, they had to learn to build the permanent and semi-permanent bridges which formed the bulk of their tasks in Macedonia. In the words of their Journal: 'These achievements have been made possible largely by the fine spirit and determination of all ranks to see the job through in the face of considerable difficulties.' After such efforts they could see the fruits of their labours – unlike so many British advisers in other fields who worked hard but to little avail.

Tribute must also be paid to a small band of very courageous British Red Cross women who struggled valiantly to ensure that food and supplies were distributed fairly, conscious that many village committees favoured their friends and discriminated against their old political enemies. Occasionally, when feelings became too heated, supplies had to be withheld for a period, but this measure could be of a temporary duration only because the ladies realized that, inevitably, the poorest would suffer if nothing whatever was given out. The dilemma that faced these ladies, the Red Cross and UNRRA officials, as well as British troops, was that an equitable distribution was difficult to achieve: as far as most village elders were concerned, the political persuasion of the supplicants was the overriding factor, not the degree of hunger.

During spring 1945 the political situation appeared to show some improvement, with units of the Greek National Guard beginning to establish themselves in most parts of the country. One ELAS *kapetano* who refused to compromise was Aris Veloukhiotis, whose verdict on the Varkiza Treaty was, 'We have been betrayed.' Thereafter he took to the mountains with a small band of devoted followers to continue to defy his enemies. There were occasional clashes, once near the Albanian border when his group lost nine killed, with a further eight captured. Until he himself was killed on 16 July, Aris operated either from Albanian territory or hugged the border, continually hounded by the National Guard, occasionally betrayed and eventually shot.

The bodies of Aris and his adjutant were handed over to the police at Trikkala. Two days later, when R.H.A. Cockburn was passing through the town square, he noticed two heads on a lamp post. On inquiring of the police the reason for the macabre display, he was told in French (which most educated Greeks spoke) and with a smile: '*Ah, monsieur – pour encourager les autres.*' Whether it did or not is debatable; certainly it was a custom adopted in other towns and villages during the Civil War after 1946.

By the time of his death Aris, although a legend in ELAS circles, had been disowned by Siantos and his colleagues. Then it was Siantos' turn for demotion when, without warning, he found himself superceded because, after being a prisoner for nearly ten years and surviving the horrors of Dachau, Nikos Zachariades had re-emerged from obscurity to return to Greece and take up his old post of Secretary-General of the Communist Party.

Trained in the USSR, Zachariades was a true Stalinist by belief and conviction. After resuming power in KKE, he made it clear that he was against an organized return to the mountains, prior to a renewal of nationwide guerrilla activity. Zachariades felt it was better to delay any insurrection until the British forces had withdrawn, which, with the war in Europe ending on VE Day, seemed a distinct possibility in the very near future. His hopes were raised, too, when in July Winston Churchill was defeated at the polls in the British election and a Labour Government took office.

Prior to the British election, the Right in Greece had hoped for a Conservative victory, while the Left looked to Labour, not only to win but to make radical changes in British policy towards Greece. In the event, although Attlee's victory was received with open jubilation by the Left, both sides were to be disappointed because, gradually it became apparent that British foreign policy would not change overnight. The political defeat of the Conservatives did not mean that they were to be subjected to intimidation – or that 'the old man, Churchill' would have to take to the hills, the normal fate of displaced politicians in Greece at that time! John Hudson, CO 1/9 GR, has recounted that, after the defeat of Churchill in the General Election, the commanding officer of the nearest Greek battalion sent a message asking him if any of the officers were to be shot, and did he want any help!

It was yet another illustration of Greek politics, whose extremes the average British observer in the country, be he politician, soldier or journalist, found it difficult to understand – and more especially if they tried to equate the opposing Left and Right factions in Greece with British political parties. James Thomson of the Queen's Own Camerons summed it up: 'Politics are their hobby, their passion. When a Government changes, all the local officials change too – even down to a lavatory attendant!'

The red-hot intensity of Greek politics was something that amazed the British troops who served in Greece after the Second Round was over. J.R. Probyn of 2/7 GR recalls that, 'In one village, north of Kilkis in Macedonia, political feelings went so deep that the Nationalists colour-washed their houses blue and the Communists pink: when the Gurkha company was there, an uneasy peace prevailed, with the two factions drinking at separate cafés … it was obvious that the main talk was about politics. That point was brought home to me, once more, when we were on patrol and came across a boy who was wandering and found that he had been disowned by his family because he was a Boy Scout. This was a Communist family, and Boy Scouts owed allegiance to the King! How deeply rooted politics were in Greece was brought home to me by that example!'

One other sphere in which the British played a major part was the remodelling of the Greek Army. To build up a strong and efficient army in a country which had known 3½ years of Axis domination was no easy task. Towards the end of 1944 hastily formed units were recruited and sent out to various parts of the country to help restore law and order. Inevitably, their standard of discipline and training varied considerably, and improvement could be made only if operational circumstances so allowed and there were British instructors available locally. To illustrate the problem at the top: in the spring of 1945, ten out of sixteen generals on the active list had not served with the Army for the past seven to twelve years, and it was not until May 1946 that most of those were retired. Moreover, successive War Ministers moved units around for political rather than military reasons so that indifferent leadership in the senior ranks contributed to morale which was volatile, fickle and often poor, thus resulting in desertions.

Communism within the ranks of the Greek Army was another serious danger, and for this the British must take some of the blame. After assessing the position from the viewpoint of Western-style of democracy, the Labour Government in London advised the Greeks against political discrimination in recruiting, advice that the Greek General Staff accepted with loyalty but genuine misgivings. EAM/ELAS took advantage of the situation and as a result there were Communists serving in the Army whose only purpose was to undermine discipline, spread disloyalty and eventually organize mutinies. It has been assessed by a British source that ten per cent of the National Gendarmerie, responsible for internal security, were Communist, and later in the Civil War, during the Third Round, this canker spread, especially when there were military setbacks.

A large British Military Mission had been established in 1945 to lay the foundations from which a new Greek Army would spring. One of its first tasks was to establish a really sound system of recruit training all over the country. Whether the tactical doctrine, taught by the Military Mission was best suited to a country like Greece, four-fifths of which was mountainous, with primitive communications, is debatable. Oliver Plant, serving as a junior officer with the Military Mission, has stated that some of the programmes were based on the RMA Sandhurst curriculum and seemed to him inappropriate for operations against partisan irregulars, operating in the mountains. He also recalls that the Greek War Office files were in a chaotic state – as was to be expected after the turmoil of the 1940-41 war, followed by the Axis Occupation and the Second Round.

As the end of 1945 approached, the activities of left-wing armed bands and an increasing number of armed civilians of right-wing sympathy increased. Despite the Varzika Agreement, between February and late summer it is estimated that 20,000 ex-guerrillas were arrested, and EAM was to claim that over 500 of that number were murdered, and nearly 3,000 condemned to death. The word 'compromise' was rarely, if ever, heard. One notable exception to this extremism was Archbishop Damaskinos, who had inherited a crown of thorns as regent and, with a great sense of duty towards his countrymen, strove for reconciliation.

The British Government continued to press for an early plebiscite, disliking their indefinite responsibility for Greek affairs, especially when peacetime austerity measures had to be enforced in the United Kingdom by the Labour Government. It was understandable that the cost of stationing over 16,000 British troops in Greece, plus all the other forms of aid given the country, was being increasingly questioned by the Cabinet.

Admiral Voulgaris, who took over in April, remained Prime Minister for about six months. Like his predecessor, Plastiras, he had no political experience. His 'Service Government' consisted of Army and Navy officers and professional men. The Right Wing, who had assisted in the downfall of Plastiras, welcomed it as the next step to the return of the King, while the Left, who had previously abused Plastiras, now praised him and lamented his going. Irrespective of who was Prime Minister, there is little doubt that the average Greek citizen moved further to the right than the Greek Government ever intended and, by so doing, provided martyrs for ELAS to proclaim, as well as giving their newspapers ammunition for violent attacks against 'The British Army of Occupation and the Greek Fascist Government'. In truth, the one thing in common that appeared in the speeches made by the politicians of both sides was that there was a distinct absence of any constructive programme, because they spent most of the time attacking each other virulently and complaining that the other side had no programme whatever! The deposed General Plastiras made a tour, trying to rally the support of moderates, while he attacked the Communists and Monarchists with equal fervour and declared his aim was to see a democratic republic. The old general attracted large audiences, but few influential figures had the courage to support him publicly in his proposed middle way.

In such an atmosphere, Grivas, at the head of X Organization, stepped up an extensive 'white terror' campaign against the Communists, 'the Red Fascists of Moscow', and in certain towns, particularly Verioa and Kozani, X began to show its strength for the first time. Of even more concern was the fact that National Guardsmen were to be seen wearing its badges and openly demonstrating their allegiance to the organization.

As Prime Minister, Voulgaris, some of whose policies were

sound and sensible, failed to get his way by persuasion, and in
September he too was forced to resign. By the end of the year
Kanellopoulos, for a few days only, and Sophoulos had both
been given mandates. The appointment of Sophoulos, an old
Republican Liberal, as Prime Minister was welcomed by the
Left so that temporarily they decided to give his Cabinet their
support; for a few weeks, agitation against the Government
and the British Labour Party ceased. Meanwhile, at their
Seventh Congress, the Greek Communist Party admitted past
mistakes, including the abduction of hostages earlier that
year.

Although no decision was taken to begin another
insurrection, armed resistance ('self-defence' being the
phrase) was permitted 'against the Right's carnage in the
countryside' (Markos Vapheiadis). It appeared that no one
wanted the Civil War to break out by deliberate intent,
although the impossibility of a true compromise or
reconciliation between the extremes, on the right and left,
brought violence ever nearer with an air of inevitability.

Some commentators have accused the British Government
of having brought about this sort of climate. Their case is
that, the British having taken up arms against the Left and
won the Second Round, late 1945 saw the new Labour
Government adopting a *laisser-faire* policy. While prepared to
give advice and, in fairness, to grant generous financial help
at a time of grave stringency in Britain, there was marked
indecision, vacillation and deep-seated reluctance to interfere
in the affairs of a friendly foreign country. Their argument is
that British influence could have been used to ensure that the
rebellion, which began to spread especially in Macedonia and
along the Greek-Yugoslav border, was checked before it
became a full-scale civil war. The British policy, or lack of it,
puzzled the Greeks because, just as long as British troops
remained in the country, there seemed to be a clear duty to
help the Greek Government in every way – the sensible
alternative being to withdraw all the fighting formations of
the Army at once. This lack of effectiveness won the British
few friends, as they were accused by the Right of restraining
their efforts to destroy the Communists, while the Left held
them guilty of supporting the Monarchists, accusing them of
being an army of occupation.

Zachariades began to preach his doctrine of 'Mass Popular Self-Defence', stopping just short of calling for an all-out war. By the end of 1945 over 4,000 armed Greek Communist guerrillas, many of them trained in Yugoslavia, had gained control in the mountain villages of north Macedonia and Thessaly. As ELAS had done before them, in the areas under their jurisdiction special tribunals were set up to try and punish their Nationalist opponents, schools were re-opened under Communist teachers, and young men were forced to join their bands of partisans.

During December 1945 there was a startling increase in guerrilla activity throughout Thrace where road and telephone communications were cut until, in modern parlance, there were several Communist 'no-go' areas. At a time when the 4th Indian Division was preparing to return to India, the British 13th Infantry Division arrived under Major-General Allan Adair. The 13th Division and other British troops stationed in Greece at that time were given orders to be prepared to deter any foreign aggression, and to support the government of the day in the maintenance of law and order. Any other assistance which might be requested in an internal security situation could be provided if necessary but orders given the senior commanders were specific: Greek forces were to be used in the first instance and only if required were the British to act in support of them. A hope was expressed that they '… would in no way interfere with political activity and would treat all Greeks alike without discrimination on political grounds'. They did *try* to comply!

When Russia complained in the Security Council that British troops were being used in order to shape the political future of Greece, the British Government replied that they were there in response to the wishes of the Greek Government and that after free democratic elections, followed by a plebiscite, had been held, the British Army would be withdrawn. Although the unrest in the countryside once more provided strong arguments for the postponement of the election, a date was fixed, 31 March 1946, and to this end the Allied Mission for Observing the Greek elections (AMFOGE) began to arrive in December, consisting of British, French and American members who would remain in the country until after the elections had been held. In an atmosphere of continuing unrest and open clashes between the Nationalists and Communists, EAM and KKE finally announced that they would abstain from taking any part in the elections. They alleged that their followers had been persecuted so that a fair result would be impossible, as well as accusing the Government of compiling electoral rolls which were inaccurate.

Behind the scenes the decision not to participate in the elections was taken on the advice of Zachariades – although the majority of Communist Party organizers favoured participation. Years later Thanasis Hajis (Secretary-General of EAM, 1941-4), was to state: 'But Zachariades thought the situation was revolutionary and did not want to get entangled in parliamentary procedures. He thought that this would alienate people from the prospect of an armed confrontation which they wanted and at the same time block that prospect.' From the statement it would appear that the Stalinist Zachariades wanted revolution rather than ballot-box democracy – even if it risked open warfare.

On 31 March the elections duly took place, carefully observed by the 1,200 members of AMFOGE, and apart from one major incident in Macedonia, the day passed quietly. With the Left abstaining, the result was a foregone conclusion: out of the 354 seats, the right-wing parties won 231 seats. Arguments about the election, and in particular about the numbers who had abstained, continued for many weeks after the event – until silenced, to a certain extent, when observers reported that, 'On the whole, the elections had been free and fair and, as far as they could ascertain, represented a true and valid verdict of the Greek people.' Forty-nine per cent of the total electorate voted and none could say how many people had abstained for political reasons. Once again there was a change of Prime Minister: Constantine Tsaldaris, leader of the Populist Party, took over.

Prior to Tsaldaris' taking up the appointment, the first phase of the Third Round of the Greek Civil War had begun, although initially attacks were limited to hit-and-run raids on isolated villages and small units of Government troops. This phase was to continue until mid 1947.

The rebels, now called the Democratic Army, were

commanded by Markos, and it was not long before he became 'King of the Mountains'. In retrospect it is strange that Sarafis was not invited to return in any capacity but in the eyes of Zachariades and, possibly, Markos, he was not a true Communist for he had never joined the Party.

Although the insurrection began in the rural areas, and especially the more remote parts of the mountainous country, Zachariades remained convinced that the decisive struggle for power would take place in the cities. Unlike Markos, he had been away from Greece during the Occupation and had not seen how successful small groups of ELAS guerrillas could be when operating as irregulars in the rural areas. Nor was he present when that same ELAS movement had attempted to take on a conventional army in Athens and had suffered accordingly after the British had flown in reinforcements. For Zachariades, any guerrilla campaign in the mountains could only be a diversion, designed to create a climate of uncertainty that would undermine the people's trust in the ever-changing governments in Athens.

The power-struggle between Markos and Zachariades started in October 1945 at the 7th Communist Congress, when it was decided to dismantle the KKE/EAM structure in the countryside, an order that disorganized the Party in the rural areas at a time when its branches should have been strengthened in every way possible. With the comfort of hindsight, it can be concluded that the orthodox KKE leadership had become increasingly suspicious of the *kapetanios*, beginning with Aris and finally focusing on Markos himself.

Although the Russians had refused to send observers to the General Election in Greece in March, Zachariades still hoped they would come to the assistance of Greek Communists. Stalin was out of touch, however, and against meddling in Greek affairs after having agreed with Churchill that it was to remain a British prerogative. Later, Tempo, a Communist, was to write: 'The leadership of the Soviet Union had no interest whatever in the victory of the People's Revolutionary Movement in Greece, because Greece was geographically remote from the Soviet Union (hence intervention of the Soviet Army was out of the question), because it was outside the sphere of interest of the Soviet Union (by agreement between the Governments of the Soviet Union and the Western Imperialists).'

The Royalists having won a handsome victory at the elections, which were devoid of violence, it was a mere formality that the King would win a parliamentary majority when the plebiscite was held in September, and King George II returned after six years in exile. Inevitably, his return was the signal for increased violence, with raid after raid launched against police or isolated National Guard posts. By the end of the year there was open revolution in the country – apart from southern Greece and the islands, which were comparatively free from armed bands – in which the British were loath to get involved. Understandably they did not want to have to put down another left-wing-inspired insurrection.

During all this period, senior members of the KKE continued to live ostensibly blameless lives in Athens while their Communist newspapers pumped out anti-British propaganda with unabating vigour. The Left wanted the British out, and by this time the British too wanted to depart: they had spent over £28 million and by now the Labour Government thought that enough was enough.

1947 was a bad year for Greece as the Civil War gained momentum and as hopes of a quick, bloodless ending steadily receded. On 21 February the British Government announced that it could not provide equipment or supplies for the Greek armed forces beyond 31 March – although, fortunately for Western-style democracy in Greece, the Americans decided to fill the gap when President Truman persuaded the US Congress to provide the necessary funds. The British Military Mission remained behind but by now the responsibility for bolstering the Greek armed forces against the Democratic Army lay with the Americans. Nevertheless, it must not be forgotten that the basic foundations on which the new Greek Army was built, and eventually proved victorious, were laid by a dedicated band of British advisers and instructors who had helped to raise and train the Greek Army after Varkiza in February 1945.

10 Epilogue – The Third Round

'Among those who dislike oppression are many who like to oppress'

Napoleon

King George II, a correct, dutiful but colourless monarch who lacked the common touch, died in April 1947. He was succeeded by his brother Paul, who was not much more forthcoming, but fortunately for Greece his consort, Queen Frederika was a fearless woman, with an outgoing personality, who was not afraid to mix with anyone. While her opponents called her overbearing, in time she even received tributes from the revolutionary spirits of the International Press!

Seven weeks after the passing of George II, the king he had hated, George Siantos died, leaving Nikos Zachariades undisputed leader of the rebel government in Greece, one that was never to be recognized by the Soviet Union. Zachariades continued his purges of the *kapetanios* while exhorting his Communist followers with the cry, 'Everyone to arms – all for victory.'

In the end, 150,000 Greeks died in the civil war, with another 100,000 homeless, destitute people forced to be refugees, the flotsam of man's inhumanity to man. The fact that there were so many refugees was caused by the burning of houses, and sometimes complete villages, by both sides, an act of barbarity carried out on several occasions by the Germans which was subsequently practised and improved upon by the Greek protagonists. Needless to say, both factions denied ever carrying out such acts and could claim

243

that they had documentary evidence to show who was to blame.

With direct British involvement in 'the Third Round' being minimal – even though it was a drama in which Anglo-Greek interests were inextricably linked – its details are not part of this book. Briefly, the war itself fell into three stages, the first being from February 1946 to midsummer 1947, when the Democratic Army's activities were confined to hit-and-run raids against isolated villages and small-scale actions against Government troops. By the end of that stage, Markos had about 8,000 *andartes* under his command so that, when August 1947 arrived, the guerrilla leader felt he was strong enough to intensify operations on a much wider scale. During the following year his army's effective strength rose to as many as 25,000, and attacks were launched against large provincial centres such as Florina, Konitsa, Grevena and Alexandroupolis, his aim being to capture a town of respectable size so that a rival Greek administration could be set up, one that he and Zachariades hoped would be recognized by the Communist bloc. After heavy fighting and considerable losses, all these attacks failed, so that once more Markos decided to return to more orthodox guerrilla tactics, whose success induced the Greek Government to declare a state of martial law on 19 October 1948.

By that time American aid was pouring into the country, and General Van Fleet, an able and vigorous soldier who played a big part in events until the end of the civil war, came to co-ordinate, advise and often cajole the Greek General Staff into action. American soldiers did not take up arms against the rebels, but counter-insurgency operations were co-ordinated by the Joint United States Military Advisory and Planning Group, a highly efficient organization even if at times its members were somewhat naïve and insensitive to Greek pride. When the Americans criticized the rather conventional, orthodox tactical doctrines the British Military Mission had been teaching, there was some validity in their strictures, especially as most of the action was fought in the mountains. The guerrillas built up fairly secure bases in the mountainous areas of Grammos and Vitsi and, whenever they suffered a severe reverse, the majority of the partisans withdrew across the frontier to find sanctuary in Yugoslavia,

Bulgaria or Albania. Those friendly Communist neighbours also served as a source of supplies and as a training ground for new recruits, volunteers as well as those who had been forcibly coerced into joining the Democratic Army.

By late 1948 the situation began to change in the Government's favour, with much-needed Army reorganization being effected under General Papagos, recalled from retirement for the first time since 1941, when he was Commander-in-Chief during the Axis invasion. In the late summer of 1948 the National Army mounted a succession of attacks on Grammos, which is more than a mountain – a succession of peaks 4,000-7,000 feet in height, a forbidding bastion to have to carry by storm. Markos' *andartes* were supported by up to forty artillery pieces on the mountain, and although the weight of attack by ground and air eventually drove them back from peak to peak, Markos was able to conduct a successful retreat and save all his guns. Once again, most of the vanquished crossed the border into Albania, only a few weeks later to infiltrate back and re-form in the forests around Mount Vitsi.

Despite the vast numerical superiority of the National Army, which had increased its overall strength to 250,000 men, largely by the creation of new battalions for the National Defence Corps, the likelihood of the war's continuing for months, even years to come, still prevailed. Two events, however, changed the situation radically. First, increasing disputes between Tito and Stalin led to a total breakdown of Russo-Yugoslav relations and eventually to Tito's expulsion from the Comintern, and on 10 July 1949 Tito closed the Yugoslav border to the Democratic Army, which thus lost one of its main sources of supplies. It was a crippling blow. The second major factor was the indifferent leadership of Zachariades, who decided that larger formations should be created, thus making the fatal mistake of thinking that his partisans were capable of fighting in open country, against a conventional army, supported by an air force. In contrast, Markos had always realized that the Democratic Army's only hope was to operate in small, independent mobile units, and for such a reason his largest unit was a battalion of only about 500 men. As to why Zachariades changed that well-proven system of operating is difficult to say, unless he had been swayed by the example of Tito and Mao Tse-Tung in their respective campaigns. Markos protested to no avail: brigades, and then divisions, were formed before he himself was dismissed – 'for health reasons' – and Zachariades took over personal command.

In August 1949 the revitalized National Army, under the field command of General Tsakalotas, an egoistic, impetuous but brilliant soldier, once more stormed partisan bases in the Grammos and Vitsi mountains. In face of the overwhelming superiority of the National Army in all aspects, desertions increased and were one way only. On 15 August Tsakalotas reported to King Paul, who had come to witness the final throes of the Democratic Army: 'Your Majesty, Grammos has fallen. You can start on your return journey whenever you decide.' On 16 October 1949 the Communists announced a ceasefire with the words, 'We have decided to discontinue the armed struggle for the time being.' They had been defeated even if they were never going to admit it.

It had been a costly war – for everyone. In terms of military aid, the Americans had contributed 140 aircraft, about 4,000 artillery pieces and mortars, nearly 100,000 rifles and small arms, and over 10,000 motor vehicles. Their financial contribution reached the staggering total of $260 million, and it is estimated that the elimination of each Greek *andarte* during the war had cost the American people $19,000.

Important though the American contribution had been, there was also a dramatic transformation in the National Army, which suddenly found its spirit as real leaders emerged. Papagos, who was a superlative staff officer and planner – which he backed with the necessary seniority, played a big part in the final stages: he could be called the Eisenhower of the Greek Civil War. However, the paramount factor was that the Greek rebellion, fermented and sustained by its Communist neighbours, fell apart when that alliance ended. It was the death blow to the Third Round. It also marked the end of an era for the British Army: after being stationed in Greece for five years, the last British troops left the country in November 1949.

As far as most British soldiers were concerned, Greece between 1945 and 1949 had been but one of several world-wide postings which involved them in insurgency and counter-insurgency operations. There was one difference, though: instead of feelings of enmity towards the majority of the Greek people, there were strong ties of affection and respect. Those who have returned to their old haunts in Greece, and renewed old friendships, have been much moved by the welcome given them, undimmed by the years and by doubts about the British Mission to Greece expressed by modern left-wing writers. Not surprisingly, those British participants take a very different view of events in which they played a part, insignificant though it might have appeared at the time.

In the words of Theodore Roosevelt: 'It is not the critic who counts nor the man who points out how the strong man stumbled, or where the doer of deeds could have done them better. The credit belongs to the man who is actually in the arena, whose face is marred by dust and sweat and blood; who knows the great enthusiasms, the great devotions, and spends himself in a worthy cause; who at the best knows in the end the triumph of high achievement; and who at the worst, if he fails, at least fails while daring greatly so that his place shall never be with those cold and timid souls who know neither victory nor defeat.'

11 Judgement

'And the brave victories that seem so splendid are
never really won.'

Sara Teasdale

When viewing Britain's decision to go to the aid of Greece, at
first with limited assistance against the Italians and then with
the ill-fated Imperial Expeditionary Force in spring 1941, it
is important to remember how badly affairs were going in the
war against the Axis at that time. Until Mussolini decided to
attack Greece in October 1940, Britain stood alone and even
the most optimistic of her sons and daughters could see little
chance of victory, even if they were determined not to submit
to Fascist dictators.

Against such a background, it is ludicrous to claim, as
Andreas Kedros has in *The Mistakes of the Allies and the Mistakes
of the Resistance*, that, 'Churchill was taking a risk – he was
launching a "take-over bid" against post-war Greece. In his
eyes, undoubtedly, this gesture apparently gratuitous (but
very expensive in human lives) justified in advance the fact
that Great Britain was to chain post-war Greece securely to
British Imperial policy.' It is impossible to take such a
statement seriously, especially when no one in early 1941,
including Churchill, could have foretold that both the USSR
and USA would be in the war, on Britain's side, before the
end of the year. Andreas Kedros also states that, 'He
[Churchill] had probably foreseen what was going to happen
as he was a political and military genius.' Great war leader
though he was, Churchill did not possess the gift of foresight
and, as for being a military genius, those officers who served
as his Chiefs of Staff in Whitehall would have combined to

refute such a claim: indeed, their recorded comments indicate that Churchill was the opposite of a military genius.

The truth was that Churchill was guided by reports from Athens, sent by Eden and his delegation, before he was able to persuade a reluctant War Cabinet to agree to the BEF's being despatched from Egypt. It was more than taking a risk: it was a decision that was to have far-reaching, disastrous military consequences for the Desert Campaign, as well as clouding the relationship between 'the Old Country' and the Dominions of Australia and New Zealand. Another serious upshot was the loss of invaluable ships of the Royal Navy in the waters around Greece and Crete, ships that were badly needed in the struggle to keep the maritime communications open in the Mediterranean and elsewhere.

However, while it can hardly be denied that, from a purely military point of view, it was a bad decision, the despatch of the BEF represented an act of British faith and humanity towards a country that Britain owed much for her refusal to submit to the bullying of Benito Mussolini – and in 1941 that debt of gratitude was repaid, to some extent, even if the outcome was a resounding defeat. With all the burdens on Churchill at that time, it was a brave decision, one that won British countless friends in neutral countries and especially in the USA.

Critics like Kedros tend to look through retrospective glasses at the political consequences stemming from that decision and forget that Britain stood alone in 1941, staring defeat in the face. It would have been impossible for Churchill, with all the pressures on him, to have spent time devising schemes for the long-term future of the British Empire after the war, while Greece and its post-war status were well down his priority list.

Where we can agree with Kedros is that, as a direct result of British intervention in 1941, the links between Greece and Britain continued to be as strong as in the past. Unfortunately those ties were viewed in different ways by the FO, SOE (Cairo) and GHQ Middle East Command. The FO, with Churchill's support, especially at the beginning, assumed that King George II would automatically return to Greece after the war was over and take up where he had left off in 1941. On the other hand, the handful of British officers who parachuted into Greece on the orders of SOE (Cairo) appreciated that feeling against the King's return was about the only political issue on which there was overwhelming agreement – the King was depicted as the main supporter of the old Fascist regime of Metaxas, the bogy-man being returned to Greece at the instigation of Churchill and the British, against the democratic wishes of the people. Belated efforts to ameliorate the situation with promises by the King of a plebiscite came far too late and were not taken seriously by the majority of the Greek people, and especially by left-wing politicians.

The decision to defend Crete in 1941 had no political undertones and was taken for military reasons only. Looking back at the battle for Crete after nearly forty-eight years, there seem to be three factors of paramount importance. First, it was a battle the British might just have won, but even if they had defeated Student's airborne invasion, the cost in ships, aircraft and men, while trying to retain the island against any further invasions, would have been prohibitive, to say the least. That begs the question as to whether Crete was worth fighting for in the first place, during May of that year.

Second, the enormous advantages that the code-breaker Ultra in London gave the British Chiefs of Staff proved counter-productive in the battle for Crete because, while the planners in Whitehall were able to peer into the minds of the enemy, they were unable to appreciate that their own commander on the spot – in this case, General Freyberg – did not have the means to deal with the invasion and, in particular, lacked adequate support from fighter aircraft and anti-aircraft guns, to offset the Luftwaffe's overwhelming superiority.

Third, the Luftwaffe alone stood between Student and a costly defeat, and when the pendulum swung violently against the defenders, it was the German airmen who exacted such a heavy toll of RN ships – but at a cost to themselves. Although this factor did not directly concern Greece's future, the heavy German losses in Crete certainly had a long-term effect on Hitler's strategy in other theatres because it spelt the end of massive airborne assaults by the Germans. The British gambled with such a concept when they launched their ill-fated airborne armada to seize Arnhem in 1944, with dire results, to confirm what the Germans had learnt in Crete three years before.

King George of the Hellenes just managed to evade capture in Crete and after escaping to the Middle East became the symbol of the legitimate Greek Government in Exile, even though he and his ministers ceased to have any jurisdiction in Greece itself. If the King had been captured by the Germans, would the subsequent story of the Resistance, the 1944 Liberation and the Civil War have been different? Would King George II, in captivity, possibly as a puppet-monarch, have attracted more sympathy than he did living comfortably in Cairo at a time when his countrymen were groaning in torment under the Axis occupiers? No one can answer such questions without indulging in the realms of fiction. It must be stressed, though, that it was not the Resistance that polarized Greece into factions: the country had been divided before Metaxas assumed power. His autocratic regime only served to take reconciliation beyond the realms of possibility during the lives of the generation who survived that unsettled era.

As my aim has been to examine Britain's mission to Greece between 1941 and 1946, one of the most difficult questions to answer concerns the Resistance Movement, in particular to assess the importance of the role played by Britain. To what extent did the SOE initiate and inspire resistance and, as the movement grew, co-ordinate action? What would have happened had there been no Operation Harling, no Brigadier Eddie Myers, no BMM or AMM? In order to consider those questions, we have to remember that several Greek writers, and especially those who were participants serving with EAM and ELAS, claim that the movement was more than just resistance to oppression: it was a wide-spread expression of national liberation.

That the people of Greece – and not just the politically minded members of KKE/EAM Central Committees – held firm against the Axis occupiers is a fact that cannot be disputed. We remember BLO John Mulgan's tribute when he wrote, 'The real heroes of the Greek War of Resistance were the common people of the hills. It was on them, with their bitter, uncomplaining endurance, that the German terror broke. They produced no traitors.' Such a people would have opposed the Germans and Italians, with or without outside help, although for specific operations British leadership and professional expertise (for example, in demolition and communication skills) were vital ingredients, over and above the arms, ammunition, supplies and scores of gold sovereigns that were provided by GHQ Middle East Command.

We can conclude that there would have been a reasonably effective resistance without the British officers who parachuted in, but its achievements would have been of a different nature. One example springs to mind: no large-scale destruction of the Asopos viaduct. Be that as it may, Resistance in Greece did present the occupiers with grave problems, and it was not surprising that the Germans took full advantage of the bitter feuds between ELAS on the one hand, and EKKA and EDES on the other. It was in their best interest that Greek fought Greek rather than the *andartes* combining to harass German garrisons and cut road and rail communications outside Athens. The Germans adopted a divide-and-rule strategy such as the British had themselves employed in the past to secure and retain their Empire.

Like the Germans in Greece, the British have been accused of deliberately dividing the Resistance, by dint of their full-hearted support for EDES, especially during the winter months of the First Round, when their intervention undoubtedly saved Zervas from overwhelming defeat. Left-wing adherents claim that without British intervention EDES would have been unable to continue as a separate force which, in time, would have meant a single National Liberation Army, so that, after the Germans had pulled their forces out of Greece, there would have been no Civil War. In such an eventuality, they argue, the British could not possibly have brought back the Government in Exile to Greece against the wishes of the whole nation, especially if the country was under the control of one unified army.

All this sounds plausible enough until an important question is posed: did the majority of the Greek people want to become citizens of a Communist People's Democracy? To such a question a variety of answers will be obtained, reflecting the differing political views of those asked. One fact that cannot be denied is that the reaction against

EAM/ELAS after Varkiza in 1945 was so strong that the pendulum of terrorization and intimidation began to swing the other way, something that can be explained to a certain extent by the atrocities previously committed by ELAS, culminating in the abduction of hostages from Athens which sent shockwaves through the nation. Of all the mistakes EAM/ELAS made, including vacillation and several changes of policy by their Central Committees, the one that cost them the support of the more moderate section of the Greek community resulted from the indiscriminately brutal acts carried out by some of their more irresponsible members.

KKE's subsequent allegations that the British Government decided to intervene in 1944 with a view to bringing Greece within its sphere of influence do not stand serious scrutiny, especially when it is remembered that the limited Operation Manna was mounted with the primary task of rehabilitation and help for the starving nation. The original composition of Scobie's force would have been far different had the British anticipated stiff resistance from the Germans before they evacuated the country, or had they expected to be involved in an armed struggle with ELAS. With British forces stretched to the limit in the Mediterranean theatre, neither of those options was anticipated or sought; indeed, with the battle for the Gothic Line in North Italy in full swing, the last thing Field Marshal Alexander wanted was a campaign in Greece or to be asked to divert badly needed troops and aircraft to that country. For such a reason, it is true that the British saw little merit in harassing the German Army to a major degree during their withdrawal before Liberation – both countries wanted to avoid excessive casualties, and under the circumstances that prevailed at the time such restraint was sensible even if subsequently open to misinterpretation by those who claimed that there was an unofficial agreement between the British and Germans. There never was one but assuredly it was in the interests of both Powers to avoid large-scale fighting at a time when the Germans had to evacuate Greece as a result of the Soviet Army's advance towards East Prussia.

If the motives of the British for not making serious attempts to stop the German evacuation are clear, then by the same token ELAS should not be blamed unduly for holding back in several parts of the country: with the hour of liberation at hand, surely it was a sensible decision not to risk unnecessary lives in operations which in the end would have done little to delay the departure of the German Army? This did not stop BLOs from accusing ELAS of holding back deliberately and jockeying for power, of moving partisan groups to certain strategic positions, ready for a take-over. In one or two areas ELAS accepted arms and ammunition from the Germans as payment for their non-intervention while the Nazi occupiers moved out of Greece. There is an element of truth in these allegations even if we accept that the primary reason was to avoid casualties as the hour of liberation approached.

Inevitably the passing years have softened, to a certain extent, the black-and-white opinions many of the participants had of the tragic period when the British fought alongside Greeks against Greeks. Nevertheless, the vast majority of ex-servicemen contacted while writing this book believes with great sincerity that the British Army's intervention saved Greece from a blood-bath and gave that nation a breathing space. F.J. Salfield, in the late autumn of 1945 when serving with the Royal Navy, wrote these words: 'Those Greeks, who gave us so much when they had so little, do not merely pray that we give back justice and freedom ... they take it for granted. If we fail them, it would be a betrayal of lovers.'

For different reasons such words might have earned the approbation of EAM/ELAS supporters too, because in their eyes there could be no justice and freedom if the King and the old-style politicians were restored to their pre-war positions of pre-eminence. With little common ground for constructive dialogue, the opposing politicians' arguments deteriorated into highly emotional outbursts, with such words as 'collaborator', 'intimidation', 'terrorization' and 'democracy' being bandied around until they ceased to mean anything except to the speaker. The Reverend H.T.L. Lees, an RAF chaplain taken prisoner at Kifissia by ELAS, had this to say about his captors: 'They spoilt their claim by wholesale denunciation of all but themselves as collaborators.'

Even when there was a period of comparative peace for a few months after Varkiza in February 1945, the war of words did not cease. In the eyes of the Nationalists, 'Skompie' (Scobie) and his small force had saved Greece from becoming a 'People's Democracy', and they assumed that the British Army would continue to help them until the Communist threat, posed by KKE/EAM/ELAS, had been totally eliminated. At the same time as right-wing newspapers were praising 'our glorious Ally', the Communist Press was conducting a vicious campaign against the British 'Occupation Army', seizing on any misdemeanours committed by its members and stating that the British alone were keeping the 'Fascist collaborators' in power.

In the welter of accusations and counter-accusations, it was, and still is, difficult to separate truth from myth, facts from fables. There were those like Aris who were convinced that force alone would bring about a new Socialist Greece and that, to achieve that end, the ugly weapons of physical coercion, including on occasions torture, were justified. Even if such methods won over adherents to the Communist Party, at the same time the support of countless moderates was lost, switching their allegiance to the King because they feared the KKE and its followers. With hatred of the Left increasing, the infamous X organization had no problem in finding recruits, especially from those who had lost close relatives or friends at the hands of ELAS. Everywhere violence began to increase in a rapid spiral until the Civil War affected every part of the land.

By that time the primary role of the British troops was to defend Greece against foreign aggression, and only if asked for assistance by the lawfully constituted Greek Government were they required to help the police local *gendarmerie* with the enforcement of law and order. The British Government expected Greece to stand on its own feet far too quickly after Varkiza, failing to realize that her internal wounds were too deep and recent for any sort of reconciliation. The British should and could have used their influence more. For example, sanctions could have been used to influence the Greek Government into speeding up trials of those held in custody for months on end, more often than not without formal charges being levelled against them. But by failing to exert pressure and trying to maintain the myth that they should not interfere in the affairs of a friendly country, the Labour Government in Britain allowed the Greek Government to indulge in acts which did enormous harm. One example was in July 1947 when the Government panicked and mass arrests were made; in August, twenty-four executions were carried out in one day. In the eyes of countless Greek citizens, those acts were conducted with the connivance of Britain, because the British Army stood by and did nothing.

Why did Communism not spread when, in theory, there was so much in Greece to make that country a perfect target for the creed of envy and class-hatred? The division between the rich in Athens and the poor in 'ELAS land', the social inequalities, the injustices that had existed for years, the bitter controversy over those who collaborated with the Axis and those innocent citizens who were accused of doing so: in theory, all these factors should have made a strong contribution to a swing towards Communism. That Greece hesitated was due to an excessive use of force by the Communists, not only while recruiting 'volunteers' but in their intimidatory methods while trying to persuade others to help establish a 'People's Democracy'. In far too many parts of Greece they failed to win the local people over willingly to their cause; instead the hard-core KKE pressed on with intimidation, unplanned for the most part, which drove many villagers in the mountains into direct opposition to the Communist regime.

However, that was not the only reason for the majority of the Greeks' finally deciding to reject Communism. The Greeks are great individualists – hence the saying, 'Every Greek a *kapetan*' ('Every soldier a commander-in-chief'). That is why Greeks say they need a dictator to achieve anything, someone powerful enough to direct their natural vitality before it dissipates like the autumn rains which flood the arid soil before disappearing.

'War abolishes the ease of ordinary life, is a hard master and shapes men's characters in their circumstances,' wrote Thucydides. Certainly the succession of tragic events that shook Greece from 1941 onwards shaped the lives of its citizens and inevitably drove a kindly people into committing acts which, under normal circumstances, they would not have contemplated. For example, the practice of burning houses and isolated villages, demonstrated by the Germans, was continued by both sides during the Civil War, despite vigorous denials at the time. 'In a civil war men are killed for their religion, their politics, their wealth or simply because they are in the way: the noble and ignoble perish together.' By the end of 1949 the total number of casualties, noble and ignoble, had run into thousands.

Another practice learnt from the Germans and carried out by the Nationalist Government during the Third Round was the detention of the families of partisans in order to induce the surrender of their menfolk. *Tromokatris* (terrorism) was used by both sides, and every act only added to the impossibility of reconciliation; mutual hatred was stronger than reason. The depth of the hatred was something the British never really understood; they expected moderates to emerge who would begin discussing matters rationally, as if the opponents were akin to the Conservative and Labour Parties in the United Kingdom. A Greek colonel, when comparing British politicians with those in his own country, summed up in these words: 'In Greece, it isn't like that. My politician is in power – I eat, you starve. Your politician is in power – you eat, I starve.'

Whilst the British Government's policy of *laisser-faire* during 1945 and 1946 has been queried – perhaps with justification – so too, must the strong pressure exerted on Scobie to make a precipitate peace at Varkiza, which came from the USA and for which President Roosevelt must be singled out for blame. In direct contrast, his successor, President Harry Truman, recognized that an armed Communist take-over of Greece would put the Eastern Mediterranean firmly behind the Iron Curtain, so that in 1947 the Truman Doctrine meant the despatch of vast quantities of American aid, especially money, arms and aircraft, to the assistance of the Greek Government. American intervention changed the balance of power and ensured that the Greek Armed Forces would never lack support from the air or from heavy weapons – unlike the Democratic Army, which mistakenly took on their opponents in open warfare against the advice of Markos. By jettisoning their experienced ex-ELAS officers and concentrating on a class-based struggle, Zachariades and his Committee played into the hands of the Nationalists.

During the years between 1941 and 1946, the British sent

some of their finest men to the assistance of Greece. The small band of gallant RAF aviators during the winter of 1940; the forlorn attempt by the Imperial Expeditionary Force in spring 1941; Eddie Myers, Chris Woodhouse and their dedicated band of BLOs; 'the great escaper', Frank Macaskie; Don Stott and his fellow saboteurs at the Asopos viaduct; the list is a long and honourable one. To select the *victor ludorum* from such distinguished company inevitably invites criticism, but I would nominate Ronald Scobie for that trophy. Largely unknown and a comparatively junior general, Scobie was given a task of great magnitude which he carried out despite the organized campaign of vilification against him from the politicians of the Left in Greece and the United Kingdom, supported by a large section of the American and British Press. He never wavered and, without being in the least flamboyant, impressed the Greeks with his dignity, calmness and unshakeable determination to achieve what he had been appointed to do. Even when, in December 1944, the situation appeared to be hopeless, Scobie never wavered.

A few years later, on the occasion of the dedication of the British War Cemetery at Phaliron, Scobie received a tumultuous welcome from an enormous crowd of people, men and women, who shouted '*Scompie! Scompie! Zito Scompie!*', recognizing that he and the British Army had saved them from a fate that would have seemed hideous to the majority. At the same time, in the cheering crowd must have been those who liked to oppress as well as those who feared oppression. The scars remained – and are there to this day, scars that time alone can heal.

'The path of duty lies in the thing nearby, but men seek it in things far off.' The path of duty led thousands of British to Greece, there to play a part, however small, in bringing about a victory that was never really won.

Chronology

Good Friday, April 1939	Mussolini's forces invaded Albania. Great Britain guarantees Greece support in the event of Axis aggression.
28 October 1940	Italy launched attack on Greece from Albania.
November 1940	RAF detachments, supported by British Army administrative personnel, began arriving in Greece.
January 1941	Greek Government under Metaxas refused British offer of help in event of German invasion. Germany continued build-up of forces in Romania.
23 February 1941	Greek PM Koryzis formally accepted British aid.
4 March 1941	General Maitland Wilson, Commander BEF, arrived in Athens to begin preparations for defence of Greece.
27 March 1941	*Coup* in Belgrade. King Peter of Yugoslavia's accession proclaimed.
6 April 1941	Germany attacked Greece and Yugoslavia.
12 April 1941	Yugoslavia surrendered.
20 April 1941	Greece decided to surrender. Decision made to evacuate the Imperial Expeditionary Force.
29 April 1941	Main evacuation completed.
20 May 1941	Germans invaded Crete.

1 June 1941	Last lift of Crete evacuation completed.
27 September 1941	Formation of EAM proclaimed publicly.
30 September 1942	First SOE parachuted in for 'Operation Harling' (destruction of Gorgopotamus viaduct).
June and early July 1943	'Operation Animals', deception plan of intense sabotage and guerrilla activity throughout Greece before Allied landings in Sicily.
Night 20/21 June 1943	Sabotage of Asopos viaduct by SOE party.
7 August 1943	First RAF Dakota landed in Occupied Greece to take Brigadier Myers and Resistance leaders to Cairo.
September 1943	Italians surrendered to Allies, including majority of their Occupying Force in Greece.
Winter 1943 – Spring 1944	'First Round', waged by EAM/ELAS against EDES and EKKA – which ended with the destruction of EKKA and death of Psarros, its leader.
March 1944	Formation of Political Committee of National Liberation (EAM Shadow Government, PEEA).
May 1944	Lebanon Conference under Greek PM George Papendreou, attended by Resistance leaders.
26 September 1944	Caserta Conference: placed ELAS and EDES under Greek Government, and Resistance organizations under General Scobie.
12 October 1944	Germans evacuated Athens, prior to complete withdrawal from Greece.
3 December 1944	'Second Round' began between ELAS and Government Forces, primarily British, Indian and Gurkha.
30 December 1944	Final defeat of EDES by ELAS.

11 January 1945	Truce ended 'Second Round' with military defeat of ELAS.
12 February 1945	Varkiza Agreement, formal end to fighting between Government and EAM/ELAS.
Late winter 1945	'Mass Popular Self-Defence' started by KKE under Zachariades.
31 March 1946	National elections under supervision of Allied Mission.
September 1946	King George II returned after plebiscite.
Winter 1946 – Autumn 1949	'The Third Round' of the Greek Civil War, which ended with final defeat of the Communist-controlled Democratic Army.

Bibliography

While writing this book, I have consulted and read with profit many works, and I would like to make grateful acknowledgement to those concerned who published, wrote or contributed to the following:

Archer, Laird, *Balkan Journal*. W.W. Norton (New York), 1944

Baerentzen, L. (extract from *Scandinavian Studies*), *Anglo-German Negotiations during the German Retreat from Greece, 1944*, 1980

Beevor, S.J.G., *SOE Recollections and Reflections*

Byford-Jones, W., *The Greek Trilogy*. Hutchinson, 1946

Capell, Richard, *Simiomata*. Macdonald & Co Ltd., 1946

Casson, Stanley, *Greece Against the Axis*. Hamish Hamilton, 1941

Chandler, Geoffrey, *The Divided Land*. Macmillan, 1959

Churchill, W.S., *The Second World War, Vols V-VII*. Cassell, 1950

Clark, Alan, *The Fall of Crete*. Anthony Blond Ltd., 1962

Collier, Richard, *1941*. Hamish Hamilton, 1981

Crisp, R., *The Gods Were Neutral*. Frederick Muller Ltd., 1960

Cunningham, A.B. (Admiral of the Fleet), *A Sailor's Odyssey*. Hutchinson, 1951

Dahl, Roald, *Going Solo*. Jonathan Cape, 1986

Eudes, Dominique, *The Kapetanios*. NLB, 1972

Ellis, John, *A Short History of Guerrilla Warfare*. Ian Allan Ltd., 1975

Gardner, H.H., *Guerrilla and Counter-Guerrilla Warfare in Greece (1941-46)*. Dept. of US Army, 1962

Gilbert, Martin, *Road to Victory*, Heinemann, 1986

Hanson, D., *We Fell Among Greeks*. Jonathan Cape, 1946

Heckstall-Smith, A., and Vice-Admiral H.T. Baillie-Gromer, *Greek Tragedy*. Anthony Blond Ltd., 1951

Hunt, John, *Life is Meeting*. Hodder & Stoughton, 1978

Jordan, W., *Conquest Without Victory*, Hodder & Stoughton, 1969

Laffin, John, *Digger*. Macmillan (Australia), 1986

Latrides, J.O. (editor), *Greece in the 1940s*. University Press of England, 1981

Leeper, Reginald, *When Greek Meets Greek*. Chatto & Windus, 1950

Lewin, Ronald, *The Chief* (biography of FM Lord Wavell). Hutchinson, 1980

Lindsay, Oliver (editor), *A Guards General*. Hamish Hamilton, 1986

MacKenzie, Compton, *Wind of Freedom*. Chatto & Windus, 1943

McNeil, W.H., *The Greek Dilemma*. Victor Gollancz, 1947

Matthews, Kenneth, *Memories of a Mountain War 1944-49*. Longman, 1972

Maule, Henry, *Scobie, Hero of Greece*. Arthur Barker Ltd., 1975

Myers, E.C.W., *Greek Entanglement*. Rupert Hart-Davis, 1955

O'Balance, E., *The Greek Civil War (1944-1949)*. Faber and Faber, 1966

Ovelman, R.C., *The British Decision to Send Troops to Greece, January to April 1941*. Dissertation for Notre Dame University, 1979

Pack, S.W.C., *Battle for Crete*. Ian Allan Ltd., 1953

Papagos, General A., *The German Attack on Greece*. The Greek Office of Information, 1946

Papastatris, Procopis, *British Policy towards Greece during the Second World War*. Cambridge University Press, 1984

Pravel, K.C., *The Red Eagles*. Vision Books Ltd. (India), 1982

Sarafis, Marian (editor), *Greece from Resistance to Civil War*. Spokesman Books (Notts.), 1980

Sarafis, Stephanos, *The Greek Resistance Army, ELAS*. Birch Books, 1951

Smith, E.D., *Even the Brave Falter*. Robert Hale, 1978

Thomas, W.B., *Dare to be Free*. Reader's Union & Allan Wingate, 1953

Tsatsos, Jeanne, *The Sword's Fierce Edge*. Vanderbilt University Press, 1969

Turner, Don, *Kiriakos*. Robert Hale, 1982

Wilson of Libya, *Eight Years Overseas*. Hutchinson & Co., 1950

Wisdom, T.H., *Wings over Olympus*. George Allen and Unwin, 1942

Woodhouse, C.M., *Struggle for Greece*. Hart-Davis, 1976
                    Something Ventured. Granada, 1982

Official/Semi-Official Documents Consulted

British State Papers, FO371/37201, FO Papers Vol. 511, FO141/871, FO800/276, FO837

Cabinet Papers, Vol. CAA65/40/43

War Office Papers
  WO193/48/971
  WO1707530-7531, 7707
  WO178 57-63
  WO202892-908
  WO204 10624
  WO261 139, 637, 655, 684, 686, 771/772
  WO262 40-41

Air Historical Branch Narrative
  The Middle East Campaign, Vol. VII
  The Campaign in Crete, 1941
  Special Duty Operations in Europe
  History of the Balkan Air Force and SOE in the Mediterranean Theatre

Report by the Supreme Allied Commander, Mediterranean, Field-Marshal Sir H.R.L.G. Alexander to the Chiefs of Staff (12th December 1944 to 3rd May 1945). (CAB106/469)

Cunningham of Hyndham, The Battle of Crete (London Gazette Supplement, 1941)

Wavell, Field Marshal Sir A., Operations in the Middle East from 7th February 1941 to 15th July 1941, *London Gazette Supplement*, 1946)

The Mediterranean Fleet, Greece to Tripoli, Admiralty MOI Booklet

D'Albiac Sir J.H., Air Operations in Greece, 1940/41 (*London Gazette Supplement*, 1947)

Formation and Regimental Histories

46th Division, *The Story of 46 Division 1939/1948*
23 Armoured Brigade Operations (WO 106/3185)
War Diary, 1st Field Regiment RA
A Short History of the 57th LAA Regiment RA
The Royal Engineers Journal 1985 – extract, The Destruction of the Asopos Viaduct in enemy occupied Greece by Brigadier Myers
Short History of the 4th Indian Division Engineers
Wood, Herbert Fairlie, *The King's Royal Rifle Corps*
Fergusson, Bernard, *The Black Watch and the King's Enemies*
The Essex Regimental History
Central India Horse Newsletter, 1-18
The Second Gurkha Rifles
The Seventh Gurkha Rifles, plus *War Diary* 2/7 Gurkha Rifles
The Ninth Gurkha Rifles
Extracts from *3/10 Baluch Regimental History*

Index

by Jill Smith